In Hiding

The Life of Manuel Cortes

RONALD FRASER

Allen Lane The Penguin Press

Allen Lane The Penguin Press
74 Grosvenor Street, London W1

ISBN 0 7139 0280 9

Printed in Great Britain by
The Whitefriars Press Ltd, London and Tonbridge
Set in Monotype Times

CONTENTS

INTRODUCTION

In April 1969 Manuel Cortes, the last republican mayor of a small Spanish village before it fell to the Franco forces during the civil war, emerged after thirty years' hiding from the regime. Helped by his wife, Juliana, and daughter, Maria, he had hidden in the village since the end of the war. A few days before his release, the regime, celebrating the thirtieth anniversary of its victory in the war, had declared an amnesty for offences committed or alleged to have been committed during the war. For the first time in a generation, Manuel Cortes, barber by profession and lifelong socialist, felt free to come out of hiding.

The following pages are his and his wife's and their daughter's account of those years. They speak for themselves, evoking the trials and hardships they have been through, the narrow escapes, the moments when everything seemed lost. To stay hidden in a small village where (as in villages the world over) people make it their business to know their neighbours' affairs, is in itself a considerable achievement. To do so in the face of searches, interrogations, economic hardship and the pervasive fear of illness – Manuel was thirty-four when he went into hiding, sixty-four when he came out – is even more so. Much of the credit must go to his wife. It was she who, during those long years, bore the brunt of protecting her husband, of earning the family livelihood, of schooling her daughter and her daughter's daughters in the art of silence – and this in a family where most of the relatives were kept from knowing the secret. It is a story of personal fortitude, intelligence and sacrifice. Re-living it, reminding oneself of what thirty years means in a life, one can do little more than echo the sentiments expressed by Juliana: 'Thirty years – it's quick to say, you've got to live them to know what it's like.'

Their story, however, is more than an account of these long years in hiding. Manuel's, above all, is a vivid memoir of the most momentous years in recent Spanish history: the fall of the monarchy, the advent of the Republic, the Popular Front, the military uprising, the revolution and civil war. The decade, 1930–39, which witnessed these events, is probably one of the best documented periods in contemporary history: more than ten thousand books have been written about it and new ones appear every year. But very little if anything has ever appeared on how these events were *lived* by working-class Spaniards, especially in the countryside.

Spain, it must be remembered, was (and indeed remained until the sixties) predominantly agrarian. The rural proletariat (mainly landless day-labourers) was in the thirties approximately as large as the industrial proletariat – between two and three million each. Over and above this, there were another two million peasants who share-cropped, rented or owned small holdings – at a time when the middle classes and petite bourgeoisie numbered no more than these peasants alone. Above them, fifty thousand large land-owners owned more than half the soil of Spain. In Andalusia, the classic region of *latifundia*, large estates, the situation was yet more extreme: in Seville, for example, five per cent of land-owners produced seventy-two per cent of the province's total agricultural wealth.*

The land problem – for so many centuries without solution that it began to appear 'eternal' – was at the root of almost every political problem. In hundreds upon hundreds of villages, peasants awaited a solution from the Republic in the shape of a meaningful agrarian reform – waited and were disappointed. The failure of the republican middle classes and petite bourgeoisie to consolidate their revolution and create a stable parliamentary democracy can in large measure be ascribed to their failure to resolve the land problem. Tired of waiting, the peasantry moved to the left, and seized the land on the big estates. The military rising in 1936 triggered off the greatest revolutionary upsurge seen in the West in the twentieth century. The outcome needs no repeating: the failure of the working classes and peasants to win their revolution and, *simultaneously*, a civil war; the success of the military, landed oligarchy and church in defeating their enemies and installing a dictatorship which, excepting the late Salazar's, has lasted longer than any in Europe this century. The land problem remained, receiving its 'final solution' only in the sixties with the mass exodus

* Gerald Brenan, *The Spanish Labyrinth* (Cambridge, 1943), p. 117

of millions of peasants to become the new urban proletariat necessary for Spanish industrial expansion or the unskilled labour of half
a dozen west European countries.

It was through his growing awareness of the land problem and
peasant exploitation that Manuel became involved in the thirties
in the socialist movement. To understand his position it is necessary
to know something of the village and the land from which it lives.

Mijas is a small village lying across the face of a mountain
range some twenty miles west of Málaga. It looks out over the
Mediterranean. From the village the land falls away in crumpled
folds to the coastal plain on either side of Fuengirola and the
river which flows through it. On the hills and in the folds white
farmsteads are scattered in apparently random proximity. Looking down on their white walls and red-tiled roofs surrounded by a
scattered profusion of trees – olives, almonds, carobs, figs – growing along the edges of terraces which are often little more than a
few feet across, one imagines a land-owning peasantry: each
farmstead is a microcosm – a terrace of this, a terrace of that, a
little of everything and, with luck, enough of each to live from
one year to the next.

The view is deceptive. While the land, being poor, is more
equally divided than in other parts and some of these farmsteads
are peasant-owned, the bulk belong to a few landlords. They are
rented or share-cropped; if the latter, the landlord takes half of all
the crops. The farmsteads are just large enough to support a family
in a good year; in not so good years, which are frequent, the sons,
if not the fathers themselves, have to go out looking for work.

The village lives off the land. There are a few local notables:
two or three landlords, a doctor, a schoolmaster, the town clerk,
a shopkeeper or two, a priest and the commander of the Guardia
Civil post, a corporal or sergeant. In varying degrees this petite
bourgeoisie forms the ruling group which runs village life. From
time to time in the past, one of the notables would form his own
group of supporters, recruited not exclusively from his own stratum,
and this group was then known as a *camarilla*. In earlier times each
cacique, or political boss, would have his *camarilla* at his orders.

Within this petite bourgeoisie, the commander of the Guardia
Civil indisputably wields considerable power wherever this para-
military rural police force maintains a post. He is part of the local
ruling group, but he is not dependent on it for he receives his

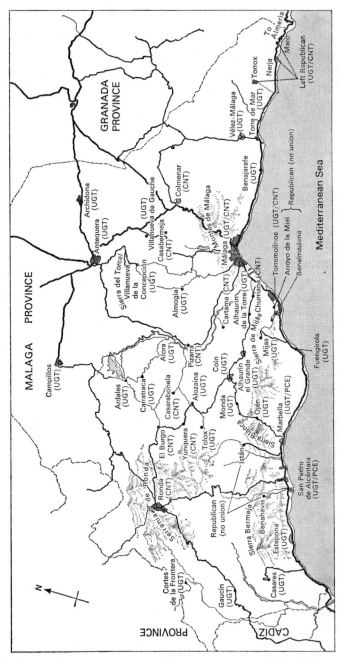

The *majority* trade union or political party indicated for villages and towns for the years 1933–6 is as given by Manuel Cortes (see note 13, p. 228).

orders through his own chain of command. He is a stranger – no *guardia* may serve in his place of birth – and must keep the distance which his authority and independence demands; at the same time he cannot distance himself entirely from it. The ruling group may be able to put some pressures on a new commander; but equally it is his right and duty to resist others which would threaten the independence in which the force's authority lies. The reader will see how these ambiguities played themselves out in Manuel's case.

Under the petite bourgeoisie there is a stratum of artisans and self-employed: a few masons, a carpenter or two, several barbers and shoe-makers, a blacksmith, esparto weavers, muleteers, fish-carriers. The village supports only a reduced number of such people. The remainder live off the land. But the land does not provide work for all. A mass of landless day-labourers get work when additional labour is needed on the farms; when there is none, which can be for as much as six months in the year, they go to the sierra for firewood or the tough esparto grass, or sit in silence at empty tables in front of the bars. Their eyes, like the eyes of the women in black at the fountains, stare at a stranger, for few come this way.

Or so it used to be. Today Mijas is 'on the map', part of the Costa del Sol: a day-tripper's venue for the hundreds of thousands of tourists who holiday among the mushroom growth of hotels, villas and apartment blocks that have sprung up in the sixties along the coast. They crowd the concreted village streets, gaze at the tourist shops that have been put there for them, ride on 'taxi' donkeys to see the sights, photograph the village and leave it by the coach and car-load. There is no unemployment, nor do many work the land any more. Behind its tourist façade, Mijas today hides its past.

*

When, in London, I read the news that Manuel had emerged from hiding, it did not come as a complete surprise. I had known the village for several years and frequently, when the talk turned to gossip, people would speculate on his wife Juliana's habit of shutting doors when anyone was about. From time to time it was suggested that Manuel was hidden in the house. Most people, I believe, at heart shared my incredulity. However, there is no doubt that many people *thought* he might be hidden there; equally certainly, no one *knew* he was there.

Three months after his emergence, on a visit to Mijas, I went to see Manuel. I found him to be a short man with grey hair and inquiring green eyes set in a face where wrinkles and smallpox scars formed an intricate web. A slight pallor was the only visible sign of his thirty years' incarceration. He was alert, cautious. Many people, including representatives of most of the world's press, had been to see him. He was the first of the half-dozen or so men reported to have come out of hiding as a result of the amnesty. It was several days before he agreed to record his life.

He talked calmly, dispassionately, without the rhetoric common among Andalusians. His main interest was politics – the politics of his youth, the socialist movement of which he had been part. Few rural socialist (or other Popular Front) leaders have survived from the thirties. They died in the war or in the repression. Of those who have survived it is probably safe to say that few if any would have so sharp a recollection of village life and politics in those turbulent years as Manuel. Always excellent, his memory has preserved, in the amber of thirty years' enforced withdrawal from active participation in the world, almost every detail of pre-war life and politics. It would not be an exaggeration to say that in many respects his memories are more real to him today than his present life. Listening to them is like listening to a voice from the past – the privileged voice of a survivor recalling what no work of history can ever fully describe: what popular life was like in those days.

With his detailed memory for local, national and international events went a vocabulary more extensive than any I had heard in the village, though it is true that I had not previously had the opportunity of questioning other people as directly. About his own suffering in hiding he was reticent: it was only after more than twenty-four hours of conversation that he mentioned how he had spent his first months of hiding.

On two scores, whenever we returned to them, his voice became charged with emotion: the execution of his friends and comrades and the killing of the local landlords during the revolution. Unjusti-fiable both, they cost him effort to recall; having done his utmost to save lives, it was evident that these deaths affected him deeply to this day.

His moderatism was evident in everything he said. Organizer and arbiter, leader and moderator – as a child the 'brain' of a boys' gang, as an adolescent the self-chosen role of referee in the football team – these, combined with a natural rebelliousness, were the qualities that struck one in him.

As Manuel recounted his life, particularly his time in hiding, the importance of Juliana's role became yet more apparent. Her (and her daughter's) accounts were necessary to complete the story. Though dubious, Manuel agreed to persuade his wife. Taller than her husband, she seemed outwardly a more forceful character than he. I soon discovered that her reputation in the village for dourness – hardly surprising in a woman who, for thirty years, had to struggle not only to keep her husband safe but the family alive – was false. The emotion of recalling events was often too much for her, and she broke down. On these occasions Manuel's presence at the interviews comforted her; on others it was noticeable, however, that she spoke more freely during his absences.

In the course of the interviews I asked hundreds, if not thousands, of questions. Since questions to some degree condition the answers, I should make my own position clear. My knowledge of the village and its recent past was fairly detailed; the same could not be said of my knowledge of Spanish history. During the course of the interviews I was both learning from Manuel and taking extensive notes (which form the basis of those appended to this book) from works on the subject. My main role was, of course, that of an investigator: to encourage Manuel, Juliana and Maria to recall every detail of their lives that had affected them. At the same time, as Manuel and I progressed, the political passions and debates of the thirties began to take hold of me who was too young to have lived them other than as a child. Frequently the interviews turned into dialogue. It became my intention to structure the book around these dialogues of discovery. I still believe this to be the correct method for I do not wish to subscribe to the pretence of having been a 'value-free' interviewer. The subjects of interest to me inevitably set the tone of our conversations; they did not, I believe, fundamentally alter the content of the answers Manuel gave. No matter how hard he was pressed, he remained good-humouredly unshakeable in the political convictions he expressed.

If I have not incorporated this aspect in the book, it is because I felt it would unnecessarily complicate a story whose interest lies in its unique combination of half a century's personal and historical narrative of Andalusian rural life. I have, instead, appended certain notes and chapter headings – which are my entire responsibility and in which none of the protagonists has had any part – in the hope that they will help clarify and amplify at the national level the local events they describe.

This then is *their* book. I have given priority (in extent if not in order) to descriptions of the first years in hiding and the section on the revolution and civil war for their intrinsic historical and dramatic interest. Otherwise my intervention in their product has been confined to ordering the work chronologically, eliminating repetitions and translating, as faithfully as possible, their spoken words.

I should like to thank all those who have helped me in this work. My special thanks are due to those, particularly Mrs Maria Acheson, who transcribed the tape recordings. The latter are available to anyone who wishes to consult the originals.

London
Mijas

GLOSSARY

abuelo, grandfather

alcalde, mayor

alberca, water reservoir

arroba, a weight of 25 lb or measure of about 4 gallons

barrio, quarter or neighbourhood of village or town

bienio negro, two-year period of right-wing government (1933-6) under
Republic

cacique, political boss

camarilla, clique around political boss

carabineros, former frontier and coastal police; republican fighting force
during civil war

chiquillo, little one (endearment)

copla, verse

cortijo, large farm

denuncia, information or charge laid against another person

falangista, member of the Falange

feria, annual village fair in honour of patron saint

granuja, rogue (derogatory)

junta, clique, faction

Mijeño, native of Mijas

novio, *novia*, boy friend, girl friend

practicante, medical assistant qualified to give injections

pueblo, village, the people

quinta, military service age group

recoveria, business of buying eggs in countryside to retail in town

señorito, master (applied to landlords, rich, etc.)

tortilla, omelette

ABBREVIATIONS

UGT   Unión General de Trabajadores, socialist trade union
CNT   Confederación Nacional del Trabajo, anarcho-syndicalist
trades-union confederation
FAI   Federación Anarquista Ibérica, semi-secret militant
anarchist federation
CEDA   Confederación Española de Derechas Autónomas, right-
wing Catholic party led by Gil Robles

One

IN HIDING
The first ten years
1939–49

Every crime alleged to have been committed
in the republican zone of Spain was
investigated. A republican mayor would
stand little chance if it were known that
murders had been committed in his village;
and in which village could this not be said?

– HUGH THOMAS, *The Spanish Civil War*

MANUEL

Although in my conscience I needed no amnesty, for I had done nothing wrong, yet I was forced to think of myself as a criminal in hiding awaiting a pardon.

The first months I spent all the time in my hiding place in the wall. It was cramped, there was room to sit facing only one way, on a small child's chair my wife had put in. My shoulders touched the walls. I could stand up but I couldn't move about. From early in the morning until after midnight I was shut up in there. My wife or my cousin brought me food and passed it down through the hole, and when I had finished they came back for the plates. Only late at night, when the front doors were shut, was it possible to come out and stretch my legs in the house a bit. My foster-father's house was a *posada*, an inn, and there were always muleteers and others coming and going, as well as people for his barber's shop, so I had to stay hidden until the front doors were shut.

The room where I had my hiding place was right next to the street entrance of the house. The room had a window onto the street, very much to hand, and because of that was less suspicious. No one would think of someone being hidden there right at street level where anyone could walk in, would they? If it had been an obscure room somewhere else in the house, that's where they would have looked if they had come to search. But here they would have opened the door and seen a bed, a chest of drawers, a couple of pictures on the wall, a chair – a very small room it was, they wouldn't have thought I was hidden in a space behind the wall. One of the pictures hid the hole by which I got in and out, a big picture my wife had put up there for that.

Those first months were bad; in reality, the first two and a half years I spent in my foster-father's house were terrible. It was worse than being in prison because in prison at least you can walk in the yard and talk to people. I was isolated, completely on my own. Still, there was nothing else to be done. I'd come back at the end of the civil war expecting to get a few years in jail because I knew that was the fate of anyone with a political past. A twelve-year sentence, that sort of thing, which would be reduced by government pardons – as happened – so that I'd be two or three years in prison and then free again. That's what I thought. But when I got here late one night without being seen and my wife told me what had been happening, I knew they would shoot me or send me to jail for thirty years if I gave myself up. That's what had happened to many who had had much less responsible positions politically than me, who had done absolutely nothing. I didn't believe it at first but as my wife went on telling me I saw it was true. More than anyone else, they were looking for me; I was the one they wanted most.

Shut in my hiding place I knew I'd have to spend several years there. Four or five, I thought, until things began to change and they said that the civil war episode was over and granted an amnesty. I was thirty-four then, in the prime of life. I never imagined that I'd have to spend the next thirty years in hiding, never. I don't know what I would have done if I had known that then. But I'm optimistic by nature, I always thought something would change, and I was right in the end – though the end has been a long time in coming.

To pass the time I would sometimes light a candle in the hiding place and put it on one of the shelves that were still there from when it had been a dresser, and I'd read. Newspapers, women's novels – anything to pass the time, I've always liked reading since I was a child. But the time went slowly, very slowly. And it wasn't much better when, after a while, it seemed safe to keep the door of my room shut during the day and for me to be out of the hiding place most of the time. Then I'd sit on the bed in the dark because the shutters couldn't be opened and I couldn't turn on the light lest someone see, and when I'd had enough of sitting I'd get up and walk a few paces back and forth, then sit down again. Then up again. . . . Day after day, more than two years like that, before my wife got a house where I could go.

I'm not one to get discouraged easily. I've faced adversity with calm, I think. But in those first two years I often got depressed. Shut in like that with nothing to do, in that small room in the dark, frightened of coughing or making a noise in case someone heard, walking the couple of steps back and forth, sitting down, up again – it was despairing. No one to talk to until late at night when I could see the family and my wife for a short time, one day on top of another and another, waiting only for night to come, and then sometimes getting back inside the wall so I could light a candle and read just to take my mind off things – well, there were times when I wished I were dead. Not to kill myself, I never thought that; I think that if someone is right in the head they wouldn't consider a madness like that. But I used to think of something happening to me, an illness perhaps. Of course, this was an aberration because at the same time I didn't want to die. And yet to die at that time would have been a relief, to have had an illness that killed me – not to be caught by them, I don't mean that. All through the civil war I was never frightened of dying, bullets whistling past me and artillery-fire, because as a medical orderly I was close to the front line, and if you're killed straight out like that it's bad luck. But it's another thing to be caught and tortured and then be killed because it's not only death but the physical suffering before. And that's what it would have been. I never once thought of giving myself up, even in the worst moments of despair, never. I knew how they would gloat over me and I've always had too much pride to bow my head in front of anyone. I thought of escaping and if they had caught me then that would have been another matter, but to turn myself in like a lamb – never.

Yet my idea on returning to the village was to give myself up. The end of the civil war found me in Valencia where my division, the 40th Carabineros, had been moved. The betrayal of the Republic by the commander of the Madrid front, Casado, ended the war. The nationalists marched into Valencia without opposition. They set up an evacuation centre in the bullring. All the republican soldiers who had disbanded and wanted to return home had to go there. Once you were in you weren't allowed out. I don't know how long some of them were shut in there without food. Ten or twelve days, at least, some of them. Those who had family or friends who could lower them down a basket with something to eat at the end of a rope from inside got by. But the others....

I was lucky. I went into the bullring one afternoon and that night there was a train. I had been waiting nearly two weeks, running round in circles selling what little I had to keep alive. They put us in cattle trucks as far as Córdoba where those of us Andalusians who were going south caught a passenger train. The safe-conduct they gave us served as a ticket. Altogether we were three days and nights travelling with only a tin of sardines and a tiny loaf each.

I got to Málaga on 16 April 1939, at dusk. We got off the train and the Guardia Civil surrounded us immediately, formed us up and marched us to a control point they had. Those of us in age groups which hadn't been mobilized in the nationalist zone were considered civilians and were told to return to our villages and report to the authorities. The others were considered military prisoners and taken to a barracks in Málaga. Although I had served in the republican army, my *quinta* hadn't been called up by the nationalists for their army and so I was free to go.

I went out of the station. I was in civilian clothes and carrying my *carabinero*'s cape. I got rid of the cape so as not to draw attention to myself. I asked a Guardia Civil patrol to direct me to the Tiro Pichon, which is an area in Málaga where I knew I could get a taxi. There were still plenty of taxis; the nationalists always had plenty of petrol from America during the civil war.

It was dark by the time we reached the road up from the coast to Mijas. It must have been 10.30 or 11. All the way from Málaga I had been thinking what to do. Well, in reality, I'd been thinking a lot longer than that. In Valencia I had tried to get a passport – you had to have a political certificate even for the photographer to take the pictures, and then get other documents, go to the commissariat and the civil governor's office – a whole business. I wanted to get to France, I would have done if I could. I'm speaking about the time before the city fell, before the war ended. During the surrender negotiations it was agreed that all those who wanted to leave would be allowed to do so. Some civilians got out on French ships in the first few days, but when the whole republican zone was firmly in the nationalists' hands no one else was allowed to leave. I hadn't a chance, being still in the army – and if I had I would have been caught in France by the Germans during the world war, no doubt. That happened to a lot of Spaniards including a boy from here who died of starvation and beatings in a Nazi concentration camp. But, of course, we didn't know that then.

In the bullring in Valencia they only asked my name, profession and home address. I could have told them I came from somewhere else, from Granada or Córdoba, and not come back to Mijas. But I had no money and to go somewhere unknown, without more identification papers than those people had given us, would have meant being picked up straightaway. With the vigilance there was in those days! The only other thing could have been to take refuge in the sierra and become an outlaw or a guerrilla; there were many who did, even in the sierra here, but I wasn't one for that. So I said to myself, I'll return to the village where I have friends and the like and I'll get sent to prison for a few years and that will be that. Not that I had ever done anything wrong during my time as mayor of the village – it was for my socialist beliefs that they would put me in jail. At that time they were saying that anyone who hadn't committed crimes of blood had nothing to fear, the war was over. My conscience was easy, I was prepared to report to the authorities. All the same, I thought, I'll take some precautions.

When the taxi was still about two kilometres from the village, down there by the Cerro Pinosa as it's called, I told the driver to stop. I pretended I lived in the country and I paid him his thirty-eight or thirty-nine pesetas, and he turned round and went back down the road to Fuengirola. I continued up the road a bit and then I cut across and up the paths by the farmsteads on this side of the Muralla, the rock promontory. That way I could get to the back of my foster-father's house without going through the village and being seen. I climbed over the wall and jumped down into the patio and knocked on the back door. To start with they didn't want to open up, they were frightened. There was my foster-father – my foster-mother died shortly after the start of the civil war in 1936 – and a cousin who had been brought up like a sister to me. Of course, they didn't know whether I was alive or dead; it was over two years since I had fled the village, and they thought I might have been killed or escaped to France or somewhere.

My cousin ran to tell my wife in the house where she was living, and she came quickly with our daughter in her arms. And her parents too. Those were the only people who knew I had come back and – with the exception of one other relative, my son-in-law and my granddaughters – those are the only people who, in the last thirty years, have known I was here. If there had been more I wouldn't be here now.

When the doors and shutters were closed I told them my plan – to report in the morning. 'Give yourself up, what do you mean?' my foster-father and wife both said. 'Don't you know they're clamouring here to catch you?' Then they started to tell me what had been happening, the people who had been denounced in the village, the sentences. Three of the four presidents of the revolutionary committee had been shot, one of them a friend and comrade of mine in the socialist party and trade union. When I heard about him I asked myself, how is it possible that they have done this to someone who did nothing, absolutely nothing. Nothing more than preside over the committee for a few weeks at the end when its importance was nothing like what it had been at the start. And then I thought it must have been a matter of personal revenge. There was a landlord here, one of the *camarilla*, and my comrade rented his farmstead from him. Under the Republic landlords weren't allowed to raise the rents as they pleased. My friend claimed his rights under the law not to have the rent raised. In consequence the landlord had it in for him and he avenged himself when he had the chance. My comrade had his chance too; if he had been a bad person he would have used his position as president of the committee to have the landlord liquidated. But he didn't, he didn't do anything to him at all – nothing more than claim his rights under the law.

As my wife and father went on telling me what had happened, I saw the danger. If my enemies in the village had kept quiet, if they had said, 'Nothing will happen to him if he returns', they might have caught me. But as they kept telling everyone what they were going to do to me when I came back, my wife knew only too well. 'You're not giving yourself up, we've got to find something else.'

We discussed it for several hours. There was no way out other than hiding; my safe-conduct wasn't valid any longer. I didn't have any money and if I gave myself up I knew what was in store. My father said I should hide in his house until my wife could get a house where I could go. Then I remembered that in the front room, right off the street and across the passage from the barber's shop where I used to work, there was a dresser built into the wall which had been bricked up. It made a hollow wall, a very narrow space that would be just big enough. I grew up in that house so I knew it well. And I thought, all it needs is a hole cut out of the wall big enough for me to get through and then covered with a picture so no one can see. I had a bad cold, so that night and the next day I hid in the attic while my wife and cousin cut the hole in the wall. Then I moved down to my hiding place.

It was just as well. A day or two later my wife talked to a *guardia civil*, a man called Garcia whose wife she knew. She pretended to be innocent, feeling out the ground. 'And if my husband should come back . . .?' she asked. 'Your husband and people like him shouldn't come back,' he replied, meaning that she should understand the danger there was. This Garcia had reason to be grateful to me for the way I acted to him before and during the civil war, and he was always ready to give my wife advice. But, of course, he didn't know I was here.

Shut up in the dark of the wall the thing that depressed me more than anything else was the news of comrades who had been shot – the majority of my comrades in the socialist party and union, the best and most generous of them, and a lot of people who weren't comrades but friends from other parties. There was the man who was mayor of the village before me. He came back to Málaga about the same time as me, a day or two later perhaps because he wrote a letter first to a sister in Málaga asking if it was all right to return. He had been a member of the radical party until he got disgusted by Lerroux's manœuvring and joined Azaña's left republicans. His sister passed the letter on to my wife who had got to know her so that she could give it to another sister in the village. This sister wrote to her brother who was in Guadalajara telling him to come back, that nothing would happen. As soon as he reached Málaga he was arrested, he never got here. He went to report to the police there, as I should have done here, and they asked for a report on him from the village. The group of men who had the village in their hands denounced him and, on the basis of that, he was court-martialled and shot a month or two later.

When the sister here heard that he had been denounced, she thought money could save him and she wanted to go to Madrid to intervene on his behalf. The men got wind of what she was up to. If she managed to get the *denuncia* lifted, they said, they would put in another. And if that failed, they'd put in yet another. They didn't have to trouble, the first one was enough.

It was these few men who most wanted to see me shot. They had the village in their grip. It needed only three people, one to sign a *denuncia* and two witnesses. They could take it in turns, between them they could accuse one of any 'crimes' they wanted. What could the courts martial do in these circumstances? They had only the *denuncias* to go on. It wasn't their fault, I want to make it clear, the fault lay in allowing people the freedom to denounce. In villages like this where there are always personal grudges. . . . Here, four landlords lost their lives during the revolution. Later a great many people were denounced and shot for taking part in their deaths. With the exception of a few, for I know very well who was responsible for those crimes, the rest had nothing to do with the killings.

Only one of the landlords was shot by people from here. The others were shot by anarchist patrols which came from Alhaurin and Los Boliches. I did my best to save them, as I'll explain. I didn't want anyone shot. In fact I saved fourteen people one night when another anarchist patrol came for them. Among the fourteen was a man who later was one of the group which most wanted to see me shot!

Even if only one landlord was killed, it was one too many for me, he shouldn't have been shot. I wouldn't have done it, whatever he was like. What is gained by killing a man?

In Málaga my brother-in-law, my wife's brother, was sentenced to death. He had worked on a farm which had been collectivized during the revolution. The landlord denounced him. But the sentence was seen as unjust and was commuted to twelve years and a day. He had served two or three years when, as a result of one of the first amnesties, he was released on conditional liberty, which meant he had to report to the authorities at specified times. There were always people in the villages ready to denounce – even those who had served in the nationalist army might, on their return from the war, be denounced locally and get sent to jail for three or four years.

Apart from one other, I think I am the only mayor of that period from the villages round here who is still alive and living here. The mayor of Fuengirola was hanged, those of Alhaurin and Benalmádena shot when their villages fell. The mayor of Los Boliches, who fled with me and returned after the war, committed suicide in jail, slashed his veins with a razor blade. Perhaps nothing would have happened to him other than a few years in prison, but he was frightened and liquidated himself rather than face the possibility of being liquidated. The mayor of Coin fled to the sierra and met his death there with the other outlaws. The mayor of Marbella, who was a communist, and the mayor of Monda, a socialist, both escaped to the republican zone. The former became a militia lieutenant and, as far as I know, escaped to France. The only one to my knowledge who is still living here is the mayor of Estepona who was released after serving a few years in jail. The only one.

I had been in hiding not more than a day or two when a man who had a shop up the street went to the Guardia Civil to inform them that he had seen me on the train coming down to Málaga. When my wife told me, I realized it was probably true because there were lots of nationalist soldiers who had been demobilized on the train. He could well have been among them. He said he had seen me get out of the train at Bobadilla, the railway junction, as in fact I did. I was dying of thirst and I remember going down the underground passage-way to the buffet for a drink. But I didn't come back the same way. I got into the carriage at the far end on the other side, and so, if he did see me, he would have lost me then. Although we were political opponents he wasn't a bad man or he would have gone to the police on the spot and told them, 'Look, there's a man who is wanted.' However, he didn't wait long after his return to inform the Guardia Civil. Garcia told my wife what this man was saying and she was called to the Guardia barracks for questioning again. She told them that if he had seen me he would have to tell them where I was because she hadn't seen me. Then she went to see the man, to sound him out. But he wouldn't tell her for sure one way or the other, he didn't want her to know that he had informed the Guardia that he had seen me for certain. In any case, he couldn't say he had seen me reach Málaga and that was the main thing. All the same, we spent several anxious days, but the Guardia didn't search.

This man went through a time of hiding himself during the revolution. His father was one of the richest men in the village when I was young. He had come from the north and got a job in a cloth shop as an assistant and after a while he took over the shop. When peasants got into difficulty he would lend them money or give them credit to buy from his shop against the surety of their title deeds. When they couldn't pay and the interest accumulated, their debt became so big that within two or three years they would have to hand over their farmsteads. In this way he became the owner of more than fifty properties which his children inherited. His daughter is one of the biggest land-owners here today.

When the military rose in 1936 and the revolution began, there were some extremists here who went after him. They didn't find him, he had a hiding place in his house. One day the militia searched his place and one of the militiamen saw him. Instead of calling the others, he turned round in the doorway and said there was no one there. The militiaman was a socialist and he came and told us, 'Look, what's his name is in his house, I saw him there, but I didn't want to say anything to the others.' So we knew all the time where he was but we didn't give him away and he came through it all right.

He was a political opponent, not an enemy of mine. As I've said, there were two or three men in the village who, more than anyone else, wanted to see an end to me. For them it wasn't only that I had been the main organizer of the socialist and trade-union movement here or mayor during the time of the Popular Front. They hated me for that and held me responsible for everything that had happened. But on top of that there were personal scores they wanted to settle. It was for this, as much as, if not more than for my political past, that my life was in danger.

These grudges arose out of things I stopped them doing in my official capacity as mayor. They thought they could carry on in their old ways, as though they were still living in the time of the *caciques*. In one of the cases, the people of the village protested at what they considered an abuse. But in spite of that it was against me personally that these men held grudges. I don't feel free to say more about the reasons than that, it might be dangerous even today. These were the only real enemies of mine, the two or three who held personal grudges. Otherwise I always had a lot of friends, not only people of my political beliefs but of other ideologies as well. Politics was one thing, friendship another – that's how I am, friendship counts a lot with me.

More than anything else, this is what I missed most – not being able to see and talk to those of my friends who were left. Being shut in alone without seeing anyone or anything is very despairing. From morning until late at night, hidden in the wall or in that small, dark room, I'd wait for the few moments when my wife or cousin brought my food and we could talk in whispers. Knowing each time that as soon as that moment was over it meant being shut in again. Two long years, the worst of my life. Day after day. Pacing the few steps across the room and back again, getting tired of that, sitting on the bed. When I'd had enough of sitting, beginning pacing again. Hour after hour. At least that way I didn't lose the power of walking. I've always been nervous, my nerves have never let me be still for long. I've always been wanting to get on with things, get them done. I'm tough in that way, very tough. I never give up once I've started something, though physically I'm not very strong. But strong-nerved, yes, because despite all the despair I never feared going mad, I never thought of it. Looking back, one could imagine it happening. Nothing to do, shut in one room in the dark – but no, to imprison myself in my brain and lose all sense of reality, no, I couldn't have done that. I was always looking for something to revive me, some hope to cling to. One day they would remember to grant an amnesty, I thought. Although in my conscience I needed no amnesty, for I had done nothing wrong. Yet I was forced to think of myself as a criminal in hiding awaiting a pardon. Until it was given I had to go on in hiding. My wife will tell you what those first years were like.

JULIANA

My husband is calm . . . he doesn't have caution. . . . I'm not like that. Walking, I'd have got across the frontier if I had been him rather than come back here.

I was in bed when they came to tell me the news, the foster-father and the cousin, that Manolo had returned. I caught up my daughter in my arms and went to the foster-father's house. It was twenty-six months since I'd seen my husband last outside Málaga that day we fled. I started to cry with the emotion and the sight of him, he was so thin and his face was livid from the journey and the hardship of it. And I was happy and sad all at the same time, happy to see him again and sad because I knew what was in store. And I cried, 'Ay! Why have you come back? What have you come back here for?' My head was bursting with the thought of what they would do to him and of trying to think how we could hide him. I felt I would go mad. He couldn't give himself up and we didn't know where to hide him and what we would do if they came looking for him. . . . Before, when sometimes I thought, if he should come, I'd imagined hiding him in Málaga; it would have been easier, in a city. But my brothers and sisters wouldn't take the responsibility. . . . I had never thought of being able to hide him here until he appeared. I'd have been glad really if he hadn't come back and had escaped instead and been able to live abroad, and I would have joined him sooner or later. That way we would have been spared these thirty years of purgatory; it's quick to say, thirty years, but to live. . . . My husband is calm, although he's a man who knows a lot more about things than anyone else, he doesn't have caution. He takes everything calmly as though there was no danger. I'm not like that. Walking, I'd have got across the frontier if I had been him rather than come back here.

That night in the foster-father's house, I explained to him everything that had happened and what they had done to his comrades, those who had returned and given themselves up, and I'd say, 'Look, that's what they've done to so-and-so', and give him the name, 'Well, that's what they'll do to you.' And as I went on telling him he became more and more downcast until at last the spirit went out of him. He saw I was telling the truth, he saw the danger at last. He'd expected something, of course, but nothing like this and he didn't know what to do. They'd get rid of him if they could, as they did only a few days later to another one who returned. He had been head of the revolutionary militia here, he'd been in the republican army too. The very day he returned I saw him in Málaga and I said, 'Where are you going?' 'To report,' he replied. He was still wearing his army beret from the other side. 'Take that thing off,' I said. He thought he was still in the other zone. 'Why are you going to report?' 'I haven't done anything, so I'm going to Mijas to report.' 'They'll seize you and then God help you,' I said, 'don't stay here, get out.' And the words were hardly out of my mouth when some people from the village arrived in the place where we were eating. 'Olá!' they said, 'so you've come back, you're here.' And he said, 'Yes, I'm going back up to Mijas in a little while,' and they said, 'Good, the lorry is outside, it's waiting for you.' We came back in the lorry too, a couple of other *recoveras* and I, and he rode up on top. He'd no sooner jumped down in the square to take the Calle San Sebastián in the direction of his house than they grabbed him. His mother hadn't even time to embrace him, they arrested him in the middle of the street. Two or three days later they took him to Málaga and that was it. When I saw what was happening, when everyone came running up, I felt something go through me, I had such an attack of nerves that I left my basket of shopping in the square and went to my house, thinking of my husband and what could happen to him.

But that night my mother was the only one of us who thought he should give himself up. Imagine her ignorance! 'They've given him a safe-conduct, that means they won't do anything to him,' she said, 'The war is over, the worst is past.' 'No, no,' I said, 'you'll see the worst isn't past if Manolo gives himself up. He isn't giving himself up.' Like the rest of us, she didn't know what to do either, where he could hide. 'It would be best', she said, 'if he gave himself up at night and not in the daytime so the people won't see.' 'He's not giving himself up by day or by night,' I replied,' we're here to see if we can find some way out.' Later, when she saw what was happening, she said, 'Ah, you did well. What they would have done to him if he had given himself up.'

The foster-father didn't want him to give himself up. 'Even if it's in the well that you have to hide, you won't report.' In the well! How could he hide there, in the water? You could stay two or three minutes in the well, perhaps, but to live. . . . And then he had this idea, Manolo, he remembered the dresser that had been bricked up. It was his idea and he told us what to do the next day, he had it worked out. And I thought, what else can we do, if it turns out well, good; and if not, what we've got now is even worse.

His cousin and I made the hiding place the next night, we got a hammer and broke through where the dresser had been bricked up, making a hole big enough for him to get through. I got a picture and took the glass out so it wouldn't be so heavy and hung it over the hole. That way he could hang up the picture from inside if he had to. I got a child's chair to put inside; that was all that would fit. Under the hole we put the chest of drawers which he could stand on to get into the place. He'd get on a chair and then onto the chest of drawers and into the hole without much trouble. No one would have thought he was there, even less because the room was so close to the street. It was safer than trying to hide him somewhere else, in the countryside. My father's house was too small anyway; sooner or later he would have been seen, and here he was close by and I could look after him.

What else could we do? He couldn't leave, there was nowhere for him to go. He wouldn't have thought of joining the outlaws in the sierra, that would have been even worse. They were people who were there because they had done something bad, and when they were caught they were shot. He has never committed a crime in his life, he's never liked things that were outside the law. Although he was a socialist, he wouldn't break the law. To have political ideas has got nothing to do with evil-doing, has it? To have such ideas is one thing, to do bad things is another. If he had gone to the sierra and been caught he would have been accused of the outlaws' crimes and that would have been worse. No, he wasn't a person for that, he would rather have given himself up, however bad the outcome might have been.

Those first months were terrible for him, you could see the effects in his face and body. He got very pale and thin. He had to stay in there squashed between the two walls from the moment of getting up until late at night. When he slept, his bed was under the window and he had to be careful not to make any noise. He wrapped the pillow round his face when he coughed. He had a candle in there to read by a bit, to see to eat, that was all. I took him his food which I cooked in my house and carried it in a basket covered with something so no one should see. If there was a neighbour in the street who stopped me to talk, I wouldn't go into the house; I'd go on up the street as though I was on my way to my parents' house. Because his father's house was an inn and people were coming and going all day, it meant that it wasn't watched. All the same, I had to be sure no neighbours noticed that I was going to the house at the same time every day. I had to be on guard the whole time, I never thought of anything else except about keeping him safe, about cooking his food, about getting it to him.

The days when I was in the countryside or in Málaga on business his cousin cooked for him. He didn't come out of the hole to eat, I passed the plates in to him and when he had finished he passed them out. Each time I went into the room I made sure that his cousin shut the street door first so that no one saw me. Once inside, I locked the door, it was only a thin one, and of course the shutters across the window were closed all the time. I'd stand and talk to him through the hole, whispering so no one should hear, like in a silent film. I'd tell him what was happening in the village so he knew the danger there was. Some days I didn't stay at all when things got very bad and it seemed dangerous and there was the chance of a search. But they never did look for him because they didn't believe he was here, they thought he was in Málaga or somewhere like that.

Sometimes he despaired – how could he not in those conditions? But he knew there was nothing else he could do, it would be worse if he tried to escape. He had to put up with it and hold out. I never doubted he would. After all, life is pleasant – too pleasant to throw away, isn't it? And the same for me, I knew I had to go through with it, what else was there to do? It was hard, very hard, but when you've got to you can do whatever circumstances require.

The night he came back I took our daughter to see him, but not after that because the next morning when I went out, she said to the cousin I'd left her with: 'Cousin, I saw my father last night and I had some chocolate to eat. . . .' It's true, that night we did have some chocolate, I think. She had stayed awake only a short time since it was so late, but she remembered enough. When I came back, my cousin – she was only ten and I often left Maria with her when I went out to work – said to me straightaway, 'Do you know what Maria just told me? That her father has come back and that he gave her some chocolate.' 'Ah,' I said, 'the poor child, she must have dreamed that last night. I never stop talking to her about her father so that she shouldn't forget. She must have got it mixed up in her dreams.' Being so young, my cousin believed the story. If it had been someone older they might have got suspicious.

As soon as the cousin was out of the house I got my daughter alone and asked her why she had said that. She wasn't quite four at the time and until the night of his return she couldn't remember having seen her father. When I used to take her through the square during the war she would point at the bar where she saw Don Lucas, the town clerk who was a friend of my husband's, and say, 'Mama, mama, there's papa there.' She was only eighteen months old when my husband fled. She was full of joy at seeing him for the first time, but I had to give her a good talking to. I told her that her father would be killed if she told anyone, that we would all go to jail, that the Guardia Civil would come for us. 'Mama, I'll never say it again, never.' The next time the cousin came, Maria told her it had been a dream. By then I had talked to her so often about having dreamed that her father had come back that she believed it herself.

I didn't let her see him again after that, I used to take her with me to the house so that, by lifting the picture up a bit, he could look at her from his hiding place, but I didn't want to run the risk of her saying something. As soon as he'd had a look at her I'd take her from the room.

Every time I went out into the country on my round to collect eggs or to Málaga to sell them I was full of fear. If they come while I'm not there, if they find him. . . . As soon as I got out of the village taxi that made the trip to Málaga each day I was all eyes, looking to see if people were looking at me. Had they caught him while I was away? Did the people know what I didn't know? A terrible anxiety filled me while I went on my rounds. I was anxious about being away from the village all day and only wanting to return. At the same time I was anxious about coming back in case something had happened. Yet I had to go to Málaga to attend to my business because that was all we had to keep us alive. When my husband fled he left me with fifty pesetas and with that I became a *recovera*, buying eggs from the farmsteads and selling them in private houses in Málaga.

I lived in fear all the time. The people in the village went round saying that the Guardia Civil had some sort of machine with which they could find anything that was hidden. I got it into my head that it was true, they had a machine like that which they could put against walls and find someone. It terrified me. I said to myself, if they come with that thing and look for him it's finished. Of course, it wasn't true, they hadn't a machine or anything like that, it was just the people talking to create fear.

The Guardia sent for me as soon as this man went to the

barracks to say he had seen my husband get off the train at Bobadilla. He was coming out of the barracks as I went in. I denied everything. 'If he says he saw him then he'll have to tell you where he is. I don't know anything because I'm in my house and he hasn't come there.' They kept saying, 'He says he saw him.' 'If he saw him, let him tell you where he is, I don't know anything,' I kept replying. They had to let me go and I came out of there red as a tomato with anger at being interrogated by them.

I went to see this man the same day. I wanted to see what he knew. He didn't seem very certain, he only thought he had seen someone get off the train who looked like him. 'Well, he hasn't come back here, and since he hasn't come back it means you must have seen someone who looked like him,' I said. 'Yes, it must have been that, there was someone there who looked like him,' he said. 'There are many coming back, it must have been someone else.' Yes,' he said, 'someone else, it must have been.'

Neither he nor the Guardia could prove that my husband had reached Málaga. As far as they knew he might have stayed in Bobadilla or somewhere round there. This man didn't put in a *denuncia* or sign anything, if he had and could have found two witnesses they could have arrested me. But all he did was to bleat out the bit of information he had. That was enough to make life difficult for me because it stirred everything up and they started calling me up to the barracks for questioning all the time. That was always the worst, when they'd get to thinking where Manolo could be. Each time the sergeant in charge of the post was changed it started again, they'd be on top of me calling me up and threatening to arrest me. It was the *camarilla* who put the pressure on each new sergeant or corporal, it was the people here who wanted to find him. After a few months when the sergeant hadn't been able to get anything out of me, they'd forget it. Then there'd be a new commander of the post and it started again. There was no end to it.

But they never searched the house for him. About the same time as my husband returned, this *guardia* called Garcia gave me a bit of advice. He said I should move into a house where four or five other women were living so that no one could suspect me of hiding him. As soon as he said that I moved – in one night I packed up the little I had and went into the new house. Although Garcia was said to be a bad man – and I won't say he was good – he was kind to me. I was friendly with his wife and she used to order things from Málaga through me and I would give her a few presents for her child from time to time. Through another woman she often sent me a message warning me the night before I was to be called to the barracks for questioning. 'Tomorrow they're coming for you, they want to give you more trouble.'

This Garcia had been here before the war, he had relatives here, and when the village was taken by the nationalists in February 1937 he came back. To begin with he was made the acting commander of the post because he knew the village and the people, and later when they sent a sergeant he stayed on as an ordinary *guardia*. He was good to me right from the start. He knew Manolo had left the village and he never bothered me, it was the *falangistas* who came searching my house. Garcia knew that in the revolution time I had never been mixed up in anything like some of the people when the church and the retired major's house were sacked. He knew I wasn't to blame for any of that. He was bad to a lot of people here but as far as I was concerned I've nothing bad to say about him.

He used to send a *guardia* to fetch me when I was called up to the barracks while he waited in his aunt's house where I would go first. Then he'd tell me how to answer the sergeant's questions. 'You know nothing of your husband's whereabouts, you don't know anything at all. You keep saying that.' His advice helped me a lot, I always kept to it. I didn't know anything, I couldn't know anything, they should stop calling me up for questioning.

Often he'd tell me that he held only one thing against my husband and he had forgiven him that. It was a May Day just before the war and the Guardia were trying to stop the demonstration. He said my husband as mayor had sided with the demonstrators against the Guardia. But he had forgiven him that incident and he wouldn't do him any harm if he saw him again. What the people in the village might do to him was another matter, he said. I let him go on like that, letting him think I believed him. Who can tell if he wouldn't have done what he said the village people would do if he had caught my husband? He's dead now, and it doesn't matter any more.

As soon as I was ready to go to the barracks he'd say, 'We'll go ahead and you come on behind so that the people don't see.'

He meant that the people shouldn't notice that I had to go with the *guardia* to the barracks again.

The morning after I moved into the house with the other women, they came for me. It must have been 8.30 and by the time I got there it was 9. I was there all morning, until 1.30 at least, being questioned. Always the same thing. Where was Manolo? He had been seen on the train, I must know where he was. Where was he hiding? On and on, the same questions over and over. That day they threatened to put me in jail if I didn't tell them where he was. 'You can question me, you can lock me up, you can do what you want, I can't tell you because I don't know. And even if I did know it would be my duty not to tell you. But as I don't, I can't tell you.' I kept repeating the same things over and over. When they said they would throw me in jail, I told them, 'You're not *caciques* here, you've got no right to throw me in jail unless you've got a signed *denuncia* and two witnesses to it saying that I know where my husband is. Until you've got that you can't arrest me.' That stopped them a bit. Playing my cards open on the table like that made them think. They were trying to frighten me into saying where he was. I was frightened every time I saw them coming for me, but once I was there I knew I could hold out against them. I'd say to myself, whatever they do, I'm not going to talk. They can jail me, they can shoot me, but they won't get a word out of me where Manolo is.

MANUEL

My despair was greatest when it seemed the Nazis might win the war. With their defeat I began to live a blind hope.

Sometimes, shut in the dark during those first two and a half years, I used to think I was born under a black star. First my mother dying when I was a baby, then my father soon afterwards, then nearly dying myself when I caught smallpox. And now this. . . . Black thoughts. I'd despair so much that the desire to flee would nearly overwhelm me. I didn't know where I could try to go, I never planned anything. Sometimes I thought I might be able to get to Barcelona, at other times I imagined reaching Gibraltar. Whenever I got these thoughts my wife would warn me: 'Where can you go without papers? Things are very bad, they'll catch you wherever you go.' She was always very pessimistic, my foster-father too.

Then I'd say to myself, if they catch me they catch me. But at the back of my mind I knew my wife and father were right. The world war had started; even if I managed by chance to get out of Spain it would be difficult to find safety abroad. And first I would have to get out of Spain! Little by little they would convince me it was impossible to escape. 'There are controls everywhere, they'll catch you at one of them and that'll be that. You won't be able to run away. In a few years things will be better and then we can see.' They said that to comfort me, they didn't believe it themselves. But I believed it because even in the worst moments I always had hope that something one day would change. My hope lay in the war. If the Nazis were defeated. . . .

After about a year in hiding the *camarilla* again started to put pressure on the Guardia Civil to find me. They thought I must be in Málaga because my wife's business took her there at least once a week and because I have relatives living there. They got the police to search the house of a cousin of mine, but they didn't find anything. What they didn't believe was that I could be here, since my wife hadn't a house of her own where she could hide me. That was what we wanted, of course.

It was one of the men with a personal grudge against me who was mainly responsible for putting pressure on the Guardia. The sergeant at the time agreed all the more easily because he had fought on the republican side and was trying to prove that it had been against his will. He was a hard devil, this sergeant, he went after anyone who might have been on the left, he was really out to ingratiate himself. And, of course, I was their number one enemy, the only one who had escaped.

To be a socialist here was to be thought worse than the devil. They had only to say, 'That was the one who organized the party and union here', for the sergeant to be ready to help them. Of course, the *camarilla*, the landlords and *caciques* weren't likely to forget what I had done. I organized a strong union in the thirties and I earned their hatred for it. They didn't like having a union where there hadn't been one. They were used to dominating the village and paying whatever wages suited them. They knew I believed the land should be nationalized, along with the banks, the key industries, transport, education. But above all the land, because Spain at that time was predominantly a peasant country. Even so I was a moderate, I believed in paying for land that was expropriated and in distributing it to the peasants in individual plots. Most of the younger militants believed in outright expropriation. But moderate as I was, it was too much for the landlords. Even the friends I had among them used to accuse me of being in it for personal gain, to take away from them what was theirs. 'No, *hombre*, no,' I'd tell them, 'it's to save you from something much worse.' But they didn't understand.

They couldn't believe that someone could do something that was not for personal gain. But I didn't go into the socialist movement to benefit myself. I went into it because I believed in social justice, in the poor having a share in the wealth of the nation, in ending the domination of the capitalist class. That was what socialism meant to me. It was through my admiration for the peasants, for their patience and their sacrifices, and through wanting to do what I could – within the limits of my understanding and culture – that I came to socialism and helped organize the party and union. For my downfall as it turned out, but how was I to know that then?

When their search of my cousin's house produced nothing, the sergeant stopped my wife going to Málaga. They thought she went every week to bring me food and clothing and that if they prevented her from going they would force me to come out of hiding. They were wrong in that, but it was a threat to our lives.

Though it was a struggle, the little my wife made as a *recovera* was enough to get by on in those days when everyone was used to living in much greater poverty than today. All the same, she had to fight very hard to make a living, especially when the government imposed a control on the sale of eggs and the free market was ended. Then she and a friend, whose husband had been killed in the repression, used to walk all night to Málaga to get their eggs through. Thirty kilometres! And then all day going back and forth between her sister's house on the outskirts and the centre of Málaga carrying the eggs basket by basket into the town as though they were housewives shopping. All this not to be caught. Imagine all the trips they had to make in a day to get rid of several hundred eggs, and that on top of walking all the way from here to Málaga. Yes, she had to struggle very hard, as hard as a man, to keep us alive.

When the sergeant stopped her going, my wife couldn't earn. We had to live on her savings. After six weeks the little she had saved was nearly gone. It couldn't go on like that, another few weeks and I don't know what we would have done. I thought, if it weren't for the *camarilla* the Guardia wouldn't be doing this, if it weren't for the sergeant and his special position, having fought on our side. All the sergeants weren't like him, the first one who came here as permanent commander of the post never bothered my wife at all, never questioned her or said anything to her, although the people here were after him to do so. He used to say that these were political matters and he wasn't here to concern himself with them. But he was soon promoted and posted to another place and then came this one who was obviously out to ingratiate himself.

At last, as the weeks went by, I said to my wife, 'You'll have to go to the barracks and tell the sergeant you're going to Málaga. Tell him to send a policeman after you if he wants to see where you go. But he can't go on cutting off your livelihood like this, he hasn't the right.' And she went and told him what I had told her to say. Of course, since I was hidden here, she could speak her mind openly, knowing that if they followed her in Málaga it would only be to the *señoritos'* houses where she sold eggs and the shops where she bought goods. The sergeant must have said to himself, I can't go on stopping her earning a peseta to keep herself and her child alive, I'll let her go; because he lifted the ban. By then he probably had understood that it was the *camarilla* which was pressuring him and that he had been taken in, because he never bothered about us again. Still, it was a very bad time.

Things were made worse because all this happened at the height of the famine. When the civil war ended in April 1939, food supplies held out for a while, at least through the summer. But as soon as winter set in and the world war started, there was nothing to buy. On top of the poverty there was near starvation. Cabbages and sweet potatoes was about all there was, there was no olive oil or fats. They were years of drought, too. People walked all over the countryside looking for food, for a cabbage to buy, while those who had a terrace of cabbages growing would sell them off one at a time to the highest bidder. Although we couldn't complain because we were a little better off than the poorest, the worst was not having olive oil or fats. Everything had to be cooked in water, a bit of boiled cabbage would be a meal. President Roosevelt sent a large gift of food – milk, flour, butter and cheese – which would have relieved much of the hunger if it had been properly distributed. But it wasn't. Some of this food reached here and a little was handed out to the few it pleased them to help. The rest was 'lost', 'eaten', shared amongst the *camarilla* who were the only ones to have food and least needed American aid. The crisis was worsened by the devastation of the war.[1]

Even worse was that it looked as though the Nazis were winning the war. Sometimes when I read the papers – they were full of nothing but Nazi victories because the people here exaggerated everything in their favour – I got so depressed that I thought I was doomed to die in hiding. If Hitler had won the war, we would have been occupied, we would have had fascism in Europe for a hundred years. There would have been no hope at all. When I read the papers my wife brought me I would be so overwhelmed with the thought of an Axis victory that I began to pace up and down in the room, thinking I might as well make a break for it and see if I could get by. Then there was the succession of Japanese victories on top of everything else.

Despite all the depressing news, I could never bring myself to believe the Nazis could win. I didn't think the Nazi–Soviet pact was anything more than a 'let's see who can cheat whom', with both sides trying to get the advantage over the other. People here were going round saying, so my family told me, that the fascists had got together with the communists. But I knew that was wrong. I knew they were mistaken in thinking that. Of course, that was what the press said too. The papers welcomed the pact because officialdom here was 'Hitlerite' and supported everything the Nazis did. The only reason Spain didn't join in on the side of the Axis was that the country had just come out of a war and was destroyed and near starvation point. Still, Stalin made a mistake in thinking he could deal with Hitler; no one could deal with him, even though it's clear why Stalin tried. The Soviet Union was in no condition to fight then and wanted to preserve its forces for the struggle that was coming. Also, it wanted to annex Poland and the other countries in the east which has always been an aspiration of Russian governments, Tsarist or whatever they are.

The press here never reported the blows the Russians were giving the Germans on the Russian steppes and the Nazi rout. They said nothing about Stalingrad. So it was difficult to get an accurate picture of the war. They were still talking about Nazi victories when the Germans were in full retreat! I had to try to piece together what I could for myself out of what the press reported because I had no contact outside the family, and no one in the family understood these things. Once in a while my wife would bring me an English or American embassy bulletin and those helped. If you were caught reading them in public they'd tear up the bulletin and break your head for you. The German embassy bulletins were all right, you could be seen reading those, but not the Allied ones. There was a lorry driver who used to bring these bulletins to my house – not for me, of course, but for my wife, because he knew we were on 'the other side'. They were typewritten and duplicated, these bulletins, and distributed from the embassies in Madrid to the consulates in Málaga and throughout the country. Officially, since Spain was a non-belligerent, these people couldn't protest, but as I say, you couldn't be caught locally reading an Allied bulletin. . . .

The Nazis were fighting from too small a base; they had too small an area to live on to win the war. Sooner or later they would have to go under economically, especially when they were blockaded as well. That's what I thought then, and I would always look for the bit of news that would point the way to an Allied victory. I would never allow myself to be depressed too long; I would always react by trying to find some good news between the lines. And when the Allies and the Soviet Union joined forces, I said to myself, 'The Nazis have lost, there's nothing they can do now, they're caught on two fronts.' When at last I heard the news of Stalingrad I knew the war was won. In my opinion, Stalingrad broke the Nazis' back, it was the real turning point. And as soon as I thought that the Nazis were going to be defeated, I began to live a blind hope, telling myself that, if the Nazis went, their allies and supporters must be defeated too. I was wrong, and so were a lot of other people. I should have known better! After all, hadn't Britain and France allowed the civil war to be lost by our side? When I say that, I don't mean that I wanted those two countries to intervene directly in our affairs – no, far from it! What I mean is that they should have prevented anyone intervening, they should have ensured that the Germans and Italians got out of Spain and left the war to the Spanish alone. We would have won the war then because all the main urban centres, the large industrial cities, the mass of the working class was with us. Madrid, Barcelona, Bilbao – just those three, not to mention the others. Within thirty-six hours the issue was clear. It might have taken us time, a month or more, to clear up the isolated centres of the military uprising, but it would have been done if Hitler and Mussolini hadn't immediately intervened with planes and arms and men as well. During the course of the war the Italians had an army corps of sixty thousand men here – volunteers they were supposed to be – fighting in divisions like the Black Arrows, the 23rd of March, the Littorio. There is no doubt in my mind, then or now, that the war was won for the nationalists by Hitler and Mussolini. Without their participation, the result would have been the opposite.

Knowing what Britain and France had done at that time – only talk about non-intervention – I hadn't much hope in what they might do at the end of the world war. But now the Soviet Union was one of the Allies and it seemed that something must be done. Britain and the U.S. were against doing anything, Britain more than the U.S. because Churchill in particular was the most conservative of all the Allied leaders and the one who least wanted anything done. Yet I still couldn't believe nothing would happen. A withdrawal of ambassadors, agreed by the United Nations – what difference did that make! An economic boycott which was supposed to be complete – and which let through as much oil and petrol as anyone wanted! Nothing more. I couldn't believe it. My worst despair in the past thirty years was at the end of the war when I saw nothing was going to happen. I kept telling myself, it's all lost, there's no hope of any sort now. I was right in a way, and also wrong. Because in the years since then, owing to the Allied victory, the present regime has evolved too, it has had to because it has to live in the world and the world has been that of the capitalist democracies. If Hitler had won, there would have been no hope at all.

By the end of the war I had moved from my father's house to No. 5 in this street which my wife had rented. The fact of being with my wife and daughter, of having the warmth of a family round me, helped me get over this very bad period. It was much worse when I was alone, shut up in that room in my father's house.

From the start, I decided that if I was going to survive in hiding it meant having no contact with anyone, direct or indirect, other than the smallest number of relatives. If I had got in touch with anyone else, however loyal he was, I wouldn't be here today. None of them would have been able to keep quiet in the end, every man has a wife or brothers or family of some sort, and sooner or later he would have told someone in confidence. That's when the trouble would have started. Women talk, they'll tell anything, and the one would have told another in strictest confidence and she would have told the next in confidence too and so on until the whole village knew. Plenty of people like to say now that they knew I was here all along – well, if they had I wouldn't be sitting here now, I'm sure of that. Even my sister, who lives in San Pedro de Alcántara, was never in the secret although she came here once or twice and I saw her through the keyhole of the door.

After a couple of years the pressure eased a bit. The *camarilla* thought I'd escaped the country or was hidden somewhere else. So it was possible for my wife to start looking for a house. Also, by then my wife had taken on an esparto business and needed help. In our own house I would be able to work. But it took her a while to find a suitable house, there weren't many available since there has always been a shortage here. At last a friend of hers, a woman who lived with her husband and family on a farmstead but kept a house here, said she could rent it. This was No. 5 Calle Capitán Cortes – the name the street has been given, though here it has always been known as the Calle Pilar – and we decided I could move.

Before moving, my wife remembered that this house had a hiding place ready-made. One of the statues from the church had appeared there when the nationalists came in. I wasn't here then but my wife remembered it; it was a hole in the wall much like

my first hiding place. This statue, a Heart of Jesus it was, had disappeared when the church was sacked during the revolution and
had been hidden there. And so I said to myself, well, if it hid the
Heart of Jesus it will hide me too!

The problem now was to move to the new house. How to do it?
It was a distance of about 250 metres along one of the busiest
streets in the village. It would have to take place at night, that
was certain, but it was my wife who had the idea that I should
dress up as an old woman. She brought some of her mother's
things and I got dressed in them as best I could with her help. Her
idea was that she should walk ahead of me down the street and if
she met anyone she would stop and talk to them while I shuffled
by as an old woman might. It was after midnight on a very dark
winter's night when we set off. We were worried that we might
meet someone, and I waited a minute while my wife began to walk
ahead. Then I came out of my father's house. There wasn't anyone in the street. I started slowly, bent over like an old woman,
walking as best I could in the unfamiliar clothes. At any minute,
if I saw someone, I was ready to start to shuffle like a tortoise as
though I couldn't carry the weight of my years. But there was no
one about at all, we met no one the whole way, and so I picked
up courage and came flying to my new home.

The civil war, the famine and the black
market have led to a social revolution in
which, all over Spain, people of energy and
determination have risen out of poverty to
affluence. . . . Like the Industrial Movement
in Victorian England, the black market
offers facilities to hard-working and
enterprising people of all classes to rise in the
social scale.

    – GERALD BRENAN, *The Face of Spain*

JULIANA

As the years went by and there was no end in sight, I no longer expected anything. Sacrifices and hard work and misfortune was all I thought of.

We nearly died of laughing that night at the sight of him dressed up as an old woman. He didn't know how to walk, the skirt kept getting tangled up in his legs and all he could do was hop. Nervous as I was, and my stomach trembling at the thought of the danger, I still couldn't help burst out laughing. He looked a sight! They were old-fashioned clothes with a long, wide skirt, petticoat, scarf and shawl for the head, and a coat. His face was almost hidden under the shawl and the umbrella I'd brought as well. No one could have told him from an old woman if it hadn't been for the way he tried to walk. We'd been waiting several nights to see what was the best way to move him to the new house. That night it started to drizzle – it was winter – and the night was dark. So I said, 'All right, we'll do it tonight because it will be less difficult.'

Now that I had him in my own house and we were all together again as a family, I was much happier. I no longer had the constant anxiety of making two or three trips a day to his father's house with his meals in a basket. I didn't have to be thinking all day, ay! his food, it's getting late. Now I could take his food up to him if someone came to the house on business at meal-time. And when I went on my egg-round I locked the front door with the big old-fashioned key – there was only that one – and took it off with me. That way I knew no one could get into the house while I was gone and that was a weight off my mind. When I came back I used to rattle the key in the door or talk to someone passing in the street to warn him to get out of the way.

By now they were convinced he was in Málaga or in the sierra or somewhere. It had been necessary to wait those two years and more to throw them off the trail. Also it took me a long time to find a house and I was lucky to get No. 5. It was a big house with three rooms, two of them bedrooms and a hiding place already made. The owners used to come there quite often on Sundays and fiestas and they stored their olive oil and things like that in the attics. But they never spent the night there and they always let me know in advance when they were coming because I had the only key. So it wasn't dangerous, he would get in his hiding place when they went upstairs and that was that.

We spent one whole night opening up and clearing out the hiding place where the saint had been kept to make it big enough for him. It had been filled with rubble and we had to deepen it. One night he had to get in there while a *guardia civil* sat almost underneath him. Ay, what a night that was!

I had been out on my egg-round and when I came back a young man who was known as El Muñon stopped me in the street. A very bad reputation he had as a thief. He stopped me and said, 'There's something I want to speak to you about in your house.' 'In my house? What about?' 'Well, I was in the sierra and I saw some men and I think one of them was your husband, though I didn't recognize him, and he asked me to bring him money and bread. . . .' I saw straightaway the trap he was trying to spring, but I let him think I'd been taken in. 'Well, look, you come about ten or half past ten tonight because there's no money in my house at the moment, all I've got is what I've collected from the eggs. But by the time you come I'll have gone out to look for some.'

I came back and told my husband. 'Go to the Guardia immediately and tell them what's happened. It's a plot,' he said. That was what I thought too. I went out and just up the street I met a *guardia* by the name of Desiderio who had a *novia* here and I told him what had happened. 'Go back to your house and I'll go and report it to the corporal immediately,' he said. Very soon he was back with another *guardia* who kept watch in the street while this Desiderio came into the house. My husband had got into his hiding place in the wall and the *guardia* hid behind the door in the same room to hear what El Muñon had to say. Two of them hidden – only the *guardia* didn't know my husband was there! When El Muñon came I said to him, 'Well, *rubio*, what is it you want? What did you say in the street? I didn't hear it too well.' 'Nothing, only that I saw someone in the sierra who asked me to come for money and bread and I think it was your husband, though I didn't recognize him. I think he told me it was him.' Then I said, 'Look here, I've got no one in the sierra, I don't know anything about any of them, do you understand? You've come to rob me, that's what it is.' At that the *guardia* came out from behind the door and caught hold of El Muñon. '*Granuja*, you've come to rob this woman,' he said. The other *guardia* came and they took him off to the barracks. But the plot wasn't over, as I soon found out.

At three in the morning I was called to the barracks to make a statement about what had happened. Because it was the middle of the night and I didn't want to leave her here as though she were alone, I took my daughter with me.

A number of *esparteros*, the men who go to the sierra for esparto, had been rounded up. El Muñon had named them and they were being interrogated to make them confess they had seen my husband among the outlaws in the sierra. One by one they were brought into the armoury of the barracks while we were made to sit outside on a bench. Through the open door we had to watch as each one was interrogated. I never thought I'd live to see what I saw that night. I can't describe it. Imagine a young girl having to watch what went on. And all the time El Muñon was standing there, accusing each of the men. 'This one brought the outlaws money . . . this one bread . . . this one wine . . .', and so on. A worse moment I don't think I've gone through in my life.

While it went on I was thinking only of my daughter and the poor men who were there. I wasn't frightened for myself, because I knew I had been cleverer than them this time. But an innocent child, the innocent men! I suffered for them because of what they were suffering there. And all through that thief El Muñon. He was the only one to whom nothing happened. That confirmed what I thought – it was a plot. If not, he would have been there like the rest of them. But no, all he had to do was to accuse each of the men of being in contact with the outlaws. Of course, the *esparteros* saw the outlaws; they had to go to the sierra nearly every day of their lives to fetch back esparto to earn themselves a living, if you can call it that. But not one of them said he had seen my husband among them.

What they were really trying to do was to get enough evidence against me to put me in jail. They didn't know where my husband was, so they said to themselves, he must be in the sierra. We can get her for giving money to the outlaws and detain her. Once we've got her like that we can get her to talk, to say where her husband is. At the same time we can get money from her. . . . That was how they thought. To implicate me in the outlaws' affairs and then lock me up so that I would give my husband away. It was a very dangerous moment for us, but for them it failed. They couldn't get anyone to confess.

After that they searched my father's house in the country to see if they could find him there. But nothing. In one way this incident helped to protect us. The people thought he couldn't be hidden here if they had ever really thought it. 'If Juliana is ready to go to the Guardia Civil it means that she doesn't know her husband's whereabouts.' That's what they thought and this lifted a big part of their suspicion from me. Having called the Guardia, having had a *guardia* in the house, the people couldn't believe my husband was hidden here. The *guardia* could have searched the house if he had wanted to, couldn't he? Yes, bad as it was, the El Muñon affair made things easier for me in this respect.

It was after this that we decided to make a new hiding place. My husband didn't trust the old one, he thought people might remember it because of the saint. One Holy Week night when the procession was out in the streets and no one could hear because of the noise we built a new one under the stairs. Every Holy Week now I think of that night! I bought him the tools he needed in Málaga, and bricks and plaster. I pretended I needed the bricks to build some rabbit hutches. I was his labourer for the job, mixing the plaster, going out to the patio for bricks and water because he couldn't go out. When I had whitewashed the wall he had built to make a space under the stairs from which he could get into from above, it looked so much part of the place that on all their visits there the owners themselves never realized we had done anything.

Although the new hiding place was safe enough, I couldn't relax. I was always thinking about precautions – much more than he ever did. He was careless, he'd be upstairs in the attic and open the door a crack to look out at the people coming into the house. It led to fights between us. I would come in and I'd see that door slightly open and I'd say, there he is again looking out, and I'd get angry. Often when I went out I'd lock him in the attic so he couldn't open the door. But if I hadn't and I saw it open I'd say to him, 'You've been opening that door again.' 'No, I haven't.' 'Yes, you have, I could see it was open from downstairs. Someone is going to see you one of these days.' 'Ech, what do the people know, they don't know anything.' That's what he always said. Almost every day we'd have a fight over his carelessness. I know that the people who came into the house didn't notice that the door was slightly open, but I could never be sure someone wouldn't come in who was looking for just such a sign. But he wasn't frightened, he had his calm as usual and never thought of such things.

And one day it happened. A young girl came to the house for something for her aunt and just at that moment he opened the door. She saw him as clearly as anything before he shut the door. Immediately I went to the girl's aunt and asked her to lend me a tin. She was the *recovera* I had walked at nights to Málaga with. 'My brother has come from Málaga and wants to take some olive oil back. I haven't got a tin. He's in the house waiting, he was there when your niece came. . . .'

It was even more dangerous when he took to looking out of the window. There was no glass in any of them and he'd open the leaf of a shutter a crack to watch the people in the street. Often, when I came back from somewhere, I'd look up at the house and there would be that tell-tale opening. 'He's at it again, looking out.' And I'd go in and say, 'Who opened the window?' 'Ech, no one can see,' he'd say, 'the people aren't thinking about that.'

All these thirty years he went on looking out of the window. When we got our own house, the one we're in now, I had glass put in the windows and bought net curtains so no one could see in. That was after I'd been out in the street one night and seen him – I was always on the look-out for the smallest sign – with the light on behind looking through the crack in the shutters. The next day I went for the material to make the curtains so as to put an end to all that. During the day then he could have the shutters open and look out through the curtains without people being able to see him. At night, when he had the light on to listen to his radio, he had the shutters closed and I checked them from the street to make sure they didn't let any light out. . . .

He made me go through some times of anger and irritation with all this, we were always fighting about it. 'They're going to see you, I can see you looking out.' Sometimes I was sure someone must have caught sight of him. 'They've seen you.' 'No, no one has seen me.' Always with the same calmness – carelessness it was. He's much more intelligent than I am and yet he doesn't have my caution. I had to protect him against himself – and suffer the consequences of his anger because I couldn't convince him to be more careful. Only last year the neighbours across the way did catch sight of him looking out through a crack in the shutters. But they thought it was my son-in-law. 'Last night,' the neighbour said to me, 'we saw Silvestre looking through the shutters at us. . . .' 'Oh yes,' I said, 'he went up there to get together some esparto plaits and he must have been looking out of the window.' They couldn't really see who it was, all they could make out was that it was a man. Of course, it was him!

Often he wasn't content to look through the curtains, he'd lift them up a bit on one side to see better. He's always liked to look at women going by as long as I can remember. He was the same as a bachelor; he'd stand in the small square at the top of the street and walk back and forth watching the women. He never tired of that, back and forth, back and forth, that was his habit, and he's not much changed now. See a woman go by the door and he's out to have a look at her. Or else he's out in the street himself walking back and forth. He's very curious and that's the truth. Sometimes I used to get fed up with him for all this looking at women, but then I'd say to myself, well, what else has he got to do, if he can take his mind off things with that so much the better. He didn't have much to distract him all these thirty years. But all the same, his carelessness made me go through some bad times.

By this time I had managed to build up my business. There was a great shortage of cloth and material for making dresses after the war. People were making clothes out of old sacks and bits of tarpaulin, the only cloth available came from Melilla and it was very bad and expensive. There was a shop in Málaga called the Costa Azul which was owned by a man who had textile factories in Barcelona. Queues would form up outside the shop every time he sent a shipment from there. On my egg-rounds I had got to know the owner's brother and every week I took him a present of two dozen eggs. Every week, whether a shipment had come or not. When a shipment came I would go up to the head of the queue and knock on the shop window. 'Let her in,' the owner's brother would tell the guard, 'she's the *recovera* of the house.' Once inside I chose whatever I wanted, material enough for ten or twelve dresses, and he packed it up and put it to one side for me to collect after the shop shut. I bought as much as my money allowed because I knew I could get double the price for the material here. If I bought silk at eight pesetas a metre, I sold it here for sixteen; if I bought something at sixteen, I sold it for thirty-two. I always doubled the price. Even then it didn't come out much more expensive than the bad cloth being imported from Melilla. And it allowed me to make some money.

As I've said, my husband left me with fifty pesetas when we parted outside Málaga and he fled for safety. Fourteen of those I spent on sandals for my daughter to replace those that got lost in our flight. I started with thirty-six pesetas – thirty-six, I'll never forget that. At first I didn't know how to support myself and my daughter. I lived with my parents for a couple of months and they helped as much as they could, but they hadn't enough to keep me for long. So I started asking around, asking other *recoveras* how much they made on their eggs. When they told me I said, 'Well, I'll go into that too, one week I'll earn more and another week less.' I spent a couple of days going round the farms collecting eggs and then walked down with the baskets to Fuengirola to take the train to Málaga. All day I was walking round the town with the baskets saying, 'Do you want to buy eggs, do you want to buy eggs?' I had only been to Málaga once before in my life and I was frightened to get too far away from the market. That was the only place I knew and I always asked someone to show me the way back there when I feared getting lost. I made sixteen pesetas that first time, which wasn't bad.

The next week I was three days collecting eggs and when I got to Málaga no one wanted them, everyone seemed to have eggs that day. I came back worn out and fed up. Eight pesetas was all I'd made – for three days in the country and one in Málaga. I decided to try one more time. With the little profit I made I went into a shop and bought hairclips, powder, soap, and when I went to the farms I took them with me so that I could sell as well as buy.

That week I made forty pesetas, and after that I stayed in the business, because I'd come to like it.

There were plenty of *recoveras* in the village then, there always have been, not only women but men too. For some of them it runs in the family, for others, especially at that time, it was a job for those whose husbands had been killed in the war; they used their compensation money to start them off. Those whose husbands had fought on the nationalist side – you didn't get compensation if your husband had died on the other side.

Every time I went for eggs it meant being gone from sunrise to nightfall. I had about fifteen farms to visit and had to walk about fifteen kilometres. I came back at night worn out with my two baskets of twenty or thirty dozen eggs.

Once a week I took the eggs to Málaga. At first I just went to likely looking houses and flats, asking if people wanted eggs. Here and there they would buy some and ask me to come back next week or tell me they had relatives and friends who were looking for eggs. That way I built up a whole number of clients all over the town and it was a day's walking to get to them all. Eventually I built up the business to about 200 dozen eggs a week. Even so, it was a year or more before I had accumulated what in those days of poverty was thought of as a fair bit of money – a thousand pesetas. And I only got that much by not spending anything on myself and working at esparto plaiting in every spare hour.

There were ten or twelve war widows who started at the same time as me, but they didn't last. They'd go to Málaga and they'd buy whatever they fancied for themselves. A tin of tuna fish, one of the good brands, a sausage – or drink a beer or a coffee, without thinking that for every peseta they'd earned they were spending two. I never did that. I'd leave my house with a small loaf and a *tortilla* and that would be all I'd eat because I could see very well that if I made five pesetas and spent two on myself I'd never get any money together. I'd work making plaits until two or three in the morning and be up at dawn to start plaiting again to help pay for food for the house so that I didn't have to touch the money I made on eggs. Yes, there were many others who started in the business with me but there's none who started with as little as me who managed to build up her business as I have. If I had had money to start with we would have had a different future today. Of course, it wasn't the same for those with several children – especially the widows – as it was for me with only one. Most of the widows of men on the left were very badly off, living by plaiting esparto or going to the sierra for esparto or firewood. There were some who had to go out begging for food, especially when they had a large family to keep.

It was with one of these widows that I walked to Málaga all night to smuggle our eggs into the town when the government fixed the price. 1941 or '42 it must have been. We would have been out of business if we hadn't smuggled our eggs, because they cost more here than you could legally sell them for there. This woman's brother loaded the eggs on his mule, we paid him forty pesetas the round trip which was four or five times more than a day labourer's wage here at the time. We'd set out at dusk and arrive before dawn at my sister's house by the Tiro Pichon outside the town. There we'd leave the big baskets and transfer a few dozen eggs into a couple of shopping baskets as though we were carrying food to someone working in the city. That way we could get through the control. We'd be all day going back and forth – after walking the thirty kilometres through the night it was tiring being on your feet all day.

I was nearly a year walking to Málaga at night. Eggs had become very scarce because there was no food for the hens. Only the farmers who grew their own grain could still keep chickens; people in the village had to kill their hens. This was during the 'hunger years' and if there was no food for us, there was even less for animals.

You couldn't buy anything. A little glass, like an anis *copita*, of olive oil cost two pesetas on the black market. A litre of oil at that rate worked out at about sixty pesetas. We couldn't afford that, no one who wasn't very rich could. I remember one day I and the *recovera* I worked with walked down nearly to Fuengirola looking for cabbages. When we found a farmer who had some to sell he charged us twenty-five pesetas for the leaves left over from a couple of heads. Twenty five pesetas for a few leaves! But there wasn't anything else. Then we walked to Osunilla to see if we could buy flour from one of the mills, but no one would sell us any. If you had forty pesetas you could buy a kilo of bread, you could buy as much as you wanted from Alhaurin at that price – but which of us had that sort of money? For myself, I'd cook a few cabbage leaves or a bit of chard with a few broad beans. At the time, a vegetable stew seemed very good but after eating nothing else I hated it so much I couldn't face it again for several years.

Whatever extra I could get I'd give to my daughter. Until the end of the war there had been food enough and she had everything she needed, her barley coffee and milk and that sort of thing. But in the 'hunger years' she had to have the same as the rest of us, a few cabbage leaves or a bit of maize bread. Only very rarely did anyone in the countryside give me a present of food, nor did I ask for it. I went for my business and that was that. Once in a while someone might say, 'Here, take this for your child', and give me a bit of bread. But it was very rare. I didn't go round telling them of my troubles, I kept them to myself. Because there were some who might be willing to share my troubles with them, but there were others who would say, 'Let her look out for herself. He shouldn't have got mixed up in politics, that was their fault.' There are all sorts in this world. So whatever there was to say, I never said it to anyone but kept it to myself.

We never thought any more about eating meat. Bread and oil, those are the two most important things for us. Only the rich ever ate meat, people like us would taste it twice a year, for Christmas and the *feria*. The people didn't eat eggs either, except during Holy Week; they had to sell their eggs to buy other things. And not only during the 'hunger years' but before.

There were some who made a fortune here out of the black market and rationing, two or three who became millionaires. Not from working but from selling on the black market the food that was supposed to be distributed to the people on their rations. Yes, in those times there was everything.

It was a bad blow when the sergeant stopped me going to Málaga. I had to start the business all over again with little more than the thirty-six pesetas I had when I first went into it. But I had contacts and was able to buy on credit. Every week I'd pay off a little bit, twenty-five pesetas in this shop, fifty in that, and this helped me build up the business. Because, if I was three or four weeks paying off what I owed, that was three or four weeks in which I was turning that money over on something else. My father used to say that I was never going to save a peseta because I was always spending the little I'd saved to buy something. But that's what seemed best to me. Money not used is money not earned. What was I going to live on if I didn't use money to make money?

As long as there was something to buy which I knew I could sell, I would buy it. Money has got to earn or else you can't live.

As soon as I started going to Málaga again they put the police onto me. I was followed around for several months. I wasn't aware of it myself, but other people told me in the houses I went to. 'Look, they've come here asking what you are doing. . . .' But that didn't worry me because I knew that as long as I could defend myself in the village, as long as they couldn't pin anything on me here, that was all that mattered.

There was a man in the village who owned a lorry and who used to buy all the esparto plaits to sell in Málaga. Since I knew something about the business I went to the shop in Málaga which was buying from him and said I could supply him for my own account. At that time all the plaits the women here could make could be sold in Málaga because they were needed for making up into donkey harnesses and paniers, mats, baskets for fish and the like. There were many uses for it. I gave him some samples which he asked for and he agreed. So I started buying esparto grass from the people who go to the sierra for it and giving it to the women to plait. If she was quick, a woman could make a length of plait in an hour or so. Even then, there wasn't much money in it, a peseta or two at the most. Every other length paid for the esparto used, so at the end of the day a woman would be left with four or five pesetas, nothing really, but there was no other work for the people to do.

With him hidden here and helping in the esparto I could go about my business more calmly than before. Not that I ever forgot the dangers, but still it wasn't the same as having him hidden in that hole in the wall in his father's house.

At the beginning, in No. 5, I used to think it would be at least another six or seven years before his hiding ended, if it ended at all. But as the years went by and there was no end in sight, I no longer expected anything. I used to pray to all the saints for a safe outcome, but I didn't believe there would ever be one. Sacrifices and hard work and misfortune was all I thought of.

The enormous number of police of all kinds is, of course, one of the things that first strikes the foreigner. In certain districts, where the Reds are active, they give the impression of an army. But the Civil Guards, who form the flower of this force . . . are not what they used to be. The visitor to Andalusia before 1936 will recollect the traditional type – grave, stern and monkish, planted in a hostile village like Knights Templar among infidels, and devoted to the tradition of their service and its code of honour. These men exist no longer. . . .

GERALD BRENAN, *The Face of Spain*

MANUEL

The Guardia Civil's searches were a form of protection for me. There wasn't a week passed without a search of our house. But they weren't looking for me.

It was having space and light around me that made the new house seem like coming out of prison. I had the upstairs floor to myself and I could move around as I wanted. It was a big house built in the old way of stone on two floors, with attic storage space and rooms on the top floor. As long as the door to the street was open that's where I stayed. By placing the shutters in such a way that the neighbours across the street couldn't see in, I could open the window slightly and look out a little. It was there I began to work as I've been doing ever since, bundling and tying up esparto, though in the past two or three years the business has fallen off since now they are making many of the things out of rubber instead. You have to have a routine when you're working and mine was to get up before sunrise and work weighing the esparto to be distributed to the women in the village for plaiting. I'd do that before anyone was around and would be finished by nine when the street door was opened and people started coming in. Then I'd go upstairs and would be tying up the plaits all morning until lunch. Some days there would be as many as twenty or twenty-five bundles to be tied and each bundle was made up of five rolls of plaits. It was a lot of work and it kept me busy without stop until lunch.

At lunchtime my wife would shut the street door and I'd come down to the kitchen for lunch. After that I'd read – newspapers, magazines, a novel, whatever my wife could get hold of for me.

Nothing much, she isn't much of an intellectual, after all, and she hasn't the education to go looking for a bookshop to buy a book. Since she was always likely to be searched, it would have been dangerous if she had been discovered with literature that wasn't to those people's tastes. I should have liked to read about economics and politics, especially Marxism. I would have liked to read *Capital*, to understand it properly for myself, because I have an idea of it from hearing other socialists talk about it. Before the war I used to read all the left-wing political magazines, including a very good one edited by Luis Araquistáin to which many Marxists contributed from all over the world. And I would also have liked to read more poetry, especially Garcia Lorca, Antonio Machado and his brother Manuel. In my opinion Lorca's writings are the height of elegance, especially his poetry about Andalusia. But I hadn't any books, and if I had had, my wife would certainly have burned them. After I fled, she burned everything, a pile of papers and books and things of no danger, but she didn't understand and was frightened. I reproached her for this afterwards, especially since they never searched the house for things like that after I left the village. She even destroyed an album of photographs of myself and my friends at the time of my military service. She put them in a box and hid it in a hole in the wall which she blocked up. When she came to take the box out the photos had disintegrated, become ashes, so I had nothing left. Most of the time I read women's novelettes, things without political or class themes – stupidities really, but even they were better than nothing. I can't sit still, doing nothing, I've always got to have something to occupy me, it doesn't matter what.

I've never needed much sleep and I've never taken a siesta, not even when I was in the army and it was obligatory. So I would read all afternoon or else make the twine for tying up the bundles of plaits or weave baskets out of palmetto. In fact I never had enough time for all the things I wanted to do, and as long as I was busy it kept me from thinking. From seven in the evening until midnight I'd listen to the radio, nothing would keep me from that and I knew the exact hour of every Spanish-language broadcast from the BBC, Radio Paris, Radio Moscow, Peking, and I'd tune in to them all. I'd always listen to the news from Madrid, specially on Fridays after the Council of Ministers' meeting in case there was something new. That's how I heard of the amnesty before anyone else in the house. But that was much later because at No. 5 I didn't have a radio. We couldn't afford one, to have spent two or three thousand pesetas on something that wasn't going to earn us money was more than we could have managed at the time. Today everyone seems to have a TV, but fifteen, twenty years ago a radio was a luxury and almost the only ones were in the bars.

Life was precarious; it was only when this man in Málaga who was in the esparto business helped us that we got under way. He gave my wife credit because he saw that she is honest and keeps her word – which of course she does, because I have instilled it into her. You've got to honour your word to do things the way they've got to be done. Seeing the sort of woman she is, he trusted her with thousands and thousands of pesetas to build up the business until it was the largest in the village.

While my wife was the head of the business outside, I directed it inside. I did all the accounts in rough and my daughter copied them out because from the age of eight or nine she has been able to write well and I could tell her what had to be done. Once in a while, if I had to, I'd fake my writing a bit to do the accounts for the man in Málaga, but that was all right because he didn't know me. But here in the village I never let anything written by me go outside the house because even the cats knew my handwriting here. Later, when we went into building materials, I'd sometimes stand behind the locked door when people came to settle up and as they listed off what they had bought I'd do the calculations in my head. When my wife came through I'd tell her the total and she'd go round and get our daughter to write out the bill.

Ever since I can remember, and probably since time immemorial, the village has lived off esparto. It's a very tough sort of grass, and it has always been one of the few things that those without work have been able to make a peseta or two from. Anyone could go to gather it, it grows wild in the sierra. In the forties and fifties, however, when no raw materials were being imported under the government's autarchy policy, and the country was supposed to live on what it produced, the esparto was needed to make clothes and sacks and that sort of thing. A factory was set up in Algeciras to process the fibre. It was then that the picking of esparto on government or private property was forbidden as all the esparto was supposed to be kept for the factories. So, very soon, there was legal and contraband esparto. A few poor people trying to earn enough to keep alive would go out to the sierra and smuggle esparto back to the village, a bundle or two at a time. This esparto was immediately distinguishable from the 'legal' esparto because, being fresh, it was green. The esparto that came with its official permit from Málaga was white and dry. To work esparto properly it has to be dry because otherwise there's a shrinkage later, but it was impossible to dry the contraband stuff since it requires a lot of room to be spread out and turned in the sun. So the contraband stuff was immediately recognizable when the Guardia Civil came on their searches.

At No. 5 they came very frequently – not looking for me but for esparto. There was a corporal in command of the detachment at that time who made esparto his speciality, so to speak. Before him, none of them had bothered – they were more concerned with the outlaws in the sierra – and after him none of them bothered either. It was just this corporal, Alonso, who went after esparto. He didn't bother about politics or things like that, he never questioned my wife about me or anyone else, but through the esparto business he put on the pressure. Any poor man caught bringing esparto back had it confiscated. So much esparto was confiscated that one year the town hall told my wife to put in a bid and they sold it all to her at auction.

All the houses which dealt in esparto were always being searched, but as ours was the biggest ours was searched most often. Frequently my wife knew in advance. Very often, if she didn't feel like it, she'd lock the door and go out somewhere on business so they couldn't get in. The Guardia would go away then. There was nothing they could do about it because in fact they required a warrant to be allowed to search a private person's house. Knowing this my wife opened the door when she wanted, not otherwise. If the door was open they would come in without asking, though they would usually stay downstairs and chat to begin with. While they passed the time of day with my wife, I had time to get into my new hiding place, at the top of the stairs. Or rather the entrance was at the top because I had cut through the corner of the slab where the stairs joined the floor and built up a hollow brick wall from below so that I could get down and hide in a sort of compartment under the stairs. There had always been a compartment there, what I in fact did was to partition it with a new wall so that the rear part became my hiding place. I made a wood cover painted to look like bricks which fitted exactly into the space which I had to get down. I could put the cover on by myself if I had to from inside, but if there was time my wife would come and cover the whole thing with straw which she used for packing the eggs she took to Málaga, so that the wood slab was even less visible. Since the slab was in a corner it never had to be stepped on and there was no danger of its being discovered as hollow. I made a wood ladder so I could get up and down inside because the compartment was quite deep and, being small, I couldn't reach the cover from inside. Many a time I've been in there under the stairs as the Guardia went up and down. They weren't coming to look for me, they certainly never thought I was there. But even if they had they wouldn't have found me, I believe. When we left there and bought this house, No. 11 in the same street, I demolished the wall and left everything as it had been.

It was the business with El Muñon which made me build the new hiding place. What a bad moment that was – for my wife and daughter especially. It was the time when the Guardia were trying to hunt down all the people in the sierra.

At that time there were outlaws in all the sierras, especially in the Sierra Morena and the Sierra Nevada where there were several bands, and also in the mountains round Ronda.[2] Some were political, yes, others were fleeing for different reasons. I can't say what happened in other places but here, from what I've heard, there were at the height about fifteen or twenty men in the sierra. The mountains immediately round here, I mean. Most of them came from Alhaurin and Coin and they were led by a man from the former whose nickname was Mandamas. I knew him from before the war because his sister was married to a blacksmith here. A beautiful woman she was, too. Mandamas used to come here often to see her, and he sorted himself out a *novia* in the village too. He was always in trouble, he had been in jail before the war for robbery or something, and at the time of the revolution he joined the FAI. His only idea then was to go from one place to another liquidating people. That was the trouble with the anarchists, they'd let anyone into the FAI to get hold of a gun and 'kill fascists' as they said. He led a group one night from Alhaurin and they shot one of the landlords here. After that I never left the town hall at night and the next time he and his band came with a list of fourteen they wanted to shoot I turned them out of the village.

Mandamas fled to the sierra when the nationalists took Alhaurin. He had a few of his band with him there. But not all the outlaws were of that sort. There was one from Fuengirola I heard of who hadn't taken part in the revolution or anything like that but who fled to the sierra because of trouble with his wife. She turned out a whore and he said to himself, kill her or leave her, that's all that's left. A purely personal matter, looking for death. He found it in a watercourse a few hundred metres outside the village here, on a bit of land a foreigner has now bought. He and another man from Coin, who was also in the sierra for personal reasons, were ambushed and shot there by the Guardia Civil. They were the last of the band and were killed in the early fifties.

The others were betrayed. A *guardia* acted as a double agent and went into the sierra as though to join them. At that time that was all the Guardia were concerned about, liquidating the outlaws. Not that the latter ever killed anyone, but they robbed food from the farms. Many of the peasants were hostile to them for that, but there were enough who kept one eye closed for their own safety's sake and took them to their houses and fed them. There was one in particular who lived right at the foot of the sierra and who used to come here with his horse to load up with provisions. This was when food was scarce and there was rationing. The food was for them, of course. The outlaws never harmed him, he was a man who knew what was good for him. But another, who informed the Guardia Civil that a neighbour had sheltered the outlaws, had his house burnt down and was beaten nearly to death.

Mandamas was betrayed by an old woman, I've heard. The Guardia had her number and one time when he came to her farmstead looking for food she tipped them off. They surrounded the house and she shouted out. Mandamas realized what was happening. '*Granuja*, you've sold me,' he yelled and shot her dead, then turned his revolver on himself. By the time the Guardia entered the house he was dead.

During Alonso's time here he didn't concern himself with political matters. He was concerned only, as I've said, with esparto. There wasn't a week passed without him sending a patrol to search our house. Since they didn't come looking for me, their searches were a sort of protection; they made people think I couldn't be here. I never really feared they would find me, my hiding place was too good and moreover they didn't go upstairs very often. But if they had? Well, in the early years they would have taken me off to jail and those people would have come running with their *denuncias* and that would have been that – I wouldn't have got as far as a court martial in Málaga probably. Later, after eight or ten years' hiding, by which time those who held grudges were out of the way, it would have been jail, or rather the death sentence commuted to thirty years' prison which carries no remission.

Until the day before the amnesty, if they had caught me I could have been denounced and gone to jail. They would have let me out if it had been that close but. . . . After all those years in hiding, though I knew I would no longer be shot, I came to fear jail even more than shooting. The long-drawn-out torture of it and the almost certain death for me. I don't think I could have survived it and it was for that reason that I remained in hiding, even when I knew the worst was over. To have survived so long only to spend the rest of my life in jail – that was more than I could imagine being able to stand. And it only needed the slightest bit of carelessness and I might have been found. Supposing the Guardia had seen me on one of their searches, they were bound to detain me; it would have been part of their job. They couldn't have done more than detain me until a *denuncia* was presented and if one hadn't been they would have had to release me. They couldn't lay a charge against me themselves because, in cases like this, they could only arrest someone on the basis of a *denuncia* – but I was sure enough that there were people in the village always ready for that. That was the trouble, the government's latitude in allowing people to denounce in these sort of matters. It was a latitude which allowed people to go mad and commit horrors, even for personal reasons. That was why there was danger for me to the end, even if less than in the early years because things had changed, but danger all the same.

A short time after I came out of hiding, my wife met a *guardia* in Málaga who had been stationed here for many years and was a friend. He was a good man and he congratulated my wife on the news. 'And to think of all the times we searched your house,

Juliana! You paid us back well!' And then he said: 'What a position I would have been in if I'd discovered him there. I'd have had no choice but to detain him because otherwise I would have run the risk of jeopardizing my career.'

I don't believe the Guardia were interested in looking for me. It was the *camarilla*'s pressure in the first years that made them act. A lot depends on the commander of the post, there are good ones and others who aren't so good. The corporal who came after Alonso, for example, was completely different from him. When he first came, the watchmen employed by the owners to guard the sierra came to him and complained that their esparto was being stolen. He told them to tell the owners they should employ better watchmen because it was their fault if it was being stolen. 'I'm not here to guard esparto, I'm here to catch criminals and thieves. I'm not going to take an armful of esparto from some poor man whose misfortune it is to have to go to the sierra to earn enough to eat. . . .' And that was the end of the esparto business here.

The same corporal met my son-in-law in Málaga a month or two ago. Every time he goes to Málaga from wherever he's stationed now, he makes for the bar by the Málaga market where the Mijeños go. And he said to my son-in-law, 'I always had the idea your father-in-law was in the house because Juliana kept the doors shut every time I went there. But, *hombre*, it didn't make any difference to me one way or the other. My job is to catch criminals, not to hunt down people for their political ideas, least of all honourable men. They would have had to oblige me by force to search for your father-in-law.'

This corporal was here in the late fifties or early sixties, by which time most of the old guard were dead and the pressures weren't what they had been in the early forties. And the Guardia know very well the dirt there is in village politics and they don't want to get mixed up in it more than absolutely necessary.

Still, there was one other reason why the Guardia weren't really out to find me, and that was Garcia. He was here at the most critical moment for me and was the only one of them who actually knew me. He knew that I had fled the village before the nationalists entered and he always maintained that I hadn't come back after the war. He owed his neck to me and he was returning the favour I'd done him. During the revolutionary period after the military uprising people went from here to Málaga to try to get him. The people hated him for the way he had acted here before. But they couldn't find him. I knew where he was and a word or two from me to the Committee of Public Safety in Málaga would have had him and a couple of others shot. But I never did anything. He used to say so himself. 'As far as Manuel Cortes is concerned, we've got nothing against him because he behaved well when the others came looking to shoot me. He never did anything.' That was what he said. He had known the village a long time and because of that his words carried weight with the sergeants who commanded the post. Just as, I should say, the words of the people who held grudges against me had the opposite effect. Whatever they said, everyone repeated. If they had said, 'This man Manuel mustn't be harmed, he's a good man', everyone would have repeated, 'A good man he is', and wouldn't have wanted me found and shot. And when they said the contrary, the contrary it was. That is what *caciquismo* really means, a tyranny over the people and village. They were *caciques* of the sort that existed here and everywhere in Spain until the Republic, the sort I had known all my youth, each with his *camarilla* round him doing his bidding and tyrannizing the village. Poverty, illiteracy and *caciques* – that's all we knew in villages like this when I was young.

JULIANA

Some days I could almost manage
not to think of our situation, other days
I thought of nothing else. You could never
tell where the danger was coming from
next. . . .

Above all else, I was always worried that he might fall ill. That would have been the worst thing that could have happened. I used to think, if he falls sick and is on the point of dying, the only thing I can do is go and confess to the priest. Who else? Because if he had died here they would have got hold of me and said, 'You let him die without calling a doctor or confessing', and put me in jail. But if I had confessed to the priest the responsibility wouldn't have been entirely mine.

Once in a while when we talked about it and I said, 'If this happens there's only one solution,' he'd say, 'I want no confession.' He wouldn't have absolution while he was conscious. I'm not in favour of confession either, but what else was there to do? Any other way the risk would have been too great and we were taking enough risks as it was. But he was worried too that if I confessed and then he got better, there would be one more person in the know. It didn't trouble him if he had to be buried in unhallowed ground because he hadn't had absolution. 'What do I care where they bury me once I'm dead? It's all the same to me whether I'm buried in the cemetery or under an olive on a terrace,' he always said. That was all right for him, but for the rest of us, his family? He would have had to give up his foolishness if it came down to that.

If he had fallen ill I'd have tried one way or another to get him to Málaga in secret. But believe it or not he was really ill only twice and today he's a lot healthier than I am, except for his teeth.

Once he caught 'flu so badly and had such a high fever that for several days he couldn't eat anything. I went to Málaga to buy medicine for him. I pretended it was for a brother of mine. 'Why don't you take him to the doctor?' the pharmacist asked. 'Ay! he's such a cranky old bachelor and we live in the country and you know what these men are like, he doesn't want me to call the doctor.' I told him more or less his age and then he prescribed penicillin and suppositories. Penicillin was the only thing that did any good and brought down his fever.

I had to give him the injections in his backside. I bought needles and a syringe in a pharmacy in Málaga. There was no problem about that, plenty of people give themselves injections. But it used to frighten me having to give him one. The needle scared me. If it had been in the arm, he could have done it himself. But in the backside. . . . He'd get the needle ready, sterilize it and prepare the syringe, because he knows all about that from being a medical orderly in the war. I'd take the needle and then I'd get frightened, I'd say, 'This is going to hurt a lot', and he'd say, 'Come on, do it quick.' I'd push the needle in and once it was in I'd push it a bit more; it's better if you can do it in one go because there's less bleeding, but I was too scared. Once the needle was in I still had to fix the syringe onto it. Sometimes my hands trembled so much that the liquid spilt and he'd start going on, 'Ech, you don't know how to do it', and I'd say, 'I know I don't, but what do you want me to do?' If the syringe gets air in it then the liquid won't go in at all, it comes back out. That used to make him annoyed. But little by little I learnt how to do it, and in all these years an injection I gave never became infected. Not a single one. That's more than you can say for the best of *practicantes*.

If he didn't get ill more – there was only one other time, it was terrible, but for my daughter we would have been lost – it was because he took good care of himself. He liked to smoke and all the smoking made him cough a lot. It used to frighten me because I always thought someone would hear. There was only a thin wall between our bedroom and the house next door and when the neighbours coughed we could hear them. Every time he coughed at night I'd wake and start to cough too. That way, my coughing mixed with his and the neighbours didn't hear his alone. Well, one day he realized the smoking was doing him harm and he gave it up. He had a pile of tobacco on his table, every time I went to Málaga I had to buy him a supply, and he said, 'I'm not smoking any more.' That was that, he never smoked again. The same with the glass of *aguardiente* he used to take every morning before breakfast. When he saw it was upsetting his stomach, he said, 'Don't bring me any more, I don't want it.' He had a lot of control over himself, he was very self-willed like that. If he hadn't been he would have been a lot worse off from the point of view of getting ill.

His health was preserved by being in the warm, by not having to go out in the cold and the rain or the heat any time. Each morning in winter I'd see to it that he had the brazier lit upstairs and that his room was warm. On the mornings when I went to Málaga I had the charcoal broken up into small bits and the kindling wood ready in the patio by six. By the time I left at eight the brazier was burning and I had his food ready for him to heat up at noon. I didn't overlook anything, there was nothing he lacked. And if ever I got a cold he'd worry about catching it from me. 'Ah, you'll give me your cold,' he'd say, so I'd tell him he'd better sleep in the bed upstairs and I'd sleep alone. For me there was always some cure or other, but for him there mightn't be one. . . .

Yes, he lacked nothing, I made sure of that – and yet he wanted everything his way! It couldn't always be, I had to cross him sometimes, it was for his good. He used to get annoyed when my daughter's girl friends came to visit her in the house; it meant he had to stay shut in the room upstairs. 'What do they have to come for?' he'd say. 'But, *chiquillo*,' I'd say, 'they've got to be able to come to keep people from getting suspicious. What will the people say if our daughter never has anyone come to the house?' Another quarrel! In all these thirty years we've been through everything. 'This woman is always crossing me.' 'But no, I'm not crossing you, and that's the truth, we've got to face realities, that's all.'

He knew it was for his good, his safety. But that's what happens with men. All his anger would fall on me. I felt for him, I knew he was bored and fed up – so many years shut in without being able to talk to anyone but us. But I got fed up and worn out too. Not everyone would do what I was ready to do, not every woman was ready to make the sacrifices I made. And today, as people are, even less. But I had to put up with it, it was my duty to do so. If I hadn't, if I had undone what had been done – well, he wouldn't have got through these thirty years, would he?

When he got in one of his moods I'd try to calm him down. He'd bite our heads off, my daughter's and mine, and there was nothing you could say to put it right. It wasn't our fault he had to stay hidden, it was his for coming back here in the first place. When things are all right he's very good, but when they're not – uf! – there's no one who can say anything to him. That's how he has always been. He'll get very angry and bite your head off and five minutes later it's as though nothing had happened. But even at the worst moments of despair he never thought seriously of trying to leave.

It was I who always wanted to leave. I wanted to sell up everything here and buy a house in Málaga or somewhere else and throw people off the trail. He didn't want to. 'What if things don't work out for us in the new place, we may be discovered. Here we've got things organized.' He didn't have confidence. I was quite prepared. I'd have started another business going. This was after the first few years when there wasn't such danger any more, but when it seemed there was no end to his being hidden. Life in a town is different from being in a village, in a town there's less curiosity, the people don't talk as they do here. Really I wanted to move most of all in case he fell ill; it would have been easier to get him to hospital. A long illness, how could we have managed that here?

I knew things were a bit easier in a town because there was a man, a relative of mine, who was in much the same situation as him. Just about everybody in the neighbourhood of Málaga where he lived knew about him. I don't know what he had been, in the CNT or the militia or something; anyway, they were looking for him. His wife had him hidden in a house, but not like my husband here; he went out into the patio and that sort of thing. If there was danger the neighbours used to warn his wife and no one ever said a word to the police.

He was the brother-in-law of my sister's husband and after a while his wife bought a house in a village somewhere and he disappeared. She must have managed to get him a false identity card. When she died he came back to Málaga. I used to see him selling tobacco outside the bar where the Mijeños go. But I never greeted him because he behaved as though he were someone else, he had changed his name. Once my brother-in-law met him in the street and greeted him. He denied him! Imagine that, to be as hard-faced as to deny yourself to your brother-in-law! But that's what he did.

It was about this time that Alonso came here. There was a man in the village who had an esparto business like ours. The esparto that was confiscated from the men who went to the sierra to pick it and were caught bringing it down ended up – indirectly – with him. That way he got his esparto on the cheap. Everyone knew what was going on, but all the same Alonso ordered searches for contraband esparto in houses like mine. Once a week at least there'd be the cry, 'The Guardia are coming, the Guardia are coming.' Usually I had been warned in advance by one of the *guardia's* wives and I'd throw all the green esparto over the wall into my neighbour's patio or hide it under a pile of firewood in ours.

It went on for about seven years. Sometimes if I was going to

Málaga I'd tell my daughter, 'If they come today you tell them that I'm not here and no one is allowed into the house. If they catch you with the door open you say, "My mother isn't at home, and as she isn't at home she told me no one is to come in and search."' While she was alone they had no right to enter, since she was a minor; the head of the family had to be present.

Many's the time when I knew they were coming and I'd lock the door and go off into the countryside with the key in my pocket. Then there was nothing they could do, they'd come to the door and my daughter would say, 'My mother isn't here, she's gone for eggs', and that would be it. They always went away.

One day, though, they caught me by surprise; I hadn't had any warning. Alonso must have got the idea in his head that morning and acted on it straightaway. I had a lot of plaits lying in the patio to dry. The Guardia came to the door and I said, 'Where are you going?' and they said, 'To search for plaits.' 'There'll be no searching my house today,' I replied. 'You can tell the corporal that to search my house he'll have to give the order that so-and-so's house – and I said the name straight out – will have to be searched first. When you've searched his house then you can search mine. But not before.' I'd had enough. This other man's house was full of contraband esparto, the same as mine. But they never searched his place. No, it was time they left us all alone or searched his house too. The *guardia* looked at me and said, 'Yes, it's the truth, you're doing the right thing. I'll tell the corporal that's what you've said.' 'You tell him,' I answered. 'Why is my house always being searched and the other not?'

The next day I was in Málaga when the corporal stepped out of a car he was getting a ride in. He put on a very serious look. 'I'm very annoyed with you,' he said. 'Why?' 'Because yesterday you didn't let your house be searched and you told them that first they would have to search the other house.' 'Well,' I replied, 'if one is to be punished the other should be punished too. Just because he's one of the big men in the village is no reason. . . .' 'No, no, no,' he said, 'you should have let yourself be fined and later I would have cancelled it.' 'No, señor. What one *guardia* does another cannot undo. If the Guardia yesterday had denounced me you couldn't have lifted the *denuncia*. Moreover, if you are going to fine me you had better fine him as well, as long as he is buying esparto from where I get mine.' Every time he tried to get round this I came back to the same point. 'You won't search my house and fine me unless you search his house and fine him.' I told him to his face. There was nothing he could reply. He knew that what was going on wasn't right. I wanted to have it out straight with him so he could see I meant it. This was a matter of the law and the law applied as much to the big men as to me.

He never had the other's house searched, but he gave up sending his men to my house. He saw that the affair was serious and that I was fed up. It wasn't many days before he came round to my house as though nothing had happened asking me to bring him something or other from Málaga the next time I went!

Every Christmas it was my custom to make a present of a chicken to the commander of the post. Not out of fear for my husband's safety, but – during the time of the esparto searches especially – for a bit of peace and calm. I had to be careful about giving presents, otherwise they might have got suspicious and said I was acting out of fear. I had always to make them believe I was strong, not afraid, to have shown fear would have been very bad. They would have said, 'She's giving presents because she's afraid and if she's afraid it's because she's got something to hide.' I had to defend myself against them by strength.

Knowing the village the way I do, I always agreed with my husband about one thing – the fewer people who knew, the better for us. That's why after a time I gave his cousin to understand that he had left the village. Not that we didn't trust her, he and she had been brought up like brother and sister by their foster-parents, she would never have talked. But her daughters were growing up and had *novios* and I was frightened that the secret would be discovered because of them. So I told her I had managed to get him a safe-conduct and he had left because that way he could be freer. It was at the time when I was trying to arrange false papers for him to escape – the only time he ever tried to leave. But it failed, the man who was going to get the papers for us was killed. Anyway, his cousin made out that she believed me and from then on she never once asked after him. Not once, though she often came to the house for this or that; for her it was as though he were dead. She must have told her daughters he'd gone, which was what I wanted. If they had told their *novios*, we might have been lost – a *novio* is nothing, the couple could fall out and then there'd be a young man in the know who had no reason for not giving away the secret.

As I started to make a bit of money the people in the village began to say, 'Of course, Juliana has got some money together. Her husband sends it to her from abroad. . . .' The way people talk in a small village like this! To some of them when they asked, I replied that I had once had a letter from him from France, but after that I hadn't heard any more. And to others I'd say, 'Of course he is', when they went on about the people saying he was sending me money. I'd tell each one whatever I thought was good for them to hear, depending on what they asked. 'He left Valencia on a ship with his captain for France at the end of the war,' I'd tell some, and to others I'd say, 'Perhaps he managed to get to Gibraltar or Africa, because a lot of ships went there.' I didn't care what I told them as long as it threw them off his trail. Not all of them believed it; there were plenty who thought he was hidden in Málaga or staying at his sister's in San Pedro de Alcántara. Once someone in Málaga said to me, 'Your husband has been seen. I don't know exactly where, but round Campanillas, working in a barber's shop.' 'Ah,' I said, 'then you know more than me. That's very good if he's alive.' Another time someone in the village said, 'Your husband has got a barber's shop set up in Málaga and when you go there it's to see him.' 'Ay, he's living there, is he? and without my knowing it!' Today everyone has their story about him, how they saw him in this place or that, how they knew he was here. Well, none of them knew where he was and he's been here all these past thirty years, and that's the truth. Gossip, village talk! The things people invent, it's beyond belief the lies some of them make up.

The people were envious of me, of the money I'd got; they talked about me because I was a woman alone. They have a bad way of thinking, bad tongues. But they could say what they liked about me, I've suffered enough, all I cared about was that they didn't get suspicious and think about him. My conscience was easy, thanks to God, and if anyone wanted to single me out or hate me, I took no notice. My life was full enough without bothering about what people said. What more should I worry about than the tragedy of having to go to Málaga, to the countryside, of living in fear that they were coming for him – the rest didn't concern me. When I knew they were jealous, I always said to myself, well, never mind, God is above everything and everyone must act according to his conscience in God's sight. For the rest, I didn't bother.

A Guardia Civil sergeant whom I knew and who used to come here quite often said to me once, 'You know, people in Mijas are very jealous of you. Well, better jealousy than charity is what I say. Because if they were charitable it would mean you were in a bad way. . . .' He was right, better envy than charity any day. They never thought of the hard work and sacrifices that made me my money. In front of my daughter the people would say, 'Yes, Juliana has a lot of money. Where can it come from?' And my daughter replied, 'It's cost my mother a lot of hard work to make what she has and, thanks to God, we're all working here.' That was the truth because not only I and my husband but she also worked, as young as she was. Inside the house it was my husband who was in charge, it was he who had the ideas about expanding our business, he thought everything out very well. I wouldn't take a decision without consulting him, he was the head of the family even if in secret. My daughter plaited esparto and the money we saved to buy her a scarlet dress she had as a child. That was in those early years when we were badly off; later she didn't have to work for a living. Outside the house it was I who had to do everything. God at least gave me the luck of being healthy and having the strength to do what had to be done. Not everyone in the world is capable of that.

Some days I could almost manage not to think of our situation, other days I thought of nothing else. You could never tell where the danger was coming from next, like the time when El Muñon suddenly appeared. Or the day the house nearly caught fire and with him hiding upstairs. There was never a day in the past thirty years when I could be sure we were safe and that there was nothing to worry about.

But the worst days of all were the two of El Muñon and the fire. If one was bad the other was worse. It happened one summer when it was so hot I decided to cook outside in the patio. I put up a shelter of brushwood to give shade; cooking indoors was too hot and the firewood made the house so dirty. One noon I left my daughter to fry the tomatoes and things for a soup. Instead of taking the frying pan off the fire before putting in the vegetables, she threw them into the hot oil. She was only eight or nine at the time, poor thing. Immediately a flame flew up and caught the brushwood roof.

You've never seen anything like it, everything was so dry that in an instant the whole thing was alight. We cried out and people came running. The patio was full of people shouting and bringing buckets of water from wells and the fountain. There was no water piped in the houses as there is now. Everyone was throwing buckets up at the brushwood, which did no good at all. I could see the flames going into the small attic window and I was nearly out of my mind. None of the water was putting the fire out. I could only think of him upstairs and of the flames going in the window and of the roof which would catch alight. Sooner or later someone was going to think of going up to the attic to throw water down from above or to put the fire out if it caught the wood beams of the roof. Everything was so dry it would have taken only a spark to set them alight. Ay! Just at that moment this man – the owner's brother, it was – came running and saw what to do. He got hold of the posts of the shelter and pulled them down so that the whole thing collapsed and lay burning on the ground where we could put it out.

When at last the people had gone and we were alone I ran to see my husband. He was as white as the wall of the house with fear, and no wonder. If the fire had taken hold everything would have been lost. We were all so sick with fear that none of us ate anything that day. I never put up another shade. We'll asphyxiate of heat and the house can get dirty, I thought, anything rather than go through another day like that.

MARIA

All my childhood I lived with fear. . . .

It was late at night and my mother picked me up from the bed and took me in her arms. I was about four years old, the same as my youngest daughter today. I didn't know what was happening.

My mother carried me to my grandfather's house and when we got there I saw my father for the first time I can remember. He took me in his arms and kissed me. It's the first memory I have in life. It was the night he came back to the village, and I can't remember more than that I saw him and he kissed me. Then I suppose I fell asleep in my mother's arms.

I couldn't remember any more what he looked like, when three years later he came to live with us in No. 5 and I saw him again it was as though it was for the first time.

I used to see my mother preparing food and putting it in a basket and taking it to grandfather's house, but I couldn't explain to myself who it was for. She had put so much fear into me that I had forgotten he was there. I knew something was going on but I didn't know what. My mother would often take me with her to my grandfather's house. 'Let's go and have a look at the cat, it's got kittens now,' she'd say – and, of course, it wasn't for me to play with the kittens but so that my father could see me. I never saw him. Sometimes I'd get bored and say, 'Let's go home now', and my mother would say, 'No, we'll stay a bit longer', and I'd have to wait. Why does she want me to go to grandfather's house all the time? I'd ask myself, but I couldn't discover the reason.

My mother was always talking to me about my father, as though he were abroad or somewhere, never that he was here. She'd tell me, 'Daughter, pray to our Lord that nothing bad happens to papa, pray to Him to keep him from harm.' Every time I saw a statue of a saint or a holy picture I would get down on my knees to pray for my father. . . . I did it so often that my friends used to laugh at me, but I went on all the same. My mother had instilled it into me – and my grandmother, too, she was very religious. 'You must always be praying to the Lord that no harm comes to your father.'

When I was about seven my father came to live with us. That was a happy moment and also when fear became a part of my life. Before he came my mother gave me a long talking to. She said he was going to come, that we were going to see him, that he was in the house. She put real fear into me, she kept on saying that I mustn't tell anyone or else the Guardia would come and he would be killed and they'd lock us up. I remember saying I'd never talk and then she took me to see him and he caught me up in his arms as I'm holding my daughter now and kissed me. I knew straight-away that he was my father, I wasn't surprised. Although I couldn't remember his face, yet I recognized him – perhaps after all I remembered something from having seen him when he came back. I don't know how I knew him, but immediately I recognized him.

Up to then I hadn't been frightened. I'd been a child, playing, eating, sleeping like any five- or six-year-old. But from that moment on, all I knew was fear. My mother was always warning me, 'If anyone asks, you don't know anything, you don't know anything. . . .' I was so full of fear that when I saw anyone even looking at me I thought they were going to stop me and ask questions. The Guardia's barracks were right by the school and at playtime I was too frightened to go out into the playground in case they questioned me. And when I saw them coming along the street to search our house I'd get so nervous that often I'd vomit. A trembling inside that went straight to the stomach and I'd feel so ill that I thought I was dying. It's the same now, I still get sick that way, my stomach won't hold anything down.

I lived with this fear all my childhood. Of course, I was happy to know that my father was in our house, that we were all to-gether as a family. But at the same time I could never talk about him. There were ten or twelve other girls in the school whose fathers had died in the war and, like them, I used to feel pain when other girls talked about what they were going to do with their fathers, the places their fathers were going to take them and that sort of thing. And I had to keep quiet about him. Sometimes it seemed worse having him here and not being able to say any-thing than if he had been away. But I never talked.

I couldn't bring friends home from school, my mother didn't like it. I had one very close friend in particular and she used to come home now and again with me. Then my mother would say, 'Don't bring her here so much, your father is shut up enough as it is.' I'd have to make excuses why she couldn't come, I'd tell her I had to work helping my mother, anything to keep her away. Though she and the others used to get fed up with me, it was my mother they really blamed. 'We can't go to Maria's house because Juliana complains so much,' they'd say.

The house was small and in bad condition; with the wood floor-boards you could hear the slightest movement from upstairs. So if I brought anyone home it meant my father couldn't move. Instead, I went to my friends' houses or to my grandmother's. My mother was always saying, 'Yes, you go to your grandmother's or to your friends' to play.'

I loved school. I was like my father. A day that broke raining would find me on the doorstep ready to go, just waiting for the rain to stop. My mother would grumble about my going off in the wet and my father too, but there was nothing that could keep me back.

There were plenty of girls who never went to school at all because they didn't have clothes or shoes and also because there weren't enough classrooms. As it was, there were forty or more girls in a class. I was one of the lucky ones. I learnt to read in three or four months, though learning to write came a lot harder; and as for arithmetic – uf! that was always a problem. My father had tried to teach me to read a bit before I started school, showing me the letters. But when I made a mistake he'd say, 'Ah, you're no good, you're too slow', and I got fed up. He gave it up. He didn't have a lot of patience for teaching, no more than I've had with my children!

As soon as I could read I went up into the older girls' class. I learnt very little there because the mistress was away a lot of the time. She'd go for a week to Málaga or somewhere and she'd leave us in charge of some woman who wasn't a teacher, who knew nothing. There wasn't anything that could be done about it. If a teacher wanted to go off she could put someone in her place and that was that. I had another teacher whose husband was transferred to Seville and she went with him and was gone a couple of years without another teacher taking her place. She gave her job to a woman here who hadn't studied any more than any of us, who couldn't teach us anything. It was a complete waste of time going to school then.

At last my mother got fed up and spoke to the teacher in the next class who allowed me to move up into her class. She was here permanently and she was the only one I really learnt something from. I started with her when I was about ten and stayed until I left school just before my fifteenth birthday.

Religious history and catechism, those were the main subjects we learnt every day. Every afternoon we spent learning the catechism while we sewed. The mistress would read it out and we repeated it after her. Every Thursday morning the priest came to the school and we had to repeat the catechism from memory. That day we had no play-time. After school the same day we had to go to church for more catechism and talks by the priest. I'd escape when I could, like many of the girls. The mistress got cross and asked me why I didn't attend, and I'd tell her my mother had to go to the countryside and I had to stay in the house. 'How is it that your mother has always to go to the countryside on a Thursday?' she'd ask then. Other times the priest would stand in the square and catch us. I'd get home late and my mother would grumble because she had had to wait for me before being able to leave the house.

Sometimes, when I came home, my father would tell me about all the books he had read on religious history and the Church, and that he knew all about it – Jesus Christ was a man who had been born and who had died, and that was that. But I had so much in my head from what we were taught at school and from what my grandmother kept telling me that I didn't really believe him. That's why I'm more of a believer than he is. He'd tell me what he thought but he'd never stop me going to mass. He'd laugh at me and other times he'd get irritated and say, 'Look at you, to think that a daughter of mine should have turned out like this', but he never stopped me. As a child I quite liked to go to mass, but even so I didn't go often enough to please the teacher. 'Look at you,' she'd say, 'you've got the best marks of anyone in school, but the worst of all in religion. All the others haven't a fault for attendance and you. . . .' I'd tell her my mother hadn't let me go to mass because it was raining, which was true enough as a rule. 'Going to mass in the rain – put it out of your mind,' my mother would tell me. But the others went, whether it was raining or not. During the morning class the mistress used to announce, 'Maria Cortes didn't attend mass today.' At the end of the year I had the worst marks of anyone for attendance and the best for all other subjects.

My father could have taught me a lot if he had wanted to, but he hadn't the patience. Except one time, I remember, a Sunday it was, when he wouldn't let me go out of the house until I had learnt my seven times table. Sunday – the only day my mother would let me go out! I couldn't get it, each time I thought I had it and turned the board over to repeat it to him I forgot it. I got angry but I wouldn't show anger to him, I kept it inside me. At last I got it right and he let me go.

But usually he'd get upset and start to grumble. Instead, when my mother went out and the street door was locked, he'd tell me stories about the history of our country, about the Visigoths and all those sorts of things. I liked him to tell me stories more than anything else. He could tell them like no one I know, adventure stories, jokes, he could keep me amused all afternoon. Ay! I wish I could remember all the things he used to tell me. There was one I liked so much that I used to try to get him to tell it to me over and over again until he got tired of repeating it. He knew so many things, he had such a store of stories, he could tell you from the time God made the world until the death of Jesus Christ – I wish I could remember it all. My friends used to say, 'Aren't you scared staying shut in your house when your mother goes off to the countryside? Aren't you frightened?' And I'd say, 'No, I'm not frightened', and that was because he was there and I knew he would be telling me stories. We had to keep very quiet, of course, we had to whisper almost.

He taught me to play cards, too, I learnt that quicker than anything else. He could keep me occupied for hours one way or another.

Because I was slow at arithmetic, my father suggested to my mother that she send me to a man who gave private lessons outside school hours. When the schoolmistress found out she said, 'School or private lessons, one or the other, but not both.' I told her it was because I wanted to get on. 'Do you mean you're not learning arithmetic in school?' she replied. I had to give up private lessons because of her opposition. What she feared was that I would tell people afterwards that I had learnt nothing from her.

When I was about eleven or twelve the mistress said that I should start studying at home after school from textbooks – history, geography, grammar. . . . She said my mother should buy the books. But my mother couldn't afford them. My father got out his school books which had been saved. Five there were in all and I took them to the mistress. She looked at them and said, 'No, no, you can't use these, they're old, you've got to buy new books.' Well, as my father said, geometry hasn't changed, grammar hasn't changed, arithmetic is the same, the old books would have done as well as the new. Especially as I couldn't have any of the new school books she had to sell. But she didn't think so, she reproached my mother for not making sacrifices to buy me the books. There weren't any other girls I knew whose parents could afford to buy them school books either, so we did without. We just had the books she handed out for each lesson in class, but we couldn't take them home to study.

Most of the girls I knew were worse off than I. My mother worked very hard and she looked after me as best she could. I always had clothes and food. There were plenty who hadn't as much. My mother always prepared a sandwich for me to take to school to eat in the break. I was one of the few who had anything to eat. Those were bad times, the 'hunger years'. Often I wouldn't take my sandwich. I preferred to take nothing because I couldn't stand the others watching while I ate on my own. Some of the girls brought a lemon, one of those lemons with the thick skin, to eat in the break. They'd eat the skin as well. It used to upset my stomach just to see them eating it.

The mistress didn't seem to notice these sorts of things. Most of her lessons were about the well-being of Spain. How well off we were now because the regime had saved religion in Spain, because religion and everything else had nearly been lost. I was too young to understand all the reasons, but I can see now that this was why she didn't like my father's school books – they didn't say all the things she thought. At the time I just kept quiet, but to myself I said, yes, this regime may be very good but it is because of them that my father has to hide. Despite the little understanding one has as a child, that much I understood. Every time the mistress went on about how well off we were now, I said to myself, yes, but my father can't come out of hiding.

I always knew my father was innocent. I knew it from my mother, from my grandparents. My grandmother often used to say, 'Look at this poor man who is shut up here – he never did anything to deserve it. He never did anything wrong.' Many people in the village asked me if I remembered my father and I'd always say the same thing, 'No, no, I was too young. . . .' Then they'd say, 'What a shame! Your father was a good man. What a shame he isn't here, because he never did anything bad.' Hundreds of people have said this to me, people who thought he had died in the war or disappeared.

I left school when I was just fifteen. By that time I quite often helped the mistress in class. 'Maria, I've got a headache, you take the younger ones for reading today.' She wanted me to stay on another year to study more, but what was the point? I was a woman already, I wasn't going on to further studies. If I had been able to, I would have liked to stay on. I should have liked to study pharmacy. But we hadn't the means.

When I left school I stayed at home helping my mother in the house. I'd been helping her since I was a child. I can remember I was so small when she first put me to washing dishes that the plates used to fall out of my hands! She grumbled a lot because I was always breaking them, but there was nothing she could do, she could see I was too small. It was because she was out of the house so much earning a living that I had to start so young. I had to make a roll of esparto plait every afternoon after coming home from school. She wouldn't let me out to play until I had finished the roll. I used to stretch the plait to get the roll finished quicker.

By the age of ten or so I was cooking, although my mother wouldn't leave me alone all day in the house at that age because the people would have talked. 'Fancy leaving the child alone when she goes off all day,' they would have said; it would have looked suspicious. When I was twelve or thirteen I was old enough to be left on my own.

Now that I was helping my mother all the time, I did all the house-cleaning, washing the floors, whitewashing the walls. My mother washed the clothes, she liked doing that, going out to the irrigation channel where all the women wash, and she liked ironing too. So I didn't have to help her with that. Nor did I have to help her any more with the esparto plaits.

When I'd finished cleaning the house, I listened to the radio and sewed. I like sewing. Then, if I had any time over, I'd read, magazines, especially ones about the cinema, novels and that sort of thing.

There wasn't much to do in the village in those days. There was the cinema once a week, but at three pesetas a seat we couldn't afford to go more than a few times a year. If we saw a car in those days it was a thing of great excitement. 'A car's coming, a car. Who can be in it? Someone must be ill. . . .' Almost the only time a car came to the village it was to fetch someone to go to hospital in Málaga. Or to collect a newly married couple who were going to Málaga on their honeymoon. Otherwise – except for the taxi and the lorry which left every morning and came back in the evening – we wouldn't see a car for months on end.

In the summer my girl friends would sometimes want me to go with them for a walk in the fresh of evening. My mother never let me go. 'There's no going out in the evenings,' she'd say, 'it's enough to go out on Sundays.' She kept me very shut in, very oppressed. It wasn't because she was frightened I'd talk; from the age of nine or ten she didn't have to remind me. No one would have got the secret out of me. No, she said it wasn't decent for a young girl to show herself outside. She talks about the things her mother used to stop her doing; well, she did much the same to me! My friends' mothers didn't stop their daughters going out on a summer evening. Not at night, I wouldn't have wanted to go out at night. But what was wrong about going out for a walk with my girl friends in the evening? Nothing that I could see, but she always refused. 'No, no, young girls shouldn't be seen walking in the square or the Compas in the evenings. . . .'

But I shouldn't complain. In comparison with most of my friends – in comparison with anyone except the children of the rich – I was better off than them. My mother made every sacrifice to see that nothing was lacking in the house. It's impossible to tell how hard she worked, up before dawn making plaits, walking round the farmsteads collecting eggs, going to Málaga. Sometimes she'd take me with her when I was small and I'd drop nearly dead from the walking we had to do in the town going from one house to another. No, if anything was lacking it wasn't her fault, it was because in those years there wasn't any food. We all went hungry then. Sometimes I'd be so hungry I'd say, 'Mama, I'm going to eat a bit of bread.' 'Daughter, there isn't any, what can I do?' My grandmother had to suffer a lot from my complaints. But she couldn't do anything either, there wasn't any food. I'd try to play to forget how hungry I was.

Hunger and fear. Of the two, fear was the worst. Every time I saw the Guardia coming I began to tremble and my stomach turned over. They came all the time looking for esparto. One day my mother had gone to Málaga and a neighbour came running in all of a sudden saying they were coming. The patio was full of green esparto which was what they were looking for. She wanted to help me hide it, I was only nine or ten at the time. And immediately I thought, if she stays here and the Guardia come my father won't have time to hide. . . .' 'No, no,' I said to her, 'you go, I'll shut the door and they won't come in.' 'But I've come to help you,' she said. 'No, no', and I managed to get her out of the house. I shut the street door and ran to warn my father. I helped him into the hiding place in the wall. He jumped up on the bed, took down the picture that covered the hole and got in. I hung the picture back up in its place. It was all done in a minute or so. Whenever someone knocked at the door and my mother wasn't there I'd help him to hide. When the Guardia knocked I opened the door. 'Your mother?' they asked. 'She's in Málaga.' 'Ah well, we'll come back tomorrow,' they said. They didn't come in. I was trembling with fear and trying to hide it at the same time. But they didn't notice.

I felt safer when he had his new hiding place. He made it after that night El Muñon came to the house. Ay, I'll never forget that! I was in such a state of nerves and crying, seeing what was going on to try to get those men to admit they had seen my father in the sierra. The middle of the night, three or four in the morning. I must have been about ten at the time. I was so distraught that my mother had to carry me home in her arms. Coming on top of seeing the *guardia* come rushing out of the room where he had been hiding and pointing his revolver at El Muñon, I couldn't stand any more. I don't even want to try to remember it now.

The same with the time I set fire to the roof in the patio. Ay! What a day! It was my fault, my grandfather was picking carobs that day and we had to take his lunch down to him and it was getting late. 'Come on,' my mother said, 'put more wood on the fire, otherwise the meal is going to be late.' I put on more than I should have and suddenly a flame shot up and caught the brush-wood. When I saw what had happened I ran shouting for help. My mother came running. 'The house is going to catch alight,' she shouted. We were terrified, thinking of my father upstairs. People came running from all over. We couldn't say anything to each other because of the people there. Luckily this man had the idea of knocking down the supports. If he hadn't, I think the house would have burnt down.

Misfortunes of one sort or another – that was my childhood, the childhood of anyone of my age here.

Two

MANUEL AND JULIANA
Youth, pueblo and politics
1905–30

Rural politics was controlled by local bosses
known as *caciques*, from the Indian word
for the chieftains through whom the
Spaniards had ruled their American empire.
The term is indicative of the political
psychology of the Spanish ruling class.
Having lost their American empire early
in the nineteenth century, they ruled rural
Spain, especially in the south, as they had
once ruled naïve and ignorant Indians.

– GABRIEL JACKSON
The Spanish Republic and the Civil War

There were, in 1931, two million landless
agricultural labourers in Spain, while
50,000 landlords owned half the agricultural
land. . . . In Andalusia, classic region of
latifundia, the annual average income of a
large land-owner was 18,000 pesetas and that
of a small-holder 161 pesetas. But the
majority were not land-owners at all – they
were *braceros*, day-labourers who were
lucky if they worked one day out of two.

– PIERRE BROUÉ AND ÉMILE TÉMIME
La Révolution et la Guerre d'Espagne

MANUEL

The first time I saw social injustice
was at school. Of course, it was around me
all the time, it was the air we breathed.
But when I saw the favouritism the
schoolmaster showed the sons of the
rich, it stank to heaven, it made me more
rebellious than ever.

I have always been a rebel, I suppose it has to do with my life as
a child.

The year I was born, 1905, was the worst year in living memory.
There have been plenty of bad years since, but they have come
because of war or mis-government. 1905 was a natural disaster.

For several years it hadn't rained much. That year it didn't
rain at all. Everything dried up, no crops were harvested. Imagine
that here, where everyone lived off the land, where everything
depended on the land! The landless day-labourers and the poor
were virtually starving, they couldn't get work. There was a great
deal of unrest. People emigrated by the score. To relieve the situation the authorities had to ask the government for help and it
was then that the road from Mijas to Fuengirola was built. In
part this helped ease the worst effects of the drought.

My mother died when I was seventeen months old. I don't
know what of, and I've never found out because my brothers and
sister all left the village when I was still small. My three brothers
went to Brazil and I haven't had news of them since long before
the war, I don't know whether they are alive or dead. After my
mother's death, the woman who was to become my foster-mother

said to my father, 'If you like, I'll take care of the child.' And my father said, 'I don't want to get rid of him, but I see you have raised my niece very well, you can take him, never forgetting that I am his father and shall come to see him. . . .' Five months later he died himself; he had been ill a long time with bronchial trouble. So I stayed in the house of my foster-parents.

My own father's small-holding rarely provided for the family. Half the time he had to be out looking for work. There were five of us in the family. My eldest brother was fifteen years older than me, and when my father fell ill it was he who went out looking for work to support us. Sometimes he would find work in the vineyards between here and the coast, but at other times he'd have to go as far as San Pedro de Alcántara. My two other brothers were eleven and eight years older than me and my sister, who now lives in San Pedro, three years older. I was the only one of the family who was left in Mijas, and because of that my foster-father went to the municipal judge and held a family council to have my father's small-holding made over to me. Because, later, I was always mixed up in politics I put it in my wife's name to be on the safe side, which was just as well since she could manage it without difficulty while I was in hiding. When the foreigners started to come, we sold it to one of them.

My foster-father was a barber and he lived and had his barber's shop in the house where I hid for the first two years. It was the house where I was brought up. His name was Fernando and he owned a small-holding which a sharecropper worked. A foreigner has bought that now, too, to build a villa on. With the barber's shop and the bit of land, my foster-parents weren't too badly off in comparison with the poverty that was general then. The barber's shop always had lots of work, mainly people from the countryside. We didn't have many *señoritos* among our clients.

My foster-father was one of those old-style men with whom you had to be very formal and correct. He had a very bad temper and liked to shout a lot, tell people off and that sort of thing. Otherwise he was a good man, but his temper was terrible. All the same he didn't hit me much, a lot less than my foster-mother at any rate. They had a lot to bear between them, twelve children they'd had and not one of them survived beyond the age of a few months. They would die a month or two after birth, as a rule. Now and again one would live to six or seven months, that was all. Twelve children! That's why they were willing to raise my cousin and myself as their own, because they liked children very much. Not that either of them ever pretended I was their natural child. As soon as I was old enough to think for myself, they told me that my parents had died and that they were my foster-parents. I was still quite small when I learnt that.

I respected my foster-father the way one respects a father. I never smoked in front of him. I never went to the same bar. I'd be working alongside him in the barber's shop and I'd get a longing to smoke and I'd go out of the door before lighting up. He knew I smoked because, though he didn't smoke much, he'd sometimes want a cigarette and he'd ask my mother: 'Has Manolo got a cigarette there for me?' And if I happened to walk into a bar where he was I would leave immediately. These were marks of respect a son pays to a father. A son would never talk about anything impolite, about women or things like that, to his father. And, of course, he was always addressed by the formal *Usted* and not *tu*. For both parents that was the custom, though it's dying out like most of the respect for one's parents. These were patriarchal habits and things have changed, especially with the foreigners coming. I'm not sure I like the changes altogether. To compare oneself to one's creator as equal – father and son as equals – no, that doesn't seem right to me. One's father is always one's father and one should show him the respect of *Usted* rather than the equality of *tu*. But there's no going back on these changes.

I was about five when I got smallpox. Medicine at that time, not only here but in the whole of Spain, was very backward, and there were big epidemics of typhus and smallpox. People died like flies, especially the young, because there were no vaccines as there are now. No one dies as young now, but then it was common.

I caught the sickness playing with a neighbour's little girl. I remember playing at her house and getting into her bed and soon afterwards I had the illness. They thought I was dying. My foster-mother had been in Málaga for the death of a relative and when she returned in the evening she found me on the point of death. The doctor didn't know what to do. He wasn't really a doctor, he was more of a quack. There wasn't even a chemist in the village and so he had to do a bit of everything. He had a medicine chest in his house and if he ran out of one medicine he'd prescribe something else. He charged a peseta a visit, and as there was no other doctor in the village it was him or nothing. If it hadn't been for my foster-mother I should certainly have died, because the doctor had no idea what to do. As soon as she saw what I'd got she set to work to scrub me with a liquid. I've never found out what it was. She rubbed very hard in order to break open the pox and let the pus come out. In fact she really tore off the pox. Once the pus came out, the infection went and my life was saved. To prevent me scratching the infection she tied my hands to the bed-stead and my father told her off. 'Let him scratch if he wants to. What difference does it make if he's ugly?' But she kept my hands tied, though it didn't do that much good; my face remains marked anyway from the places where she tore the scabs off.

I was lucky to escape, there were plenty of others who weren't so lucky. The village was quite isolated at that time and only those with some money could get to Málaga if they were ill. And even then, they'd have to manage the trip on a donkey or mule. The only form of transport between Mijas and Málaga was a mule cart which went two or three times a week. It needed a team of five mules to get it up here, and it used to leave Mijas at dusk and get to Málaga by sunrise. It spent the day in Málaga loading pro-visions for the shops here – there were five or six permanent shops then – and at nightfall leave there on the return journey to arrive here at dawn. Málaga and back was a thirty-six-hour journey until they built the railway to Fuengirola shortly before the First World War and a regular cart went from Mijas down to the coast.

One of the regular clients at my father's barber's shop was the schoolmaster, Don José. He came every day to be shaved, but he didn't have money enough to pay. He and my father were friends, and one day my father told him that something ought to be done for me. My father wanted me to learn. 'I don't want what happened to me to happen to you,' he used to say to me. 'I've learnt very little.' He had never been to school. As soon as he had been old enough to leave home his father sent him from Los Boliches, where they lived, up to his grandfather's farm at Osunilla to be raised. No one taught him anything. When he was grown up a bit he got a place in a barber's shop in the village to learn the trade. It was only when he was a man that he got a little education, taking lessons from a private teacher and learning to read. He never really learnt to write very much – at that age it's too late – though he could get by for the little he needed. But he was determined that I shouldn't be like him on that score and later, during school holidays, he would pay for a private teacher for me, a man in the town hall who spent his spare time giving lessons round the village. An hour or two with me and he'd go to another house down the street.

When my father spoke to the schoolmaster, Don José said: 'Let him come to my school if you want.' I was six, and I should have started in the other school for boys of my age. Instead, I went straight into the older boys' school where, because he was a friend of my father's, Don José took an interest in me.

For those he wanted to trouble himself with he was a good enough teacher, Don José. I was lucky because otherwise the only children he took an interest in were the sons of the rich. The sons of the poor he left to themselves and they didn't learn anything. It didn't matter whether they were intelligent or not. There were plenty of them who were intelligent, a lot more so than any of the sons of the rich. There was one in particular – a genius, I believe, who could have become almost anything, he was so bright – but like the rest of us he couldn't afford to study for a career. Through his friendship with a doctor later he became a *practicante*, that was as far as he could go. Of the children of my age among the poor there were a number who were of the same level as me or probably better. But there wasn't one among the *señoritos'* sons. Only one of them in my time went on to study for a career as a schoolmaster, and he was no great intellectual star. An intellectual calamity rather, I'd say, but by force of years he managed to struggle through. All the others did their primary education and that was all, no one studied here, rich or poor. In that we were all the same. Those of us who were of the same age and at school together called each other *tu*, rich and poor alike, for the rest of our lives. We all played together. I had friends among the *señoritos'* sons as I had among the poor. There wasn't any distance between us, because of our different backgrounds. Among my friends was the nephew of the old *cacique*, and I was often in his house as a young man. Of course, once we had left school, the *señoritos'* sons would look down on the people who lived at the top of the village, the poorest of the poor. But not on those of us who came from the intermediary level. Even when one of them went away to study, there was no distance between us when he came back. But then no one went away. . . .

Later on, some of the younger ones went to the seminary in Málaga to become priests, although none of them finished. It was one possible way of getting to study, but it meant recommendations from the local priest and that sort of thing, documents and papers – it meant being well in with the Church to be admitted.

The schoolmaster's favouritism for the sons of the rich was the first time I came up against injustice. Of course, it was around me all the time, it was the air we breathed, but this was the first time I'd come up against it myself. There was nothing that could be done about it. I was lucky, but I could see what would have happened to me if my father hadn't been friendly with Don José. It stank to heaven, the injustice of it, and it made me more rebellious than ever.

Despite that, I loved school. I used to cry if I wasn't allowed to go, if my foster-father said I had to go out into the countryside for something or other. It didn't happen often, not like the majority of children who never went to school at all because their fathers put them onto herding goats or pigs as soon as they were old enough to go to school. I learnt to read without any difficulty and soon I had all sorts of books in my hands. One I remember especially, a novel about some bandits who were famous in olden times called the *Niños de Écija*. I liked the story so much that I organized half a dozen of my schoolmates into a band and instructed and drilled them with rifles and machetes. Once I had them trained – we were all about eight or ten years old – and the *feria* came round, we set out like bandits to rob the various stalls of peanuts and sweets and whatever there was. I was the captain because I knew more than the others and used to tell them where to go and what to rob. I remained in the rearguard, keeping watch up by the church over the stores that had been stolen. Then I'd divide the spoils among the band and we'd eat our fill.

There wasn't much for kids to do in the village when I was young. Today every day is like a fiesta, and the boys play football and that sort of thing. Football wasn't known here until I was about eighteen or twenty, when we formed a village team. I was the referee; I preferred that to playing in the team. But as a kid there wasn't much else to do than play in the squares and in summer go down in bands looking for early figs or whatever fruit was in season to steal. Sometimes we'd look for an *alberca* in which to swim and I can remember once having to run half-way back up to the village with our clothes in our hands because the sharecropper chased us off, thinking we'd come to steal fruit. The water was close to where there were some good figs and he always thought we were going to rob them. He was usually right!

People had to organize their own amusements in those days and most of them revolved round festivals of one sort or another. Christmas, carnival, the *feria*, those were the principal ones. The best time of the year, the time I enjoyed most, was carnival. What a good time that used to be! The whole village came alive and took part. Groups of twenty people or more would get together and go round the village streets playing all sorts of musical instruments, dancing and singing songs about the government or the local authorities. Critical songs, satirical verses, about this or that wrong, making fun of the authorities. There were poets, natural poets who made up the verses. Two brothers in particular here who had a real gift for making up *coplas* satirizing the government and also individuals who had done wrong. They would add whatever music seemed appropriate to their verses and copy them out for the people to learn at nights a couple of weeks before carnival began. Technically they weren't very accomplished, no doubt, these two brothers hadn't the culture for that, but all the same their *coplas* were always a delight. And when the groups went round singing them, it was like having walking critics at large in the streets.

In my youth people used to wear masks at carnival time and they could say and do pretty much what they liked. Things got to such a state in the towns though that they forbade masks. That must have been a few years before the Primo de Rivera dictatorship, because I can remember people still wearing them. Before the dictatorship there was a certain amount of freedom of criticism – despite the *caciques* – and especially at carnival time. But the dictatorship put an end to all that.

As I got older, the injustice I felt at school became evident to me in other ways. There are thousands of incidents I could speak of, but one in particular has always stuck in my memory. I must have been about twelve when one day the *cacique*'s toughs brought up a small-holder half dead on the back of a mule from the beating they'd given him. They had his hands tied together with rope, and they made sure the people would see him to awaken terror in the village. They said he hadn't paid the taxes the town hall claimed he owed and they had gone down to seize his property. The *cacique*'s toughs went armed with shotguns to protect the town hall officials on jobs like this. This time, when they tried to take the man's yoke of ploughing cows, he resisted. It was the only yoke he owned, it was his living. They beat him until he was half dead and brought him up for everyone to see. I don't mention it because it was an uncommon event but because I can still see it so clearly. It was the sort of thing that happened often enough when there were *caciques* because the people submitted to their terror. There were some who rebelled and said, 'Why should they take what is mine, my children's food?' But it didn't do them any good. What could they do against the terror a *cacique* used against them? They weren't organized, the union didn't exist or was weak, it was the system – an undemocratic system, without real political parties and with a *camarilla* at the top manipulating everything through a *cacique* in each village.

My foster-father was like many of the villagers at the time. When there was an election he'd say, 'What do I want to vote for? They'll take what they want anyway, whether I vote or not. I'm not going to.' He knew that it was a game in which every four years the parties in power changed, the conservatives coming in now and the liberals next time round. After one party's term of office the king gave the government to the other. The new government called elections and these were sometimes held though they were caricatures of real elections. What happened more often was that only one candidate – usually of the party to be elected to office – would stand and he would be declared winner without election under article 29 of the electoral law. If there was for some reason more than one candidate, then the comedy of elections took place. The *cacique* would get busy, the civil governor would name a government delegate who came to the village and jailed all the leading members of the opposing party for the whole of election day. It wasn't an election, it was a form of terror. The people were told how to vote and since they lacked culture and education and because they were frightened, they did as they were told. The *cacique* gave them their ballot slips and that was it. I can remember votes being bought – for five pesetas a time – and the people would sell themselves without a shred of political awareness. They say things were even worse in the old days before my time.

For as long as I can remember, there was one *cacique* here most of the time until the Republic. In villages like this where there were no political organizations locally, the *cacique* would call himself a conservative or a liberal as it suited him and as the parties changed office. He would change allegiance the way a man changes his shirt. What mattered was to retain power. To be a *cacique* you had to have money, and to become rich in a village in those days it was necessary to be in politics, to be close to someone who was manipulating the situation. The parties didn't pay the *caciques*, but there was enough to be got out of politics to make it worth while for them. Each *cacique* gathered his *camarilla* round him and when he was in power, as this landlord was most of the time, he would run the village pretty much as he wanted. Usually he would appoint himself mayor or judge, but sometimes he would appoint one of his *camarilla* so that he could run things better from behind the scenes.

I can remember a time when there was another *cacique* who wouldn't let anyone stay in the square when he was there. 'Get to your house,' he would shout at anyone who came into the square. Only he and his *camarilla* could be there, no one else would dare stay, let alone go into the bar where they were. Once a *cacique* appointed a relative of his as mayor to help him out, and when the latter's term ended he hadn't paid the town hall staff for over six months. He had 'eaten' all the money himself and had nothing left for wages. Even for here that was an outstanding swindle – though it was customary for the mayor to 'eat' what he could. And yet no one said anything, no one protested. That was fear. . . .

It was the poverty and lack of education of the people that made all this possible. And also the respect inculcated from father to son for the *señorito* – as though he were a god or a demi-god at least. What they should have been told was that there was a man like themselves who had had the luck to make more money than they, that's all. But that was part of the patriarchal system.

The poverty was so great that most of the houses in the top part of the village were no more than huts or shacks. The village was rachitic in its poverty, even most of the rich had left to live in

Fuengirola because it was more comfortable and convenient for them.

Apart from the land and the vineyards there was only esparto. And to live off esparto meant the worst sort of poverty.

There was one other way of earning a little money – smuggling. Around here there has always been a lot of smuggling, mainly because of Gibraltar. I can remember strings of horses and 'haversack' men coming into the village at night laden down with contraband tobacco when I was young. The house next to ours was owned by the man who bought the tobacco, and when someone informed on him and the *carabineros* came to search, all the tobacco was passed over from his patio to ours. The man was a friend of the judge's and at that time, unlike later on, the *carabineros* needed a warrant to be able to search a house. As the judge was in the plot, he used to take his time about making out the warrant to allow his friend, with our help, to clear the tobacco out of his patio into ours. When the *carabineros* searched, they would find nothing and they never bothered to search ours. It would have meant getting a new warrant and, moreover, as they weren't from the village, they didn't know the patios. More or less everyone was in the business in one way or another. As long as you were well in with the *cacique* you could get away with pretty much anything, and everyone kept their eyes closed to the smuggling. It was only if you were opposed to the *cacique* that the trouble began.

Except for a few, smuggling wasn't a regular way of earning a living. And there were always at least 800 landless day-labourers looking for work, out of about 1,700 directly employed on the land! You can see the scale of unemployment from that. Many of these landless labourers didn't live in the village itself, but in the huts and hovels in the countryside. The majority of the other 900 farmers didn't own the land they worked but share-cropped or rented it.[3] The landless were the poorest of the poor. Slightly better off were the artisans and people who had permanent jobs – there were about 200 of them, out of a village population of 2,300 – as well as those who owned and worked their own plot of land. And yet, as in my own father's case, owning a plot was no guarantee of being able to maintain a family. Around here the soil is too poor and too hilly, that's why the big land-owners didn't bother with it.

If it weren't for the fact that the village is rich in water, who knows whether the land would have been worked at all. But yes, the land would have been worked because what alternative was there? Emigration was about all, and there were at least two massive waves that I can remember, the first when my brothers left in 1911 and the second about nine or ten years later when I was almost a man. The people left for South America in their scores; it was always South America they went to. Some made their fortunes there and came back later, but not many. Brazil at that time was as poor as Spain, if not poorer. But no matter how many people went, there were always more wanting land.

Having a small-holding over and above what the barber's shop brought in certainly helped my foster-parents a great deal. But not enough by any means to let me go on studying. When I was about twelve Don José said to my father, 'Fernando, you should let the boy study for a career, he could do it.' And my father replied, 'Don José, we haven't the means, it's impossible.' That was quite true, he hadn't the means and, though I always liked to study, I knew it was impossible for me to go on. So my father put another chair in the barber's shop and I left school and began work. I was thirteen. The school-leaving age was fourteen, but my father said to the schoolmaster, 'What's the good of him coming any more? If he were going to study for a career or something. . . .'

I'd been working in the barber's shop since the age of ten in my time off from school. By the time I was thirteen I could look after myself, I could earn my own living. Not that I earned anything for myself, everything that came in was for the house. There were no fixed prices in a barber's shop in those days; it all depended on what the customer wanted to give. Two reales, fifty centimos, was customary for a haircut and shave, but sometimes you'd get only forty. Sometimes for a shave alone you'd get a real. It all depended. At that time a kilo of bread cost two reales and a packet of sugar fifteen centimos, so things were fairly even. All the same, it was hard work to bring in five pesetas a day. There were no fixed hours – as long as there were customers we went on working, seven days a week. Often we didn't stop to eat – or rather my father didn't because I, when it was time, would always eat, being more modern than him about these things. As long as there was a customer in the shop my father wouldn't leave; he would be there on his feet working all day and not even stop to relieve himself. He would rather contain himself than put a customer out by leaving him for a moment. I'd tell him, 'You're very backward in your way of thinking, that's not the way to be', but he took no notice. It was idiotic, but that's how he was. And he was relatively independent, he didn't have to bow his head in front of anyone. All the same, it was the sort of upbringing he had had, the respect. . . .

There were two other barber's shops in the village. The barber who later became my comrade in the party had more *señoritos* than us among his customers. But they began to leave him because of his ideas. They went to the third barber who was completely servile. We also lost customers because of political differences – not only *señoritos* by a long shot – but my father who wasn't very political didn't trouble: 'Those who don't want to come needn't bother,' he used to say.

I'd been working a couple of years when some of my schoolmates, who hadn't learnt anything because of the schoolmaster's attitude towards them, asked me to give them lessons. So I said, 'All right, come to my house', and I found I had started a private school. At first most of the pupils were people who had been at school with me, but later, when word got around, children of eight and ten and twelve also joined. Their fathers would hear that I was giving lessons and come to see me. 'My son wants you to teach him too,' they'd say, and that was how I came to have more than twenty pupils. Of all ages, some older and some younger than me.

I used to charge them three pesetas a month, which meant that I got about sixty pesetas a month out of it. That wasn't much, but even so it was a lot more than today when you can spend that much just in buying a round of drinks! Though the money came in useful for clothes, it wasn't that which interested me most, it was the enjoyment I got out of it. Though some of the children weren't as clever as the others and didn't learn much, there were enough who learnt everything they know today from me. And I used to feel that, in some way, within the limits of my own intelligence and learning, I was righting the injustice which I had first come to see and understand at school.

All the same, I never believed that I would remain a barber all my life. The very first idea I had of what I might become was a soldier. Legally I could have been excused my period of military service because I was an only son – even if adopted – and my father's support. But I waived that and joined the army. I was twenty. The stupidities of youth – and even more so for someone having a bit of education! And yet I imagined myself rising from the ranks to become an officer – not a colonel or anything, but at least a lieutenant, as did many of my age. In fact I made the first rung up the ladder almost immediately, because before we had even sworn the oath I was promoted to acting corporal. After only thirty-six days! I was in a mountain infantry regiment stationed in Ronda and I was very enthusiastic at the beginning. It didn't last long. I soon became disillusioned. They would tell you white was black and black white when you could see that it wasn't and I couldn't stand that. I'm too rebellious. It was the system of unthinking respect for authority I couldn't take – I've never been able to take it, here or in the army.

Though the fault among the NCOs lay in their lack of education and culture, the same couldn't be said of the officers. There was one who used to inspect our quarters and if he found a speck of dirt somewhere on a bed or a wall, he would fine the whole company on the spot twenty-five centimos per man. That was a day's pay for a soldier. As a corporal I used to get fifty-five centimos a day. There were about 150 men in the company, so a speck of dirt brought him in 37 pesetas a time which went straight into his pocket. It didn't take long before I had had enough of all this. I decided to get out. Military service at that time was two years, but in practice you didn't have to do much more than a year, unless you were in Africa where it was the full two years. Here, at home, after a year it was the custom to give soldiers four months' leave and in my case this was twice extended. So I completed my two years' obligatory service, spending the last year of it at home in Mijas.

My father was glad to have me back. He hadn't opposed my going into the army but it had meant leaving him alone in the barber's shop because there was no one who could take my place, it would have meant bringing someone in from outside. He couldn't afford to pay a wage, so he welcomed me back.

My spell in the army influenced my political development. Before going in I'd known four years of the Primo de Rivera dictatorship, and yet my ideas were still quite different because I imagined that I could make a career out of the army. That was in 1927 and I came out the following year. In one's twenties one doesn't have the experience and understanding that comes later. But after being in the army I began to understand better the meaning of the dictatorship's oppression and, having a naturally rebellious spirit, I began to change.

Though it doesn't bear comparison with what we have known, the Primo regime, which came in in 1923, was oppressive. Under the constitutional monarchy – despite the rule of the *caciques* – there was a relative freedom of speech and criticism. That came to an end under the dictatorship. You couldn't criticize the government or anything. The union and the socialist party in the village were closed down. It was at this time that the retired major became the *cacique* here. He had served in Cuba where he had made a fortune and also become very ill during the war. He came from Granada originally and he returned there when he retired. But his health didn't improve and he came here. Soon he had bought up a number of houses and farmsteads and was one of the village *camarilla*. At first he and the old *cacique* were great friends, but after a while they fell out. No doubt there were personal as well as political reasons for this. The major had studied at the military academy with, and was a personal friend of, General Martínez Anido, who organized gunmen to shoot down CNT leaders in Barcelona where the King appointed him civil governor in the early twenties. Though the major wasn't like that, as soon as General Primo de Rivera came to power, he became the local head of the dictator's Unión Patriótica. Once he was *cacique*, he thought he would run the village like the army and that all he had to do was give orders. There were plenty of people who resented that and came to hate him for it. . . .

In the barber's shop on my return from the army I began to listen to the socialists who had been active in the party and union from the time before the dictatorship. They were very moderate most of them, followers of Pablo Iglesias, the party's founder, and had taken part in the strikes at the end of the First World War. I can remember the 1918 strike. I was a kid, about thirteen, and dozens and dozens of Guardia Civil on foot and on horseback were brought in to repress it. They surrounded the Casa del Pueblo and pursued the strikers through the streets and out into the country. It was nothing really, the strike, a simple stoppage of work, but they brought in all these Guardia in the name of the right to work. The old *cacique* was in power then and as usual he meant to show his strength. Of course, the landlords died of fright at the smallest sign of unrest. . . .

Most of these old socialists were peasants, sharecroppers or tenant farmers, and I liked to hear them talk about their problems on the land. Although my father had been a small-holding peasant, I didn't know much about the land. Soon I began to learn of the sacrifice and hard work that the land required of them. It didn't make much difference whether they owned their plots, rented or share-cropped them, they had to work all hours of the day and night, they could never just say, 'Now it's finished.' If the water reached them at midnight they would have to irrigate then. If the wind wasn't in the right direction for winnowing by day they would have to do it before dawn. If an animal was giving birth they would be up all the night. . . . All these things, they had to work harder even than the day labourer, they had to work harder than me in the barber's shop, and we worked enough hours there. This was why later, when we formed the union, I spent so much time and energy trying to get these small-holders to join to defend their interests against the landlords.

From what I had seen in the army and could see around me under the dictatorship, I began to understand these socialists' point of view. I might have become politically conscious earlier if the union and party hadn't been closed down in the village under the dictatorship which lasted until 1930. As it was, when they talked I could see that their ideas were not very developed, they lacked the culture for that, but what they had to say about the need for social justice was enough to make me think. Thereafter I worked things out for myself to the best of my ability because in fact I knew more than they, though I lacked their practical experience.

It was obvious that the first thing that was needed was to re-create the union. Since it was forbidden to organize under the dictatorship we had to act clandestinely.[4] At first there was an attempt to set up a branch of the radical socialist party but when the old *cacique* heard about it he threatened the principal organizer who got frightened and dissolved the party himself. It was then that we decided to act and we formed a branch of the newly created Landworkers' Federation which was affiliated to the socialist UGT, and a branch of the socialist party – both clandestinely. We had meetings in my house, sometimes as many as forty or fifty people came. By 1930 Primo de Rivera had fallen and we were under the 'soft' dictatorship of Berenguer. Within a month of our starting, the old monarchic constitution permitting political parties was restored and we could become legal. As soon as that happened, within a very few days, we had 500 to 600 members of the union, a membership which rose to 1,500 in July 1936, and the start of the civil war. This was out of a total population between the village and countryside of just under 7,000.[5]

The first people to join were the agricultural day-labourers, of course. Many of them had been in the union before the dictatorship and they remembered how it had protected them from the abuses of the landlords who paid them very little, a pittance. There was no need to propagandize among them. They brought their friends and relatives with them. But the tenant farmers, the sharecroppers and small-holders were always more under the control of the landlords and *caciques* and were fundamentally conservative. They didn't want to join, they couldn't see the advantage. But little by little I persuaded them, as I'll explain, and in the end I created a section of the union for them which was almost as large as that of the day-labourers.

In the following year, 1931, the monarchy fell. 12 April was the day of the municipal elections that led to the King leaving Spain.[6] Here, as in many other villages of the province, there were no elections, the result being declared under article 29 of the electoral law as I've explained. The old *cacique* was in power again and could do what he wanted. No one could protest. He proclaimed the result for his side and that was that. But it lasted only a day. On the 14th, after the results had come in from the towns, the King left and the Republic was declared. There was great joy. People crowded round radios in the bars to hear the news as it came from Madrid. Largo Caballero, Azaña, Lerroux and the many other socialist and republican leaders who had been imprisoned under the old regime were released and formed the provisional government. The whole village was in the streets to celebrate but the *cacique*'s power was still strong enough to forbid demonstrations of any sort. The people went to the bars – almost the only place where you could listen to a radio in those days because they were too expensive for us to own – to celebrate a victory that had been won without shedding a single drop of blood. Imagine it! The monarchy which had brought so many evils to the nation – backwardness, illiteracy, *caciquismo* and dictatorship – was overthrown quite normally and without loss of blood. So everyone was out in the streets and bars – with the exception of the *cacique* and his *camarilla* – to celebrate in the way these things are done, drinking and shouting '*Viva la República!*'

Once the Republic was proclaimed, the old *cacique* was ousted as mayor and an electoral commission made up of members of all the political parties was appointed to hold fresh municipal elections. These were held about a month later, in complete freedom for political parties and voters – the first time such a thing was known here. By this time our union organization and party was the strongest in the village, twice as large as our coalition partners, the radical socialists and the radicals put together. Because of our lack of political experience and because it was the first election we had fought, we were advised to join forces with the other republican parties to combat the right, which was completely defeated. I was elected a councillor and the socialist majority on the council wanted to elect me mayor. I refused. I was only twenty-six and I thought I was too young, and I had enough work to do with the trade-union and party organization, so I said to one of the older generation of socialists: 'You are well known and respected. It would be better if you became mayor.' I was elected his deputy.

Politics – me? Never. Politics, you
know what they bring in their train?
Misfortune and sorrow for the poor at the
bottom who have to pay the consequences
so that those at the top can climb even
higher.

My father worked the land, but he didn't own any land himself.
When I was about nine months old, early in 1913, he rented the
small-holding which Manolo's father had owned and we moved to
the house there. We lived there twelve years. Manolo's father was
dead by then and the land in fact belonged to Manolo. Who would
have thought that later we would get married and that that bit of
land would in the end be made over to me!

I went to school, but only a short time, two or three years in all.
There was only one school for girls in the village and they taught
very little. At the age of nine or ten I had to work, helping my
mother and father on the farmstead. It wasn't that they didn't
want me to go to school, but as we lived some way outside the
village and there was always work to do, I didn't go. Only the
privileged class went to school in those days. Also, I didn't have
much desire to go, I wasn't like my husband in that respect.

My parents never learnt to read or write, and I didn't learn
much either. I can do my accounts and that's about all. I regret
not having learnt more, but as I wasn't taught I've had to make
do with the little I know. And I've managed with that. For the
struggle I've had, a lot of learning hasn't been necessary. Many's
the time I've had to sign an instalment agreement on something
we were buying, a taxi or lorry, and I've said to the man, 'Look,
I don't know how to sign very well', and he has said, 'With what
you know, it's enough.' No, I haven't needed to know more.

At thirteen I was already earning my living, working as a
servant for some people here. I preferred that to staying at home
helping to plait *esparto*, which was the only other thing I could do.
The girls of my age at that time would ask each other, 'Have you

got work?' and if they knew of something they'd tell you, 'Look, there's this señora who's looking for someone. . . .' That's how I heard there was a job going in this house. I went to speak to the señora and she took me on. My mother and father had no part in it, it was up to me. I liked the idea of service because I would get my own money and it was better than having to work at home.

Twelve and a half pesetas a month – that was my wage when I started. For that, I worked twelve hours a day or more, from eight in the morning until eight or nine at night every day of the week. Those were the wages and hours that were customary here then. If you went to Málaga you could earn as much as forty or fifty pesetas a month, but that meant leaving the village and being away from home. Here there wasn't the climate for those sort of wages because there was nothing else for a girl to do but plait esparto or work in the fields. Hoeing, reaping, picking the olive crop for one and a half pesetas a day. Nothing really for the hard work it was, but many girls went all the same. Other women and girls went to the sierra to cut firewood which they had to bring down to the village tied to their backs, or to fetch esparto.

The first people I worked for were the town clerk and his daughter who lived in a big house in the square. There was no water in the houses then, every drop had to be fetched from the fountain in a pitcher. I was the only servant they had and I had to do everything, scrub floors, cook, whitewash the whole house, clean the underside of the roof – all that for a pittance, on top of which the clerk's daughter was always complaining. She was only happy when one had worked so hard and so many hours that one was ready to collapse. Very proud, a bad employer, that's what she was, and I wouldn't have stayed with her the two years I did if I'd had more experience and sense.

When the clerk died and the daughter left the village I went to work for an old lady who was one of the richest people in the village and who owned many farms. I got a rise there to fifteen pesetas a month and that because I had to work every hour of the clock and sleep in. I'd be at work at seven in the morning and very often I didn't end until midnight, without a moment's rest all day. There were no hours in that house. I cooked, I cleaned, I white-washed, I took the old lady to church and went to fetch her after mass – she was very old and had to hold onto my arm – I did everything. When she had company at night I'd have to wait up crucified with tiredness until they had gone to be able to lock up the house.

In both houses I got the same food as they ate. The old lady had the habit of giving me an egg every day for lunch. Every day an egg! Well, as I cooked for myself in the kitchen, I used to eat the soup and the potatoes or fish or whatever she was having – and the egg I'd put to one side. Then when she'd say to me, 'Go and buy half a dozen eggs', I'd take what I'd saved and come back with them from the shop as though I had bought them. That way I saved a bit of money for myself to buy a tablecloth or a sheet or something like that for the time when I married. . . . That's where I first learned to save!

The old lady was very good to me in her way. Not that you could ask for more money or anything like that – neither she nor anyone else would have heard of that. But for the *feria* she would always give me a dress, and on her saint's day another, not as fine, so I didn't have to buy them. Not that they cost all that much, the stuff for a dress in those days wouldn't cost more than sixteen pesetas. All the same I was happy, I'd say to myself, she's given me a present. And at other times when we went to the shop she would make me a present of a handkerchief or a packet of powder. Small things of no great importance, but after all, she wasn't obliged to do it. She was a good woman – but then in those days one earned very little.

I was with her three years. Then the clerk's daughter who was living in Málaga asked me to serve in her house. I was there only a couple of months. I didn't like it because I was away from home and without my mother . . . and also because this señora hadn't changed her ways. We were four maids in the house, but as she had known me here she wanted to go on treating me as she had done in the past. Always complaining and biting my head off. The other girls said to me, 'And you, why do you allow her to talk to you like that?' I didn't like it either, being treated as though she thought herself God, and I came away, back to the village.

It wasn't long after this that Manolo 'spoke' to me and we became *novios*. I had known him since I was a child, not only because we rented his land but also because, when we moved back into the village, he lived not far from us in the same street.

One evening – I was eighteen at the time – I went with a girl friend to buy tobacco for my father. Going out to a shop was about the only amusement there was most evenings then. As we were coming back through the small square in front of his barber's shop there he was walking back and forth as usual. We passed him and then I heard my girl friend say, 'Listen, Manolo wants to talk to you, he's following us.' And I said, 'Ech, he'll be wanting to go for a walk!' When I got to my house he turned down another street but he was still looking at me. I didn't know what he was thinking, there wasn't the freedom then that there is today. Today a girl can talk to a man but in those days you couldn't. A woman talk to a man! – no, only if she were very 'forward', and even then. . . .

When he 'spoke' to me later that evening I didn't want to accept him as my *novio*. I didn't want any more *novios* – I had had two and I'd got fed up with them both, and my mother was fed up with me for having turned them away. She thought they were good catches. 'Ay! this woman, she takes a *novio* and then sends him off', was what she said about me. So when Manolo spoke to me I didn't say yes and I didn't say no. But in those days you couldn't be long about making up your mind, because if a man came to speak to you you had to become *novios* or else turn him down, otherwise the people would say immediately that you were immoral. On the other hand, you didn't say yes straightaway, you'd let him wait a day or two or three. So it was a few days before I agreed to become his *novia*.

I liked the way he was. He was very sympathetic to me and we got on well together. He could be as serious as you know him today – but so funny too, he could keep us laughing for hours. He would come out with all sorts of things, funny stories, things that had happened to him when he was a boy, jokes – he had a very good memory and never seemed to forget anything. I remember we laughed so much one night in my house that a neighbour who was with my mother suddenly said, 'I'm not coming here any more of a night.' 'And why not?' my mother asked. 'Because they're laughing at us, your daughter is laughing at us and I'm not coming any more.' It wasn't true, we weren't laughing at them but at the stories he was telling me.

When you're young you'll laugh at anything, and he was such a good story-teller. Whenever he read something it would stay in his memory and he would explain it as easily as if he were just reading it. He had a pile of books, novels, and he could explain them all. There are enough people who know how to read but there aren't that many who understand what they read, that's how it seems to me anyway. Already when he was thirteen or fourteen people were commenting on how much he knew, and that was the truth. 'You should hear Manolo explaining about this,' the people used to say. 'Everything he reads stays in his mind.' Among the intelligent ones of his age he was the most intelligent, the cleverest of them all. That's why they used to come looking for him before anyone else if there was something they wanted to know or something they wanted writing.

It was his stories about when he was a child that made me laugh most, stories about things he remembered, jokes about priests and the like. The evenings would pass very quickly in my house when he was there. On fiestas he would come in the afternoon and again in the evening, if he could get away from the barber's shop, but that wasn't often. Other times he would come to see me at ten or later, when he had finished work, and many days he didn't finish in time to visit at all. We went out very little, he would come to my house for a while of an evening, and that was about all. The cinema – silent films they were then – once in a while, on a fiesta, or a play, there was nothing much else. Life was a slavery, nothing but work, not like today when the young go out every night, and on their own. In my time we could only go if we were accompanied by my parents or a married woman at least.

My mother was one of those old-fashioned women, very conservative, who liked nothing new. Not all mothers were like that but the majority were – they had their eyes on every small detail. To give you an idea – she wouldn't let me pass by the door of my *novio*'s house because, she said, it was an ugly thing to do. Just to pass by the door of one's *novio*! So each time I came back from the centre of the village I had to take the upper street to avoid his house. 'Don't take the lower street,' she was always telling me, 'go by the upper one or else the people will say you're going past his house to see him. And he won't see you going past his door.'

When he came to visit we had to sit inside the house. Never alone, that goes without saying. She was always there and that I can understand. But she wouldn't let me look out of the doorway when he left. That was ugly too. 'If someone saw you standing in the doorway to see him go. . . .' I used to protest. 'What harm is there in that?' I'd say. 'Mother, there's no harm in any of these things.' I couldn't stand on the doorstep to talk to him. 'Nothing good can come of that,' she would say, 'it's ugly.' Things had changed a lot by then, but she wanted everything to go on as she had known it when she was young. Then *novios* used to talk through the bars of the windows of the girl's house, him in the street and her inside, but that custom had disappeared by the time I'm talking of.

We were *novios* five years before getting married. There were plenty of *novios* who were together longer than that before marrying, fifteen or twenty years, some of them. It took me five years to buy all the things a woman has to buy to get married. All in all they wouldn't have cost more than a thousand pesetas, so you can see how much we were able to save in those days. A woman had to buy the sheets and blankets, the table linen, mattress and all the kitchen utensils. The husband had to buy the furniture, but in the poor class that wasn't much. Just the essentials, a table to eat off, chairs, a bed, a chest of drawers and a night table. Even so it took a long time to get the money together, things were cheaper than today but one earned a lot less. I also bought some pictures of saints, the very large ones they used to sell here and which I paid for by the week. A peseta a week they cost me!

If we had had the means we would have got married before. But as there wasn't the money we had to put up with it and wait. Money was the main thing.

We had a civil marriage. I don't know, I might have liked to have been married in church but he didn't want that. Moreover, the Republic had come in by then and civil marriage was more the fashion. I wore a blue dress, I remember, bought for the occasion but like any other for going out in. You wouldn't get dressed up in white for a civil marriage. But no – it didn't really make any difference to me whether I was married in church or by the magistrate, it's the same either way. As for believing in God, that's got nothing to do with priests who have their job to do, like the rest of us, to earn enough to be able to eat. It's not that I wasn't religious – I was and still am. But I'm not pious. Piety doesn't appeal to me at all, spending all day in the church and that sort of thing. But believing in God – yes, I believe. I have my own beliefs. I haven't been to confession since I was ten or eleven. I didn't confess when I got married, nor afterwards. People have said to me in these months since he came out of hiding, 'Now you'll confess, you'll go to the priest and confess all these years. . . .' And I say, 'The priest? Why does he have to know what's happened to me? Why should I go and tell him about my affairs?' I don't believe in that, in making public displays to any-one. Why tell things to a priest – he knows as much as anyone anyway, why should he know more? No, it never enters my head to go to confession. Perhaps when I'm dying I might because it will be very late then. . . . If I'm conscious, yes, I'll confess then, because I don't want to be buried outside hallowed ground. But until then I'll do what I've always done, go to mass when it suits me for a funeral or something like that, or during Holy Week when I like to see the saints got ready, but that's very rare. I've got more to do than time to lose so I don't manage to get to church very much. Not that I'm against church, no! But piety and con-fession and all that, I haven't time for.

When my daughter was born in June 1935, I saw to it that she was baptized. I shouldn't have liked not to have done so. How I got married was all the same to me, but baptism is different. . . . If one isn't baptized there are always problems – investigations and the like to get the papers to get married, that sort of thing. Things were difficult at that time and we had been waiting, day by day, to take her to church. At last, when she was three months old, my mother and I took her one day and had her baptized. In a short dress too. My husband didn't concern himself about things like that. It was all the same to him whether she was baptized at birth, or when she was older or not at all. He didn't trouble himself. If he had we would have had a quarrel, that's for sure. The child was going to be baptized, I was going to see to that. But then he always left me quite free in matters like this, he never tried to persuade me not to go to church.

We didn't go away on a honeymoon, there was no money for that. Only the very few, the rich, could afford such a luxury. We moved straight into his foster-father's house, but that didn't last long. There were always quarrels with his cousin because she wanted everything run her way. We rented a house in the *barrio* at the end of the village. When his cousin left the foster-father's house the old man came begging us to return. We did, and that's where we were living until my husband fled the village.

In those days we lived on three or four pesetas a day. You

could live on little because food wasn't too dear – but in any case you had to live on that because that's all there was. Every day he would give me what he earned, one day more, another day less, and the day he earned nothing – well, nothing. A wife had to be very careful about what she spent. Meat only very rarely, for a fiesta, at Christmas. Fish, the cheaper sorts, potatoes, vegetables, rice – the more ordinary food of the poor – was what we ate. I cooked on a tripod in the hearth, with firewood mainly. The best food of all is that cooked on firewood brought in from the mountain. It is really delicious, with a taste like nothing else.

I was happy to be in my house. There was always plenty of work. The washing, ironing, cooking, cleaning, whitewashing, caring for the child . . . there was work enough to keep anyone busy all day. I was never one of those women who likes to spend all day in the street, visiting and gossiping; no, I preferred to be cleaning my house.

I didn't want to have anything to do with politics, either. People used to come all the time to my house from the socialist party and tell me I should come to a meeting of something or other. I never went, I didn't want to know about politics. Never, no one ever saw me at that time or this having anything to do with politics. I refused to go to meetings under that regime or this, and I've lost nothing by not going, that's for sure. If I'd been a man I'd be saying the same. Politics – me? Never. Politics, you know what they bring in their train? Misfortune and sorrow for the poor at the bottom who have to pay the consequences so that those at the top can climb even higher.

My husband kept his affairs to himself, he didn't say anything to me about taking part in meetings or anything like that. Moreover, I didn't have the intelligence for it. You've got to have a lot of intelligence, like him, to understand about politics – you've got to be able to read and write at least. And as I can only read and write a little, he didn't try to tell me about politics either. We used to have our quarrels about politics because I was fed up with him being involved in the town hall and all the things he had to do, but otherwise no – my house and, when my child was born, her, that was all that concerned me.

There were many women at the time who were political, who were always going to meetings and demonstrations in the streets. There were many who put themselves forward, but not me. No,

I didn't like that commotion with the women causing a tumult in the streets – that's not right whether it is under this regime or the other.

I suppose I was like my parents. They weren't interested in politics. My father was a member of the trade union and he used to go to meetings as everyone did. But he couldn't read or write and didn't have the intelligence either for that sort of thing.

My husband was out a great deal more than he was ever in the house. That's what he liked, being out, even if it meant he had to work harder, he'd rather be out than at home. There's a saying here, 'If the roof of the house falls in it won't fall on my husband.' Well, that was him. He made up in those years for all the time he was going to be shut up, yes he certainly did – not that he would agree. But the one who wasn't able to compensate was me – I've had to go through a lot more than him in these past thirty years.

When he was elected mayor I was pleased for him and I thought, 'They've chosen him because he knows more than any of them, the socialists and the others who have voted for him.' There was a lot of joy then – but look what it brought in the end! But we couldn't know that then.

Him being mayor brought more trouble than anything else. No wage went with it and we never 'ate' a centimo from the town hall as used to happen in the time of the *caciques*. Not a centimo! He had to work for his living just the same as before. There were always people coming for him when he was working and he'd have to go off and in the meantime people would be waiting for him to give them a shave and I'd have to go to fetch him from the town hall – a mess for both of us really. When he went to Madrid for a week I had to look for someone to replace him in the barber's shop, because someone had to be earning for the house and he wasn't earning while he was gone. All he was concerned about was his political things, he wasn't worried about the house. I should have liked to have gone with him, but as he was going on his political affairs. . . .

No, I didn't want to have anything to do with politics. I didn't understand about them, I didn't want to know. . . . When the nationalists took over the village – yes, then I realized what politics meant.

Three

REPUBLIC,
REVOLUTION AND
CIVIL WAR
1931–9

Under all the unrest and revolutionary
action of the last hundred years lies the
agrarian question.

– GERALD BRENAN, *The Spanish Labyrinth*

MANUEL

There was one thing that for me outweighed everything else – to educate the
masses . . . . To make a revolution you have
to create the means that make it
possible. . . . Remember the lack of
culture, the illiteracy, the backwardness
that existed among the peasantry –
among the whole village! There existed
a revolutionary base . . . . But it was a base
that was insufficiently prepared because
of the lack of education. . . .

Agrarian reform, the end of latifundist farming, and educational
reform, the end of illiteracy – these were the two achievements
we most waited for from the Republic. In the short time between
1931 and 1933, when the elections brought the right to power, a
lot was done about education and very little about the land. All
over the country the Republic created new schools. Before, we
had had only two schools here, one for boys and the other for girls.
Now we had five schools in the village, one of them a mixed
school for boys and girls together. And there were more new
schools set up in the countryside where there was even greater
need than in the village.[7]

The new schools were set up in houses rented for the purpose
by the town hall, which also provided the furniture. Textbooks,
pencils, ink and that sort of thing were provided by the state.
The textbooks were changed and very much improved from the

ones I remembered when I was at school – there was no religion in them for one thing. Religion was no longer taught in the schools. If a father wanted his children to learn about religion he could take them to the priest to learn, this was now a matter for the Church and the individual wishes of each father. When I was at school we all had to go to church, but now schools were strictly lay educational, concerned with teaching children to read and write and arithmetic. For fifty years there had been no change in pedagogical methods but now everything was changing for the better. With double the number of new schools, double the number of children could attend. New teachers came to staff the schools and most of them were on the left, belonging to a union which was affiliated to the UGT.

Apart from agrarian and educational reform, the other import-ant changes brought in by the Republic in my opinion were the divorce and civil marriage laws and the secularization of the cemeteries. Under the latter the town hall became responsible for the cemetery instead of the priest. This was very important. Why should burial depend on the priest of only one religion, why should a Protestant or someone of some other religion have to be buried in some place apart? Up to then – and again now – only Catholics who had received the sacraments were allowed burial in the cemetery.

Under the new marriage law you no longer had to get married in church. I was married civilly in February 1935 by the municipal judge, I preferred a civil marriage to a church wedding. I haven't been to church for communion or confession since I left school. You've got to have a certain amount of determination in this environment to say 'I'm not going.' There were plenty who said it and then gave in and went all the same. Not that that made them believers, far from it! But they would give in; if church was the place to get married in they would go; if their baby was born they'd take him to the church. Often it was because of their wives that they went, because women are always more minded to that sort of thing. But I and a few others like me never gave in. I believe in freedom for people to believe what they want. If they want to go to church because they believe in that, then they should be free to go. That's how I've been with my wife, she goes to church when she feels like it because of her belief and I've never tried to stop her.

Nor did I ever try to force her to share my political beliefs. Of course, it's natural that up to a point a wife follows a husband in what he does, but she understands nothing about politics and I never tried to persuade her differently. There weren't many who thought like me, because most husbands expect their wives to follow in whatever they say, even today. But not I! My daughter has the same freedom, she was brought up freely and I never obliged her to do anything.

The new divorce laws were important, too. Of course, these weren't as free and easy as it seems from reading the papers they are in some countries today. You couldn't get divorced on a whim, you had to be able to justify the demand with some serious complaint, adultery, for example. The municipal judge could grant a divorce which meant that people didn't have to spend time and money going to Marbella, which was the judicial centre. Both of these reforms, marriage and divorce, were abolished by the present regime, naturally, along with the municipal judges. The latter have been replaced by justices of the peace with far fewer powers.

One can't talk of the Republic without saying also that it declared the state had no religion and thus separated Church from state. Article 26 of the constitution said that the religious orders weren't to be allowed to engage in education except for training priests, or in business of any sort. The orders, especially the Jesuits, had a lot of money invested in businesses. This article raised a storm when it was discussed in the Cortes.[8] It was one of the reasons, along with agrarian reform, that led to the military uprising which the clergy supported. Today the clergy has evolved differently, but at that time it was solidly behind the uprising.

Agrarian reform, the most important of all, was the area in which the least was done. The government didn't make anything like enough money available to pay for the land that should have been expropriated. Fifty million pesetas was all, when it needed ten times that amount. It wasn't, as the land-owners believed, a matter of knocking down prices but of paying whatever the land was worth on the market. But without enough money what could be done? At the pace they were going those of us who were young then would have died old before the reform that was needed would have been finished. The republican parties were the cause of the delay, they weren't sufficiently concerned about distributing the land. If the reform had been a socialist measure that would have been something else, but the socialist party was in the minority in the republican coalition, though it had more members of the Cortes than any other single party.

A commission was set up in Málaga to carry out the reform. I believe that in one or two places a start was made, but it was very small, if indeed it was begun. Around here nothing happened, of that I'm sure. This seemed bad to us, even if we were aware that the reform ought to start with large properties owned by capitalists. There were few of those round here. All the same, there were individual landlords who owned more than fifty small-holdings each and about whom something ought to have been done.[9]

There was much dispute about the sort of agrarian reform that was needed. In part the socialists wanted the expropriated land to be worked collectively, but there were many like me who thought the land should be individually owned and cooperatively worked. A number of collectives were organized by the Land-workers' Federation in the south and they worked badly. I don't know why, I had no personal experience of them, but it was probably through lack of unity and solidarity. It seemed better to me to give land to those who had none, and to those who had a little to give them more.

Once the people had land they had to be encouraged to form cooperatives, because without that they couldn't get far. But it always seemed evident to me that individual holdings would satisfy more people than collectives and would create a democracy for the first time among the peasants – an evolutionary rather than a revolutionary democracy. Remember the lack of culture, the illiteracy, the backwardness that existed among the peasantry – among the whole village! To make a revolution you have to create the means that make it possible, the psychology of the nation has to be prepared for it. There existed a revolutionary base among the land workers and peasants without any doubt – but it was a base that was insufficiently prepared because of the lack of education and culture. The masses had to be educated first. In this I agreed fully with Besteiro.[10] Which isn't to say that a lot more couldn't have been done in the way of agrarian reform. If only the large estates had been expropriated so that the landless from here and all the other poor regions could have been settled. That would have made a good start.

Of course, giving the peasants individual plots of land and not providing them with state aid to work them would have been worse than no land distribution at all. To give a landless day-labourer a small-holding and leave it at that would have been to sacrifice him to a fate worse than his previous one under a land-owner. No, the state would have had to provide a fund not only for the purchase of tools, seeds, fertilizers and that sort of thing but also create an agricultural bank to make loans to the peasants to tide them over the times between crops. That was how I and the others who thought like me saw it, and how rationally it would have had to be. To have done the contrary would have been to give the land away to no end.

My aim was always to try to form an agricultural cooperative to rid the peasants of the landlords' domination so that their crops shouldn't end up in the capitalists' hands. Especially the olive crop, since all the mills were owned by the landlords and there was nowhere else the peasants could go. The landlords paid very much what they wanted as a result. 'Look at your olives,' I'd say, 'you've got to deliver them to the landlord's mill because there's no other. . . . Through the union we shall be able to get a better price, in the end we shall have a cooperative. . . .'

As many of these small-holders used to come to our barber's shop, I had the chance of talking to them and trying to convince them there. But it took a lot of explaining, one had to be very patient; they have been taken in so many times that they trust no one. I've never liked demagogy, I'm not an orator, but I would go on repeating the same themes to these people until at last they began to join. Many of them had to go out to work as day-labourers themselves when there wasn't enough work on their plots, so they had some idea of what the union was doing in raising wages and improving conditions. But as small-holders, the immediate gains were less for them and they were frightened of what their landlords would do if they joined.

Since their interests were completely different from those of the day-labourers, the small-holders had to have their own section under their own leadership in the union – but always under the overall control of the union's central committee. Occasionally there were outbursts of disagreement between the day-labourers' section and that of the small-holders. The former, who always included a greater number of extremists, used to say that the small-holders were employers and that they were going to make trouble for them. I had to step in and tell the labourers – 'They're workers like you. Whoever works the land is a worker too, even if they have a small-holding. If you do something against them you'll be taking work away from them, preventing them earning a living by their work. The union isn't here to do that.' It was rare that this sort of thing arose, but I managed to calm the labourers down.

On wages, working conditions, hours of work – on all these we made very good progress because our union was strong and also because of the creation by Largo Caballero, the socialist Labour Minister at the time, of mixed juries in which union and employers' representatives met under the mayor. Before the Republic the average day-labourer's wage here was about 3.50 pesetas. In the mixed juries we got this raised to a minimum of 5 pesetas, with specialists getting 6.50 to 7. By 1936 we had got the minimum up to 7 pesetas a day. If there had been work enough, a day-labourer would have eaten better then than he does today, I'm sure of that, because a whole family could live on 5 pesetas a day. Bread cost 60 centimos a kilo, a kilo of rice the same, and a large paper twist of sugar was 15 centimos. . . . But the worst of it was that there wasn't enough work.

Unemployment was chronic. Two or three months' work on the land and two or three months out of work, that was the pattern. Only someone with land had work all the year round and even then. . . . Under the Republic unemployment got worse if anything.

Unlike, say, in Alhaurin, here the labourers went out to look for jobs on the farms and *cortijos*. In Alhaurin the custom was for the unemployed to gather in the square every morning and for the landlords or their bailiffs to come and pick out the men they wanted: 'You . . . you . . . you. . . .' But here the men went out on their own and as like as not they'd go all over the countryside and have to come back without finding a day's work.

One of the things we in the union did was to create a labour exchange, and the person in charge went round the farms every day finding out what labour was needed for the following day. Then at night, in the square, the labourers would come and he would allot them their work for the next day, depending on their speciality. Because on the land there are many types of work which some know how to do and others not. There's digging and preparing the land for irrigation, there's pruning, grafting, there's threshing and winnowing. And there are many different specialists needed in raisin-making which, with the many vines there used to be here, was one of the major tasks on the land, especially the muscatel raisins exported to England and the US. Each speciality had its own minimum wage rate negotiated by the union.

In the summer and early autumn of 1933, things got to such a state with the grape crop here that the village union asked the civil governor to provide special measures to get the crop in. In an attempt to boycott the labourers, the landlords were refusing to gather the crop. The civil governor ordered that the crop be brought in and that, if the landlords refused, the union should take charge. That is what happened. Portions of each vineyard were given individually to peasants who were willing to work them to get the crop in and dry the raisins. Later, this caused conflicts, too, because there were a certain number of olives amongst the vines and those peasants who had brought in the grapes thought they should be allowed to gather the olives as well. But the union had taken charge only for the grapes. . . .

The system the landlords liked best was to have their land sharecropped, since they took fifty per cent of all the crops. That was more profit than they got out of rents as a rule. It was one of our aims to abolish this type of farming, or at least improve its worst aspects.

The worst was the system called *medianería* in which the land-lord provides half the seed, fertilizer and manure and the share-cropper provides everything else. It is a system of slavery, the sharecropper even has to bring half the produce up to the land-lord's house himself. We wanted to abolish this and make it an *aparcería* instead, where the sharecropper provides only his own labour and the landlord provides all the fertilizers, seeds and extra labour that's necessary and has to fetch his half share of the produce from the farm. This aim was one of the reasons I managed to get so many *medianeros* into the union, because I argued that it was only possible to prevent the landlords from continuing the *medianería* if there was collective pressure on them. But we never succeeded entirely because time was so short.

Still, we got the working day reduced for the day-labourers who previously worked from sunrise to sunset. Every two hours, under the new agreement, they now got twenty minutes' rest, with an hour for the midday meal, a half-hour in the afternoon, and a stopping time of about five o'clock. This had the effect of reducing the working day from about twelve hours to nearer six. Before, it had been slavery and a pittance.

Defence of the peasants' interests, land reform, school reform and all the other reforms proposed by the party were, of course, very important to me. But there was one thing that for me outweighed everything else – the need to educate the masses. Because of illiteracy and lack of education the masses thought that as soon as the socialists came to power everything would be all right, without thinking of the organization that was necessary. In the party and union I was always trying to restrain those among us who were demagogic, who tried to make the masses believe everything would be solved by a socialist victory. A comrade of mine, a barber like me, was one of these – a demagogue, though it's unpleasant to say. He was very 'advanced' in the way he talked to the people – and it was all lies. You can't talk to the masses when they're uneducated in that sort of way because when the things don't turn out as they expect all you do is fill them with defeatist ideas. Where there's a higher level of culture, that's another matter. I always tried to explain things as they were, the facts, not rhetoric, because I believed that was more educative and likely to produce results in the end. Of course, what I could explain was limited by my own level of culture because I had received only a village education.

During these first two years of the Republic I was busy building up the union and party. Being general secretary of the union meant a lot of work, especially when it was necessary to go to Fuengirola or Málaga to air something or other at the union headquarters or with the civil authorities. None of the union or party posts carried a wage, and so all of us had to continue in our ordinary jobs. It meant considerable sacrifices because there was no compensation for time off from work, and many times I've paid my fare to Málaga out of my own pocket. Other times the union or party would pay travelling expenses, but somehow or other we were usually out of pocket. I would work all the hours I could in the barber's shop where a young cousin of mine was just beginning to learn the trade and was able to help out a bit, but a lot of the time it was my father on whom the extra work fell.

When the union was first set up, U G T leaders from Málaga came to the first meeting to draw up the statutes which we had to present to the civil governor's office in Málaga where they and the minutes and accounts were approved and stamped. Under our statutes the union had general meetings once a month and extra-ordinary assemblies when either one-quarter of the membership or the committee demanded one. The committee was elected for one year, although not all its members would last out the time, they'd get fed up or something. There was a quite serious problem in this. There were always people who were serious and would keep their word in carrying out the jobs they had undertaken to do, but there were many more who lacked seriousness and took everything as a joke. It's the Andaluz character. The Catalans are people who do what they say they're going to do and, although there's much I don't like about them, I admire them for that. But not here in Andalusia.

I had always to fight against this lack of seriousness, particularly at meetings. We'd be discussing something important and there would be not one but fifty maybe, cracking jokes and laughing – without realizing the importance of the situation. And I'd say to them, 'Look, we've come here to discuss the following. If you want to turn it into a fiesta, go somewhere else.' It's a negative side of the Andaluz character, it's a great defect.

The union was open to all workers, naturally. There was a charge of one peseta to become a member and thereafter fifteen centimos a week dues. At the beginning the dues were only ten centimos but that was too little, we had to raise them. Occasion-ally, if there were extraordinary expenses, an additional contribu-tion would be voted at a general assembly. Votes in the union were always by raised hand, while in the party they were secret. Because no one could be denied membership of the union, the party's main role was to provide the political leadership, to orientate the union to socialist goals, and provide political propaganda. Written propaganda was difficult because of the illiteracy, but even so those who were able would read it aloud to the others. We distributed pamphlets throughout the countryside, down as far as Calahonda where we had members. We had a branch in the country for those people who couldn't get up here except for important meetings. And often I or another of the union officials would go down there to tell them what was happening in Málaga or Madrid.

Not everyone could join the party. Only convinced socialists were admitted, not people who might want to join out of political opportunism. To be admitted, you had to have the approval of the union organization or be generally known as a true socialist, a revolutionary. Many of the union leaders were in the party but not all. Our total membership was never more than a hundred at the time when we had fifteen hundred union members. We could have had five or six times that number of party members if we had wanted, but we considered quality more important than quantity, ideological soundness the main concern. Until you had been a party member for two years you weren't allowed to hold any official post or represent the party officially, that was a national rule.

Apart from my party and union work I had my job to do at the town hall as well. Here we put an end to the practices that were common under the rule of the *caciques*. For the first time whatever money there was wasn't 'eaten' as it had been in the past. Not at any time under the Republic, even during the *bienio negro* of right-wing rule when, though freedom was much curtailed, it was still possible to protest. The *décima*, ten per cent of the village taxes which the government returned for unemployment benefits, was now paid out to unemployed day-labourers to keep paths and streets in condition, and for any other public works the town hall thought needed doing. Before this the money had always been 'eaten', the mayor and three or four cronies giving five or ten pesetas to a few workers to sign the receipts for wages paid and pocketing the thousands that ought to have been spent. The town hall was no longer a place of graft.

We faced one major problem – the village budget was always at least forty per cent short of the money it should have got in through local taxes. This was because of a law that no republican government got round to changing. The law was that, in municipalities like this, there had to be a utilities tax which applied to everyone, in the countryside as well as in the village. It was calculated on the assets of each head of family, and was made to apply to the day-labourers like everyone else, though of course they were assessed for much less. A commission made the assessments. But whatever the labourers were assessed they never paid;

they had nothing to pay with and yet, because there were seven to eight hundred of them, they were supposed to make up forty per cent of the budget. It was that forty per cent which the town hall never saw.

In consequence, the town hall was always in debt. The budgets were a fiction and a lot of things the village should have paid never were. For example, like all the others in the region, Mijas was supposed to contribute to the cost of maintaining the judiciary in Marbella. Very rarely, if ever, was that contribution paid. And the same was true of the other villages around. The town hall's priorities were its own employees' wages, and the state taxes, then the electricity company for the street lighting, then the bank's interest on the loans that had been made under the Primo dictatorship.

Like thousands of others, the village was left indebted for thirty years to the banks by the public works that the dictator organized. For all I know, the town hall may be still paying off the Guardia Civil barracks and the school and the teachers' houses next to it which were built at the time. Often there wasn't enough money to pay the interest, so we'd tell the bank to take it out of the loan made under the dictatorship to build a new cemetery. That loan was eaten up paying the interest on the other loans, and the cemetery was built – finally – only last year. Throughout the Republic these loans weighed on us, leaving the town hall in a bad financial state.

Only the government or the Cortes could have abolished the law. Meanwhile, the land-owners and others who paid their part insisted that the law be respected. 'The taxes must be apportioned as under the law,' they would say, and there was nothing we could do about it. We protested through our parliamentary representatives but nothing ever got done.

Local administrations have never had any autonomy in Spain, they've always been dependent on the authorities above. That is the defect of centralization from which we've suffered a lot. Though we drew up our own budget in the town hall, it could only be put into effect after approval by the provincial authorities. They could give their approval, it made no difference to them that it was a fiction, but it was left to us to try to manage on only sixty per cent of the total.

Our coalition partners in the town hall were the radicals, whose national leader was Lerroux, and the radical socialists.[11] The latter were a much more democratic party than Lerroux's and closer to our positions. Lerroux turned out a traitor to the Republic when he became Prime Minister in 1933 at the start of the *bienio negro*. And yet locally we got on better with the radicals than with the radical socialists. In fact, we couldn't get on with the latter at all. In Málaga no one could understand it. 'How can that be? Why can't you work with them?' the socialist leaders used to ask us. Well, it was simple enough.

I've explained that when the radical socialists first tried to form in the village the old *cacique* forbade the party's creation. Or rather he told the man who was trying to organize it that if he went ahead he personally, the *cacique*, would have it in for him. This man, Lopez, quickly gave in. This was before the Republic came in, at the time when we were forming the socialist party clandestinely. But after a while, when he saw that the Republic was there to stay and he was going to be left out of things, the old *cacique* tried to redeem the situation by getting Lopez to start the radical socialist party again. 'You begin it again and bring in all the people you can . . .', and then he got all his old followers to join the party, all the people who had been implicated with him, as well as those who had been supporters of the Primo dictatorship. The old *cacique* himself didn't join, that would have been to give the game away. He preferred to manipulate things from behind the scenes. Of course, we couldn't get on with those people at all. Lerroux's radicals, most of whom had been monarchists here before, were better to work with than them.

The coalition ended locally and nationally in 1933. At the beginning of the year the affair of Casas Viejas dealt the Republic a bad blow. Some peasants, anarcho-syndicalists, tried to take over the village which is in the province of Cadiz not so far from here. They attacked the Guardia Civil barracks, it was part of an anarchist revolutionary strike that had started in the north. The direct action the anarchists always preached! A few poor uneducated men with shotguns who thought that all they had to do to make the revolution was to take over the village!

The government sent in the Assault Guards under a certain Captain Rojas. He was an opponent of the Republic and in his desire to discredit the government he massacred who knows how many people in the village. Later he claimed he had been under orders to do so, but that was disproved. He did it because he knew the discredit it would bring to the government, the shooting down in cold blood of the villagers, innocent most of them. It was a very serious setback to the government, which was defeated at the elections later that year.

In Casas Viejas itself the people who had supported the anarcho-syndicalist CNT learnt their lesson. They saw they had been taken in by the propaganda of direct action and brute force. The socialist party and the UGT became stronger there than anywhere else in the province of Cadiz.[12]

Here the anarcho-syndicalists never had much of a following. The CNT was set up once in the thirties and had to close down because it didn't attract enough members to keep going. After the outbreak of the civil war in 1936 it was set up again, but it never had more than a hundred members in comparison to the UGT's fifteen hundred or so. Its organizers had little influence among the masses, they were people with bourgeois ideas who set it up mainly to attack our organization.

The principal activist was the manager of the agate quarry here. Imagine that, a manager! Fernando was his name. I was quite friendly with him. His brother was in the UGT. During the *bienio negro* Fernando joined a right-wing landlords' party, the Partido Agrario. The reason he formed the CNT in opposition to us was that he wanted to keep the quarry-workers under his thumb. Though he had been a worker, he had become a bourgeois from head to toe. His interests couldn't be those of the workers; but as he attracted those who thought of themselves as the most militantly revolutionary, the extremists who wanted to use brute force, they didn't see the contradiction. Of course, they weren't more revolutionary than us, they were simply more demagogic. No conscious socialist could trust them.

For me, moreover, their ideology was – and still is – completely unrealizable, the revolution in the form in which they propose it is utopian. I don't know how anyone politically formed on the left can imagine that by destroying the state you can achieve freedom and a new form of society. To destroy the state would mean turning everybody against everybody else as each one tried to appropriate what he could. But the destruction of the state was the major anarchist principle and it was anarchist ideology which motivated the CNT, though there were many members of the CNT nationally who weren't themselves anarchists.

In most of the villages round here the CNT wasn't very strong. Coin, Alhaurin, Monda, Fuengirola, Marbella – all had socialist majorities. Benalmádena was radical. Where the CNT dominated was in the mountain villages around Ronda, in the small and most backward villages where there was no politics. In Ronda itself the CNT was stronger than the UGT. There was another area stretching from Alhaurin de la Torre up to Casarabonela, Yunquera and the neighbouring villages, in which the CNT predominated. In Málaga itself, the UGT and the CNT were of about the same strength and this meant that in villages close by one or other of the two might dominate.[13]

Wherever there were republicans, or so-called republicans like Lerroux's radicals, in power, the CNT was encouraged to expand. The fact of the matter was that the radicals supported the CNT because of the latter's apolitical stand in telling its members not to vote in elections. Throughout the first two years of the Republic the employers paid the CNT many thousands of pesetas to encourage them to put forward the slogan '*No Votad*'. The money they got was spent on preparing their revolutionary strikes, all of which failed, as they were bound to. And when the general elections of 1933 took place, the anarchists didn't vote, thereby helping to give victory to the right.

But it must be admitted that the left was disunited once the socialist–republican coalition split up.

The first thing almost to happen under the right-wing government of Lerroux – he was supported by Gil Robles's CEDA – was that the minimum wage rates we had fought for were abolished. Employers could again pay what they wanted and wages went down to the levels of before the Republic. The already slow agrarian reform was slowed down even more. It was a situation that equalled that of the monarchy and *caciquismo*.

In June of the next year, 1934, there were strikes in the countryside and rumours of a right-wing *coup* which would let Gil Robles[14] into the government. Some of us were warned by directives from the provincial socialist party committees to prepare ourselves, but without any concrete details or explanations as to what was to be done. There was no mention of a date or anything like that. Then, at the beginning of October, the CEDA joined the government and a revolutionary uprising started in Asturias, Catalonia and Madrid. There was so little coordination and advance preparation that it was doomed to fail. In Madrid there were a few skirmishes of little importance; in Catalonia the movement was put down in a few days; only in Asturias did the workers fight. The newspapers were censored and we didn't get much news. But the repression ordered by Lerroux, who made his name as a politician preaching revolutionary violence, and Gil Robles was ferocious. They brought in the Foreign Legion from Morocco to put down the revolt. They claimed that the miners had killed nuns and children – the usual lies the right put out here – when what they did was to fight for as long as they could.

Asturias was the first time socialists, communists and anarchists fought together. The union brought strength – but the whole thing was isolated from the start, it was doomed to fail. It needed coordinating throughout the nation if it was to succeed. The Asturians have always been firm in their political commitment, but what could they do on their own when the army was sent in against them and the rest of the nation stood back with its arms crossed?

Nothing happened here, there were no plans, no organization, nothing. But the reaction was immediate. All socialists and true republicans in town halls and provincial governments were thrown out of office. It made no difference that we had been legally elected. The new civil governor ordered his own radical followers and CEDA members to take over the town hall. The retired major was now the leader of CEDA here and he brought into it all the elements of his time as *cacique* under the Primo dictatorship. All left-wing parties and unions were suppressed and their offices closed at local level. We continued to meet – the most militant socialists – clandestinely in my house or wherever it seemed safest. The Guardia Civil were constantly checking and searching, and if they had discovered us we should certainly have been thrown in jail.

By the end of 1935 Lerroux was forced to resign because he was involved in a financial scandal. That showed up the man for what he really was! A certain Portela Valladares, an old-style politician who had become a republican, was made caretaker Prime Minister to hold new general elections. He thought the centre forces he represented could win. So did the old *cacique*, because he now re-entered the political arena openly and became a republican. He was made mayor by the new civil governor appointed by the Portela regime. 'Don't get any ideas about voting for anyone,' he went round telling the people, 'I've been appointed for ten years.'

For the elections, all the left-wing parties joined in a Popular Front: the socialists, communists, the left republicans of Azaña, the Unión Republicana of Martinez Barrio. The programme's major point was an amnesty for all political prisoners. Thirty thousand political prisoners the right had jailed during its two years in government! First the amnesty, then speeding up land reform and abolishing all the laws that Lerroux and Gil Robles had pushed through and which had reduced the original republican reforms to nothing. Not a very advanced programme, but that was because the coalition included republicans who wouldn't accept anything more progressive. The important thing was to defeat the right.

As it was an electoral coalition, none of the parties could make their own propaganda. We had election meetings and speakers from the provincial federations of each of the parties and we put up Popular Front posters all over the village. Sunday 16 February, polling day, it rained very hard – one of those days when the rain comes in off the sea in buckets, flooding the river. The right laid on buses to ferry the people in from the country-side to vote. As soon as they got off the buses, the people made their way to the Casa del Pueblo to collect their Popular Front ballots. The *cacique* as usual did his best, he could never forget his old ways. He got his henchmen out in the streets to stop Popular Front militants from getting the vote out.

The Guardia Civil sergeant helped. He and the *cacique*'s men tried to prevent anyone making propaganda for the left in the street, and all the time they were busy making propaganda for their own side, trying to make people vote for the right. Little good it did them or the old *cacique*. We had the sympathy of the people and their votes. Although the rain cost us a lot, because much of our support came from the isolated farmsteads in the countryside and out towards the sierra – the women especially couldn't cross the flooded river to vote – it was a triumph for the Popular Front. There was great joy in the village and countryside when the results were proclaimed.

The situation in the countryside [after the elections] was revolutionary. The Popular Front had spoken of faster land reform; the peasants, hungry for land, believed their electoral victory sufficed. From the end of February in the provinces of Badajoz and Caceres, and with increasing rapidity in the succeeding months, peasants occupied land in Extremadura, Andalusia and Castille. . . . Frequently there were bloody incidents between peasants and Guardia Civil. The most serious occurred in Yeste, near Alicante, where the Guardia arrested six peasants who were cutting down trees on a large land-owner's estate. Armed with pitchforks, clubs and stones the peasants of Yeste attacked the Guardia who were marching their comrades away. In the shooting eighteen peasants were killed.

— PIERRE BROUÉ AND ÉMILE TÉMIME,
La Révolution et la Guerre d'Espagne

MANUEL

The republicans were always thinking about legality. . . . They lacked the principles and the strength to clear away everything that was old and build on new bases.

On 3 March I succeeded the old *cacique* as mayor of the village. The Popular Front town council was formed that day, and those of us who had been thrown out of office after Asturias were re-instated. Because of the uprising, the municipal elections had been put off and so we were the rightful elected representatives. There were eight socialists, four left republicans and two republicans of Martinez Barrio's party on the council.[15] In a secret ballot I was unanimously elected as mayor – no, less one vote which was mine. I thought it was a piece of good fortune – but it didn't turn out that way!

I took over the administration and started to collect the *décima* to get the unemployed work on the streets and paths, and went through all the papers of the period when we had been thrown out. There were two things I most wanted to do – to bring the telephone to Mijas and get the road between here and Benal-mádena made up. The road had fallen into such a state of dis-repair that it was impassable. If it could be repaired it would cut the journey to Málaga and make the village less isolated. It would also give work. Ever since the Republic came in, the town hall had been trying to get funds for the road but each time difficulties of one sort or another, usually financial, were put in our way by the authorities in Málaga. It seemed to me that it was no good con-tinuing to present our case in Málaga, as had been done up to then.

I would go to Madrid instead. It happened that I knew the Minister of Labour who was a Málaga deputy called Ramos Ramos. I had established a friendship with him when I was deputy mayor and had written to him asking for his help in a village matter. The mayor at that time was an old man and often absent and I used to take over when he wasn't there. And one day I thought, why not write to Ramos Ramos? He was then under-secretary to the Prime Minister, Azaña, and a left republican like him. When he came to Málaga I went to visit him and also received him in Fuengirola one day when he was visiting there. Later he became Minister of Finance in the last cabinet before the military uprising under the premiership of Casares Quiroga, whose weakness was in itself largely responsible for allowing the uprising to take place.

Thus I thought I would go to Madrid. By talking personally with Ramos Ramos I believed I could get the money approved for the road. I arranged to travel to the capital with the mayor of Fuengirola who also had projects he was trying to get through.

We left for Madrid in early April. It was the first time I had been to the capital. It was also the first time a mayor of Mijas had gone to Madrid on business. Accompanied by a deputy who was president of the Málaga Socialist Federation and a friend of mine, I went to see Ramos Ramos. He authorized the Benal-mádena road without hesitation, and I was very pleased because no one had managed that before. Then I went to see the director general of the telephone service who agreed that a line should be put in to Mijas for a payment of two thousand pesetas to the company in Seville. In a few days I had accomplished what I had set out to achieve. Little did I or anyone else know that it was for nothing, that in little more than three months the civil war would begin. There was so little time!

While in Madrid I visited the Cortes, went to see officials of the Treasury and saw many of the socialist leaders, including Largo Caballero, secretary general of the UGT.[16] The mayor of Fuengirola and I had brought with us a small present of a box of Mijas raisins to present to Caballero when we paid our courtesy call. When we got to his office the porter refused us entry. 'Leave that box there,' he said, 'that looks like a bomb.' At that time in the capital and elsewhere there had been several assassination attempts, against Caballero himself, against Jimenez de Asúa, a socialist deputy, against Eduardo Ortega y Gasset, the republican deputy and brother of the famous writer. These were attempts by the *falangistas* who were using violence against the left. In Málaga itself, the socialist president of the provincial chamber was assassinated – but this was the work of the anarchists. Members of the FAI were waiting in ambush and shot him down as he crossed the bridge just before you reach the Alameda. Roman Reina his name was, and he was a personal friend of mine. In retaliation the CNT was attacked. Communists joined with socialists in this, we always got on better with them than with the anarchists. But the *falangistas* also took their toll. They assassinated a very famous communist councillor in Málaga who was a fine person and who was always exposing injustice in the city. A municipal guard at the town hall who secretly belonged to the Falange shot and killed him. These were the sort of things that were happening for political reasons at the time.[17]

Anyway, when we explained who we were and where we came from, they let us in to see Caballero. After we had told him about things in Mijas and Fuengirola, he said, 'All right, bring in the box of raisins. . . .' Personally, I didn't find him very sympathetic as a man. He was rather cold and distant and, though more to the left than Prieto, the latter was much warmer and more cordial with party comrades. At least that's how it seemed to us, but these were only rapid impressions. . . .

I was in Madrid on 14 April for the military parade in honour of the founding of the Republic. That day a military officer was assassinated by the *falangistas* and a bomb exploded under the President's reviewing stand, without doing much damage. When I got back to Mijas on the bus from Málaga the next day I found that everyone on the right had been rounded up and was in jail! My deputy, the barber, had ordered between fifty and sixty people to be detained. An incredible state of affairs! 'You must be mad,' I said, 'you've gone out of your mind. You can't shut up everyone like that. Let them out. You put them in, you'll have to release them.'

'Ah no,' he said, 'I only did it under pressure from the labourers. You manage it now as best you can.' He had been waiting for my return to get him out of his trouble. It was true enough that the labourers had taken things into their own hands. When they heard the news from Madrid they formed their own patrols and went to round up whoever they thought was on the right. There was only one policeman as such in the village at the town hall's orders. But it was my deputy's fault for allowing it to happen. I wouldn't have permitted a folly like that because I've never been sympathetic to reprisals of that kind. And in any case, they hadn't done anything. You can't detain people simply because they happen to be on the right.

It was left to me to sort out. The 'prisoners' were in the patio of the town hall and in the large room upstairs, because they wouldn't all fit into the jail, which is no more than a cell for a single prisoner under temporary detention, or municipal arrest as it's called. I called the clerk of the town hall and said, 'Give me the list', and then to the porter I said, 'Start letting them out.' I left the leaders, those who were known to be the main right-wing activists and leaders of the CEDA in particular, till last. I wanted the people in the square to disperse before letting them out, so as to avoid the possibility of ugly incidents.

By about ten at night, when I saw that most of the people had gone to the bars or to their homes, I released the remainder. The major was one of them. He had never forgotten the time when he was *cacique* here during the Primo dictatorship and he took being detained very badly. Soon afterwards he left Mijas to live in Málaga, his pride had been wounded and wouldn't let him remain. . . .

The mayor had the right to detain a person for twenty-four hours and then release him or put him at the disposition of the judge. During this time, when the landlords were refusing to give work, preferring to leave their land uncultivated, I wasn't above detaining one or two to put pressure on them. It was an impossible situation, because when the labourers went looking for work they'd reply, 'Let the Republic find you work, let the Republic feed you.' And all the while they had land to cultivate. If they had had no work to do that would have been a different matter, because we couldn't have expected them to do the same job twice over, it wouldn't have been economic. But that wasn't the case at all. They preferred to see their crops wither rather than give the labourers work.

The government had provided for such cases. It was possible to draw up a claim against any land-owner whose land wasn't being worked and who refused jobs. To make such a claim I had to send a member of the rural police, as they were called, along with an agricultural expert who was attached to the town hall, to determine whether there was work that needed doing, to assess how much needed doing and all that sort of thing. The expert would return and make out his report: yes, it was certain that there was this and that that needed doing. I then had to make out a claim incorporating the expert's findings and send it to Málaga to the Provincial Agricultural Section to be approved by the agronomist in charge. He in turn had to send one of his specialists here to look at the land and make his own assessment of our assessment. He would go back to Málaga and make out his report and, in due course, if he had found that there was work that needed doing, we would receive his report and the authority to oblige the landlord to do it. By that time, a month or two had passed! *Hombre*, how is a man who needs a day's labour and a day's wage to keep a family alive going to wait a month or two before getting a job? That was the trouble with all the republican governments, their excessive legality, the excessive time it took to get things done.

Well, it was impossible not to take the law into our own hands from time to time. So sometimes I would say to this or that landlord, 'You give work to these men who need it or I'll clap you in jail.' Other times the union would send men to do the work the landlords weren't doing and force them to pay the labourers' wages. It was only through fear that we could get anywhere with them. Otherwise time passed, the paper work mounted up and nothing concrete happened to give people work.

I started the action of making claims out against only two, and with one of them I reached agreement in advance. I was sorry for the man and I said, 'Give us the money to cover the costs of the labour for doing the jobs that are the most important and we'll get out of the mess.' That's what he did. He gave over the money and we put the men on doing the tasks.

But the other man was a completely different type – so stubborn that he allowed his livestock to be seized rather than pay for the work that had to be done. I had him up and I said, 'I've got here the claim that has been approved in Málaga for the work that needs doing. You've got to pay now or else I'll take action.' He refused to pay. 'In that case I've no option but to send the wage list to the judge.' And the judge ordered that his two horses, a pig and a young donkey be seized to cover the costs. He was a pig-headed man who had no need to be like that, because he didn't even own the land but rented it. His landlord was the son of a count and a millionaire who lived in Málaga and who was using this tenant to his own ends.

I said to the farmer, 'Look here, all you're doing is playing your landlord's game because you've let yourself be taken in by him. Let the *señorito* look after himself, tell him to deal directly with me and get yourself out of this situation.' He refused, so I said, 'Well, get the work done yourself then.' 'I haven't the money,' he said. 'Well, what do you want then?' He didn't say anything and I felt sorry for him because it was he who had to pay, not the landlord, who could well have afforded it. But what else could I do?

In other cases I'd get hold of the land-owners and I'd send them a dozen men. 'There you are,' I'd say, 'you've got these men and you've got to pay them their day's wage tonight. Find them jobs.' It was quite illegal but there was nothing else to do. No one could wait months and months while all the legal formalities were gone through. What was important was to get the unemployed work.

The landlords were attempting to stage a boycott in order to crush the labourers. Any work they gave had to be forced out of them. If we had let them be, every vineyard in Mijas, every single vine would have been abandoned – as indeed happened after the nationalists entered. Then the landlords rooted out all their vines to prevent anything like that happening again. Of all the vineyards which used to provide the raisins we exported from here, only two or three are left now, the poorest. That's the way the bourgeoisie is here, intransigent. For them a socialist is the very devil himself. They could never understand that they were driving the masses towards violent solutions far more extreme than any the socialist party, for my part, would have advocated. But that's how they are, reactionary, traditionalist, frightened of any change – and with a terrible fear of the proletariat.

Things got to such a state that in June there was an agricultural workers' strike, called by the provincial federation of the union. The demands were for higher minimum wages and improved working conditions. The strike was complete here and almost everywhere in the province. It lasted four or five days and was completely successful, but there were several incidents between the Guardia and the strikers. There was also a lot of friction between Mijas and Fuengirola. The latter has no municipal district to speak of and thus all the day-labourers from there depended on working within the district of Mijas. There were more landless labourers in Fuengirola – about a thousand in all – than there were in Mijas. And because most of the land-owners who held land in Mijas, the rich land along the river and the vineyards, lived in Fuengirola, they were under pressure to give work to the labourers there.

During the strike I received complaints from small-holders close to Fuengirola that strike pickets had invaded their land and were trampling their crops and that sort of thing. What happened, of course, was that the pickets were out to see that no scabs got through. Here and there they'd find a small-holder irrigating or doing some chore on his land and they'd invade it in reprisal. The small-holder would complain to me and, as mayor responsible to the whole village, it was my duty to protect him. This sort of thing caused me a lot of trouble.

I had more when a hotel started to be built on the coast. It was one of the first luxury hotels to be constructed for tourists here, mainly for the English in Gibraltar but also for people coming from abroad. It's called the Hotel Alhamar and was being built by a Spanish-born Englishman within the district of Mijas. Despite its situation, not a single Mijeño was working on it. All the workers were from Fuengirola. So one day I went down there and threatened that the work would have to stop unless the position were rectified. The foreman told the owner that I was there. 'Either half the labour force here is made up of Mijeños or I'll close down the building. Fifty-fifty, exclusivity for neither one nor the other.' The owner understood and took on half his men from Mijas. But the Fuengirola workers protested and took it very badly. 'Look,' I told them, 'I've got men out of work in Mijas as well and they have more right to this job than you because it's in their municipal district.' I had to argue very hard with them to make them respect my will. Such labour disputes between workers from one village and another were quite common at the time.

However, it was with the landlords that our fight was the bitterest. If, as I've said, they were reactionary, I don't at all mean that they were fascists. There were very few true fascists in the whole of Spain at the time. Here there were three or four, no more, and the Falange was never openly set up, though the major had organized it clandestinely.[18] Of course, when these people took over, most of the conservatives, those who believe that anything liberal must be harmful, who stick to the Church and religion – most of them opportunistically became *falangistas*.

At that time there were only two young men, the doctor and the son of one of the richest landlords, who openly showed their fascist leanings. They had to leave the village quickly, after making the fascist salute in the square. They were very foolish, they ought to have known that the people wouldn't stand for that sort of thing.

Comrades came to tell me what was happening, saying there was great unrest among the people who had seen them. I had both of them detained; if I hadn't, they might well have been lynched by the crowd. I went to see them and I said, 'You can have whatever ideas you like, but if you think you can get away with demonstrations like that, when the masses are ready for anything, you've got trouble in store. They'll lynch you. . . .' I waited until the crowd had dispersed before releasing them with a warning. They took it seriously because both of them left the village.

Indirectly, out of that incident arose one of the grudges against me, though not from either of the two young men or their families, let it be said. The doctor, who got another appointment in Casarabonela, was the son-in-law of the town clerk, this Don Lucas who was a good friend of mine, although he was on the right.

The other young man, a *señorito*, was sent by his father, one of the land-owners here, to stay for his safety with his grandparents in Fuengirola. When the civil war started a couple of months later his grandparents were said to have contributed to a fund in support of the fascists. They and the lad with them – he couldn't have been more than eighteen – were taken and shot. If he had stayed up here and kept quiet he would certainly have lived, like his father. But in Fuengirola they liquidated a great many people.

It was a turbulent five months between the elections and the start of the military uprising; there were many upheavals and disturbances. One of the ugliest happened on May Day, 1936.

The government issued an order that May Day demonstrations could be held only in those places where the mayor could guarantee they would be held peacefully. It was, after all, only two and a half months before the start of the war.

At that time there was no telephone or telegraphic communication with the village, as I've said. Fuengirola was as far as the lines went. This meant that if a telegram arrived in Fuengirola after the post had been collected for Mijas, it remained there for twenty-four hours until the next postal collection. You could count on most telegrams arriving twenty-four hours late. As for the phone, there was one line which belonged to the electricity company and which, as a favour, the electrician would let people use to pass messages on to Fuengirola. Even then he wasn't supposed to, and it was a nuisance because it was a private company's line.

Anyway, a day or two before 1 May the civil governor of the province sent a telegram to me and another to the sergeant of the Guardia detachment here. Similar telegrams went out all over the province informing the local authorities of the government's order. As usual, the two telegrams for Mijas got stuck in Fuengirola, arriving here only on the evening of 30 April, too late for me to contact the civil governor's office and guarantee the demonstration. By then there wouldn't have been anyone still at work in the offices, even if I had been able to contact them. Remember, it was the first May Day since the Popular Front victory and the people were expecting to demonstrate. It was too late to get hold of people living in the farmsteads scattered over the countryside to tell them the demonstration couldn't be held, and it was in the countryside that the mass of people were mobilized.

From early on 1 May these people started to come to the village. Without any discussion with me the Guardia Civil, six men and the sergeant, all armed, had stationed themselves in the square and were trying to break up the demonstration. As the people arrived peacefully they began to try to push them out of the square. A village councillor, Antonio Ruiz, who was coming from his house in the countryside was one of those manhandled. I was at home in the *barrio* at the other end of the village. A delegation came running to find me. 'The Guardia are manhandling people in the square. They won't last a minute more because there are five hundred or a thousand of us and they're only seven. We're going to cut them up.'

So I ran to the square and said to the sergeant, 'You must be out of your mind. Get back to your barracks. You've got your orders and I've got mine. There isn't going to be a demonstration because there isn't permission, therefore there won't be one. But is that a reason for manhandling people? For laying a hand to anyone? You've come out armed against the people. Return to your barracks.' And to the people in the square I said: 'Go to the bars or the Casa del Pueblo or wherever you want, but disperse. There's no demonstration. . . .'

It was a very ugly situation that could have led to disasters like those of Castilblanco and Arnedo where the Guardia Civil fired on peasants who were trying to demonstrate. In Castilblanco four *guardias* were killed by the peasants with whatever they could lay their hands on after the Guardia opened fire. In Arnedo the Guardia shot down six people, four of them women. All this was still fresh enough in people's minds because Castilblanco and Arnedo happened in the winter of 1931–2. And the same would have happened here.

The sergeant and two other *guardias* had been particularly heavy-handed in trying to get people out of the square. One of the two was Garcia. He had been here since before the Republic was declared, which was probably why he asked to come back here after the nationalists came in. Anyway, the people's hatred for the three men was expressed by the union which wrote a letter of protest signed by hundreds of villagers and which I took to the civil governor in Málaga. The letter asked for the removal of these guards from the village. They were transferred on the governor's orders immediately. In those days the Guardia Civil came under the orders of the Ministry of the Interior and at the provincial level under the civil governor. Today the Guardia belong directly to the Army Ministry.

One of the problems at that time was that the civil governor considered the mayor of a village like this and the commander of the Guardia post as equal in authority. Both received orders from him. Yet a mayor is the elected head of the village and it is he who should receive orders and pass them on to the Guardia Civil. In normal circumstances, you would have expected the sergeant to come to me and say, 'Look, Manuel, I've received this telegram. You've received yours too, we ought to decide what we're going to do jointly. Because there can't be a demonstration tomorrow. . . .' But this sergeant would never have imagined doing anything like that. It was the same one who had acted so badly on election day. He was one of those old-style reactionaries completely lacking an open mind. In those days most Guardia Civil sergeants wouldn't lower themselves to speak to a socialist or communist mayor. If I hadn't kept my head, we would have had a massacre here.

Perhaps because of what had happened in Castilblanco and Arnedo, the civil governor agreed to transfer these guards. They were thrown out of here – not by me, I want to insist on that – but by the will of the village. In fact, I think I should have pressed the matter further and tried to have them expelled from the corps, which is what they deserved. But I didn't want to.

Instead I – or rather the town hall – paid for the removal of their furniture and things to their new posts, which we weren't obliged to do. Garcia always remembered that and was grateful to me. But more important was my attitude to them during the revolutionary period after the military uprising. As I've said, they were in Málaga and scared out of their lives. It was a good thing for them the people from here couldn't find them. . . . When, by chance, I'd see one of them in the street in Málaga, I'd turn my head so as not to see them, pass by as though I hadn't noticed. There was another sergeant I could have taken revenge on who had personally done me harm not long before. I had it in for him because during the Asturias uprising in 1934, when all socialists were forced out of municipal administrations, he took my shotgun away from me, and those of a few others, too. I had a licence for it – that wasn't the problem – but, instead of keeping the gun in the barracks, he sent it to Málaga to be sold at auction, and that was the last I saw of it. During the revolution I could have got my own back on him and given him a bad time. But when I saw him in the street I just turned my head away. . . .

Ever since the elections, we had been aware of rumours that the military planned to rise to destroy the Republic. To anyone with any political awareness at all it was clear that the Republic was weak, and that since the beginning the government had lacked the necessary vigour to pursue the right course. And that was as true, if not more so, after the Popular Front victory as before.

The government lacked the energy or the strength to deal with its enemies who were still in positions of power, traitors in their immense majority.

The republicans were always thinking about legality. Look at the business of the claims I've described. That sort of legality and paperwork existed in everything. They believed in respecting everyone's rights as they had always been, leaving everything equal. Whereas I believed that in creating a new state, a Republic, you had to throw overboard this sort of legalism and make a clean sweep. But the republicans were weak, they lacked the principles and strength to clear away everything that was old and build on new bases. If they had, the Republic would have gone forward with far greater strength. It was going forward anyway, but too slowly, with too much respect for antiquated forms. Every time I went to see the civil governor on business I ran into the old bureaucracy that was still embedded there, which seemed to exist only to think up reasons why something couldn't be done, which put blocks in one's way.

But one mustn't forget also that the Republic lasted only a short time, only five years before the uprising, and two of those were the *bienio negro* of Lerroux and Gil Robles. In that time there were several political convulsions: General Sanjurjo's military uprising in 1932, the failure of Asturias – and despite all that, the Republic was progressing. But it wasn't given a chance. On 18 July, only five months after our victory in the elections, the news came on the radio that our fears had come true. The military uprising had begun.

The rising of the masses that led to the
defeat of the insurrection in Madrid and
Barcelona carried everything before it. . . .
The workers, through their party and
trade-union organizations, became the real
rulers of the country and the organizers
of the war. This, one might say, was the
Soviet phase of the Spanish Revolution.
And yet it would, I think, be a mistake to
regard it as a purely revolutionary
phenomenon in the sense usually given to
that word. On several occasions before in
Spanish history the people have pushed
aside their weak and clumsy governments
and taken the conduct of affairs into
their own hands. This happened notably
in the war against Napoleon. . . .
That war had also been to a certain
extent a civil war just as the 1936 war
could likewise be regarded as a war of
defence against a foreign aggressor. It was
thus natural that the *juntas* of 1808 should
be reborn in the Workers' Committees of
July–October 1936.

– GERALD BRENAN, *The Spanish Labyrinth*

MANUEL

The faith of the people in victory was inexhaustible. . . . The only thing missing for victory was arms. Where were they?

We got the news over Ceuta radio on the evening of 17 July. The military had risen in Morocco! At first the radio from there broadcast the republican anthem. It said the rising was in defence of the Republic and that the army wanted to bring justice and equality to the people. The military were trying to forestall the nation's reaction because the rising on the mainland wasn't until the following day. At the beginning, we thought that it was only a minor uprising in Morocco which could be put down. But the next day the military rose throughout the country. Burgos, Salamanca, Valladolid fell. But it was mainly those cities where the CNT dominated that the military were able to take most quickly: Seville, Cadiz and especially Zaragoza, which was the main CNT stronghold – these fell immediately.[19] Málaga held out because the Assault Guards remained loyal and fought a company of soldiers which was trying to take the key points. The workers rose and attacked the soldiers from the rear. Many soldiers deserted and the people got arms from the barracks. The company commander was lynched by the crowd.

As soon as the news of what was happening became known, the people went wild. Everyone who was working away from the village started to pour back – it was harvest-time and there were many day-labourers working on estates around Málaga. The streets and square were full of people come in from the country-side. Some were fearful and others were shouting for arms. I was in the town hall all day trying to take whatever measures seemed necessary. I wanted to try to prevent any excesses which the extremists* might attempt; it was a moment when anything might have happened. I brought in all the people in whom I had most confidence, companions from the party and some left republicans – only to be disappointed. They didn't give me the collaboration I expected in trying to keep the situation in hand. Some said, 'There's nothing we can do', because they lacked the courage to face up to the situation. Others, on the contrary, incited the labourers to take things into their own hands and to do more than was already being done. 'No, *hombre*,' I told them, 'you've got to be a bit more moderate about things. . . ' If they had listened to me, the things that happened here – not so much as happened elsewhere, but all the same – wouldn't have happened, the four *señoritos* wouldn't have been killed – for nothing, really, no, I couldn't condone that.

There was never any doubt in my mind that the revolution was necessary. It had been brewing for years. The oppression of the ruling classes was so intense that they had made revolution a certainty. In other nations the bourgeoisie is more open, more ready to compromise, from what I read, than the bourgeoisie we've known here. Here no, here all the doors are shut to a worker, here the worker has the choice only of submitting or being shut out.

But what I always feared was our lack of preparation for the revolution. Here, in this village specifically, there was a group of a dozen or twenty politically conscious people at most, people who knew what ought to be done. The rest knew next to nothing of politics or revolution, even though they might be loyal trade-union members – the majority were – but they were illiterate, they didn't know what revolution meant.

What did the revolution mean to me, you ask? Well, first I was never an *exaltado*. If I had been I wouldn't have lasted out these last thirty years. The sort of revolution I wanted to see was a democratic socialist revolution – above all, democratic. With personal power to no one, with economic and political power in the hands of the nation, and an end to the domination of the capitalist class.

I'll say this straight out, I agree with the communists in this: under capitalism the class struggle is inevitable: the interests of

* In Spanish, the word used, *exaltados*, conveys a sense of extremism and violence in political beliefs.

the workers and the bourgeoisie are completely opposed. They cannot be reconciled. Until the property-owning class disappears there must be class struggle; while economic power remains in the hands of the bourgeoisie political power remains in their hands too. Political power without economic power is nothing. Without economic control of all the main industrial sectors, the banking system, transport and the land – especially the land – there is no political power. We learnt that under the Republic. Economic power remained where it had always been, with the bourgeois class, while we had political power – and for what? For nothing!

At the same time I have to say that I am absolutely opposed to communism in its politics; it has been as anti-democratic in the type of regimes it has produced as those we have suffered from here in Spain. I never wanted to see Spain become like those worker states we've seen in east Europe since the war. It's true they have achieved a great deal in overthrowing capitalism and ending the bourgeoisie's domination, but they are fundamentally anti-democratic. Let everyone be free to express their ideas, this is why I am a socialist and always have been. Nor did I want to see the results of the revolution fragmented – localized, as the anarchists with their utopian ideology proclaimed. What can be achieved at the local level alone if it isn't being done on a national scale? The revolution I wanted was democratic and national – it could have been achieved, there were plenty of people who shared my beliefs. But not the immense majority because, apart from the socialist party and the UGT, there was the CNT on the one hand and on the other the republican parties which, however left-wing, were fundamentally bourgeois.

I always believed that before the revolution I wanted could be made the masses would have to be educated. But there wasn't time! The revolution came because of the military uprising and in that situation the extremists took over. Revolutionary Popular Front committees took power everywhere. Here my position as mayor was reduced to nothing, to little more than small administrative tasks during the first stage of the revolution in which the worst excesses were committed. It lasted six to eight weeks until the central government was gradually able to get power back in its hands. At the beginning, of course, the government was left without any organization, without a regular army or a police force since, with a few exceptions, army officers and units had joined the uprising. Power was in the hands of the unions and political parties. If the government couldn't control the situation, what could a mayor do?

The Popular Front committees sprang up everywhere that hadn't fallen into the military's hands.[20] Committees in which all Popular Front parties and working-class organizations were equally represented had existed nationally and locally since the elections of February 1936. But they were simply liaison committees and had no power. As a result of the military uprising, the unions became the only real power, and the committees were reconstituted to exercise this power. The Mijas committee, which took power after a couple of days, was formed by the UGT which, because of its size, had two members, the socialist party and the two republican parties, each of which had one member. After about a month when the communist party and the CNT were set up locally, they joined the committee with a member each. That was when the trouble started again.

I never wanted to be part of the committee. I hadn't been a member before. In many places, in Coin, for example, the mayor formed the committee and became its president. But not everywhere. In Fuengirola the mayor never served on the committee. I could see the sort of thing that might happen here under pressure from the extremists who were only out to trample everything underfoot and I knew that they wouldn't listen to me. To assume responsibility for doing things that weren't done legally was more than I could accept. It was enough for me to continue in the position to which I had been elected, and in which I considered myself the legal authority of the village. I sometimes thought of resigning altogether, but my concept of party discipline and responsibility made me put aside the idea.

The delegates from the UGT and the socialist party were elected to serve on the committee by their respective assemblies. The first delegates were relatively moderate men – in particular the socialist party delegate, the only one who served continuously on the committee throughout the six and a half months of its existence. This young man remained at his post as secretary of the committee until the end. He was shot when the nationalists came in.

But behind these delegates there was always a group of fifty or more *exaltados* – I'm speaking here of the UGT, which was the biggest – who were pushing their delegates to do more. They tried to incite the committee to go after anyone they considered a rightist, to be searching houses all the time, to be throwing people in jail – 'in the cause of the revolution'. They believed simply that because a person was on the right they could do what they wanted with him even when they hadn't found him doing anything against them. There were a number of peasants who by nature were conservative, one in particular I remember, and it was these people the *exaltados* wanted to persecute. The majority of union members didn't go along with this sort of thing, being peacefully inclined, but they wouldn't stand up to the extremists and say, 'No, that's enough, we're in the majority here.' They let themselves be swayed by the loud voices of the others, let them do what they wanted.

With the union behind it, there was no power that could oppose the committee. It took over the land belonging to all large land-owners and expropriated the rents and the owner's share of the produce if the land was being sharecropped. Tenants and share-croppers would bring what they owed to the committee rather than to the landlord, as in the past. The committee became the owner and everything belonged to it – or to the whole village.[21] Of course, the tenants and sharecroppers were a bit better off than in the past because the committee gave them advantages that no landlord would have conceded. The committee didn't make it a principle of taking everything that was the landlord's. No. If a sharecropper needed part of the crop, the committee would say, 'All right, let's share out the crop, but you can keep that part which should come to us because you need it for raising that calf', or whatever it might be. But there wasn't any funda-mental change for the tenant or sharecropper, no.

To store all the produce – olive oil, wheat, figs, raisins, whatever was in season – the committee took over the church in the square. The olive oil mills were taken over, too, and the books inspected. When they found a land-owner who had so many *arrobas* marked down as his they confiscated the oil and made it available to the village. But they didn't take the four or five *arrobas* belonging to a small-holder, only the large quantities belonging to the big owners. In this way the committee became responsible for provisioning the village with food.

Not having taken any part in the decision, I can't remember

exactly on what basis the food was distributed, but it was so much per person. The labourers received their wages in food while others had to pay. I do know, though, that the rations were fixed too high, perhaps a quarter of a litre of oil per head, and that there was great wastage, also with bread. You saw bits of bread thrown down in the street – and later those bits were needed because there was a shortage. At the beginning they gave out too much, and later there wasn't enough. It wasn't properly thought out, they weren't thinking of the future.

The committee was responsible also for public order.[22] A militia was formed immediately for this purpose. The militiamen were all volunteers from the UGT and there were about fourteen in all except when, during the most critical first hours, the different organizations delegated a number of people to assist them. The militia was organized under a chief who had two lieutenants. Like the Guardia Civil, all of whom had left the village by then, they went out in pairs on patrol through the village and country-side. The militia chief was this man I've already mentioned, who was shot when he came back here soon after me. He was a year older than me, thirty-one at the time, and a day-labourer. He had been president of the union for a time and though he was firm in his convictions I never agreed with him. He had no idea of politics or organization and, though it's a shame to have to say it, lacked any sort of culture. He let himself be swayed by the extremists and their cries of 'We've got to kill.' If he had paid more heed to what I used to tell him the things that happened might not have occurred.

'Control your people more,' I told him again and again, 'other-wise there'll be trouble.' 'No, you're always going backwards, you're always against us,' he'd say. 'You're not on our side, you're on theirs.' 'No, *hombre*, you're being stupid. If you can't understand, go ahead and do it your way and then you'll see. . . .'

During those first days, 18 and 19 July, there was a militia but without any arms. The few shotguns and revolvers there had been were all being held in the Guardia Civil barracks because the government, fearing a right-wing *coup* before the uprising, had ordered all privately held arms to be turned in. I sent an order to the commander of the post to hand over the arms he was holding so as to distribute them. They were critical moments and the militia had to have arms, even if they were no more than a few old shotguns and revolvers. At that stage there were only three *guardias* left here. The sergeant, Garcia, and one other *guardia* had been transferred as a result of the village petition and one other man had been sent to Málaga. The people wanted those who remained shot right from the start, and if I had been a different sort of person that's what would have happened to them, without doubt.

I sent an official to them with orders to report to the town hall. An order from the mayor to the commander of the post, not a request from Manuel to. . . . I was trying to get them to come round of their own will rather than resist in their barracks, because then there might well have been bloodshed. When they saw that Málaga and the province was in the hands of the Republic they had second thoughts. The commander of the post and a *guardia* came to the town hall to negotiate with me. They were armed and pretty frightened. The people were waiting to see what I would do. So I told the commander of the post to hand over the arms he was holding and that I would draw up a receipt and give it to him. He wouldn't agree at first, he said he wanted to ring up Fuengirola and get orders. I let him do that on the electricity company's line and when he heard that the same situation existed there he gave in.

From that moment on I ordered the Guardia to remain confined to their barracks and sent the policeman and two or three other men up to collect the arms. We didn't disarm the Guardia; we took only the arms that belonged to the people. The Guardia stayed in their barracks until they were ordered to report to Málaga which was where the few *guardias* who hadn't gone over to the other side were stationed.

Now the militia had a few shotguns, but only a cartridge or two. There was no ammunition! The committee sent a delegate to Málaga to ask for some but he came back empty-handed. The next day I went and I got what was needed, so the militia was now equipped for its task. A short while later, when they sacked the major's house, a whole armoury was discovered. Having been an army officer he had in his house every type of arm you could think of, and these the militia took. They also took over his house as their headquarters.

The first three to four weeks were the worst. News came in almost immediately of what was happening in the cities that had fallen: Seville, Cadiz, Salamanca, Badajoz. . . . When they captured places that had been through the revolution, like Málaga, they could always say that the executions were in reprisal for something. But in Seville and Cadiz and Salamanca they hadn't that excuse.

Refugees soon began to pour out of these places bringing the news. When the people heard what was happening they became furious, their blood boiled. 'What are we going to do?' they'd say, and in their fury they'd catch hold of the first person they suspected and threaten his life. I wasn't spared either. 'You're friendly with them, you're another one of them underneath it all.' Stupidities like that. Then I'd say, 'I'm more revolutionary than you. I'm firmer in my beliefs than you. Because I've been a socialist and a militant for any number of years, since I was a young man, and you've just become revolutionaries. And you don't even know what it means, you only see what's in front of your eyes. . . .'

The first two UGT delegates resigned from the committee after only a short time. 'We can't work with these people,' they said, 'we've had enough.' The union assembly elected two of the *exaltados* who wanted to be on the committee. They lasted even less time. As soon as they found themselves burdened with responsibilities they began to change. They couldn't take it. The other extremists kept putting the pressure on them to do more and they saw it was impossible. It was one thing to talk loudly at meetings and another to have to do things. Being in power changed them. Then more moderate people were elected and the extremists would be after them again until they resigned. And so it went on, it was impossible, there were constant changes. In its six and a half months the committee had four different presidents – and towards the end its power was in decline as the government got in control of the situation.

Three of the presidents were shot. And the other, who's walking round the village today, was the one who was in charge during the first month or so, the worst time of all. He was in the UGT and fled the village, returning about the same time as me. But he had sisters in Málaga who were friendly with *señoritos* and that helped him a lot. He admits it. 'I was much more responsible for what happened than him,' he says about me. 'I was ten times more responsible than him and yet all I got was prison and that for little more than a year before I was released.'

The local bourgeoisie, those who remained, went in fear of their lives. One, as I've mentioned, went into hiding and, though he was seen by a militiaman, nothing happened to him. Nor to the father of the young man who made the fascist salute in the square, and who owned a lot of land around here. Nor to the many other people who remained in their houses. But the old *cacique* and his brother were shot, though not by people from here. The major was the only person liquidated by the local militia and some of the extremists; if it hadn't been for one of his tenant farmers they might not have got him. They knew he was living in Málaga but they didn't know where, the exact address. This tenant farmer who had been to see the major on business told them the number of the house. That was how they found him. They brought him up here and executed him at dawn outside the village. By the time I knew about it, like most people, he was already dead.

Sometimes I was able to moderate the extremists' excesses. The night of the uprising the old *cacique*'s brother and another young land-owner, who was quite a friend of mine, were in the country-side at their farms. They took fright at what the peasants might do to them and fled into the hills and up to Valtocado, a hamlet on the track to Alhaurin, where someone saw them and turned them in. It would have been better to let them escape, go wherever they could get to. What was the point of holding them if they were escaping anyway? The militia went out and brought them back and put them in jail. As mayor I was still in charge of the jail, and I went to talk to them.

I knew them both quite well. Neither of them were fascists but right-wingers of the old sort. The young land-owner was friendly with the other because the latter had a daughter he was courting and their farms were close by. The *cacique*'s brother had a lot of land, while the young man lived mainly in Fuengirola but came up to his farm in the summer-time to direct the work.

Anyway, I kept them shut up for a while to let things cool down while I got the committee's agreement.

'They're political enemies,' I told the committee, 'but nothing more, they haven't done anything.' Then I said to both of them, 'Have you got somewhere in the village to stay?' I knew they had relatives where they could lodge, and the *cacique*'s brother said, 'Yes, in my sister's house.' 'Good,' I replied, 'go there then', and I let them both out.

They went to the sister's house, both of them, and their families came to see them. The next day while I was at work in the barber's shop I heard that they had been rounded up and put back in jail. The *exaltados* had said, 'Let's go and get them', and that's what they had done. 'Who gave the orders for this?' I said. 'The committee. . . .' 'Let them out, get them back into the sister's house, that's where they are to stay.' The following day it happened again, the *exaltados* went for them and put them back in jail. Again I ordered them let out. I had the committee's agreement that they should be freed as long as they stayed where I had ordered. When the extremists saw what I had done they denounced me and the committee to the committee in Málaga.

There was one man in particular who put in the *denuncias*, a member of the FAI but without an ounce of political conscious-ness. He started off with the FAI, then he joined our union, then when the communist party was formed here he became secretary general of that. But he didn't last long, they soon threw him out and then he went back into the FAI. You couldn't do anything with him, he was a bad element.

The Málaga committee, who knew me a lot better than any of these extremists, took no notice of the first *denuncia*. But when I released the two landlords again there was another *denuncia*. Two they lodged against me. 'Up here in Mijas all the fascists are being let free, everyone is doing whatever they want.' At last the Málaga committee asked what was going on in the village. Could it be that enemies of the revolution were at large in the streets? 'We'll have to go to Mijas to see what's going on.'

So one afternoon they came up here to look into things for themselves and discuss them with the local committee. The com-mittees met in joint session in the town hall, in the room where the council meetings take place. As mayor and chief authority in the village I presided over the meeting at the request of the Málaga committee. Those who had been denouncing me and the local committee were called in to present their evidence.

'Well, and what have you got against these two men?' the Málaga committee asked. 'That they're fascists? And how do you know? What proof have you got of what you say? They're on the right, yes, is that what you mean? And do you think we're going to liquidate everyone who is on the right just for that? We'll have to kill half the nation if that's the case.' And so on.

The two committees discussed the case. I didn't take part other than as chairman. They found that we hadn't done anything wrong in releasing the two because nothing could be held against them other than the fact that they were on the right. There was agreement, however, that the best course of action was for the two men to be taken to Málaga. 'They should be got out of here because they're on the right and hated in the village.' It was as much for their safety as anything, because it was quite possible that a FAI patrol would come for them one night.

Everyone was agreed to this solution as the best way out of what had become a nightmare. The two men were to be detained until they were sent for from Málaga. It was a decision that I knew had been taken in other places like Alhaurin where people had been transferred to Málaga prison or, when that was full, to a ship in the harbour that was being used as a prison. There they were kept at the disposition of a revolutionary tribunal, as it was called, and many people who were rightists but no more were later released.

With the Málaga committee had come some people from Los Boliches who belonged to the FAI. They had joined up with the committee as it came through their village. Since the meeting was open to the public they knew very well what had been decided. They knew that the two were going to be sent for. And that night they returned to the village and said, 'We've been sent by the Málaga committee for those two. They don't trust you up here in Mijas. We're to take them to Málaga.' It wasn't true, they hadn't come on the committee's orders but of their own accord. The militia chief delivered up the two men without even questioning their claim to have orders, without asking them for any proof. Nothing had been written down during the meeting, but all the same if they had had orders they should have been made to show them. The militia chief never even asked, he simply took their word. These anarchists took the two men away and on the road a bit beyond Los Boliches they shot and robbed them of the little money they had. It was a terrible thing, so terrible that the committee in Málaga sent a judge to Boliches to arrest them, the three or four men, and they were shot. Yes, the revolution had to shoot these people who called themselves revolutionaries. Something similar happened in Marbella where more of the same sort had to be shot.

A few nights later the old *cacique* was taken from his house by a FAI patrol from Alhaurin. In a place below the village they shot him. Up to that time I'd managed to protect him a bit. The *exaltados* were always wanting to arrest him and put him in jail, if not worse. 'What for?' I said. 'He's a bad man,' they said. 'What has he done?' 'He's bad, he should be put away. . . .' 'Leave him where he is,' I said, 'leave him alone.' No one touched him, he was in his house.

That night I went home earlier than usual, about nine, with a bad headache and cold. The next morning I found he was gone. It was too late. When I heard that I said, 'All right, from now on I won't go home to sleep at night.' I spent every night from that moment on in the town hall or the square. I couldn't leave because I knew the patrols would be back, and I knew that the local militia – there was always a pair of them on patrol – would help them to pick up whoever they wanted rather than stop them. I had no confidence in them at all. So I slept only by day, a few hours in my house from dawn until ten and then I'd go back to work. That was the job in those days!

It was as well that I decided I couldn't afford to go home to sleep. One night when I was in the town hall a patrol came from Alhaurin again with a list. Fourteen people they wanted to take out and shoot. The list was the work of the man who had denounced me to the Málaga committee. He knew I was trying to prevent anyone here being shot and he went to Alhaurin and said: 'Go to Mijas. That's where the fascists are and nothing is being done about them, they're not even in jail.' Other times he went to Los Boliches on similar missions. That was his only job. The patrol of five or six men arrived and went straight to the local militia and showed their list. The militia were such cowards that they said, 'We'll let you have them, but first you'd better go to the *alcalde* and see what he says.' The militia outnumbered them, they could have thrown them out of the village. Instead a couple of militiamen came to the town hall with the patrol – they knew by that time that I spent the nights there. They came in and the militiamen said, 'They've come for so-and-so, they want them handed over. . . .' Fourteen there were, among them the clerk of the town hall, Don Lucas, who later helped my wife. He was a rightist, I knew that as did everyone, but that had nothing to do with it. On their way to the town hall they had picked up his son and he stood next to me as the list was read out. Imagine the poor boy's distress when he heard his father's name. 'That's the list of these fascist pigs.' I looked at the men. 'Here no one is going to be shot by you lot. I'll give you ten minutes to get out of the village. Get on the road out of Mijas and never come back. If you want to kill fascists go to the front. In the trenches is where you can kill fascists face to face, one against one. You're not doing any of your work here. Now get out.'

They left the town hall and got into their car and went in a hurry. They never came back. As they were fully armed they could have turned nasty and I had nothing to oppose them with except force of character and my authority. Apart from the couple of militiamen who accompanied them, I was alone against them. I hoped that if anything happened the militiamen would have stood behind me, but who can say? Anyway, they left in a hurry because I think I had frightened them.

Fourteen people saved – and among them the man who, because of his grudge, was my biggest enemy in the time when they were looking for me. Yes, I saved this man's life and he tried to repay me by getting mine! Not only him, but one or two others who were on the list and later wanted to see me killed. Pepe, the clerk's son who heard everything that night, told everyone what had happened. And even more so when they were looking for me. 'It isn't possible,' he used to say, 'you're hunting down a man, the man who saved your lives that night. . . .'

It happened again a number of times. Not the same people, they never returned, but other patrols which were trying the same thing. It's for what I did then that so many rightists have come to congratulate me on my coming out of hiding – although there are some who have come only to play a role. On the outside they've come with their good wishes, but inside they're thinking something else. . . .

The day the major was shot and his house sacked the people set about the church. A crowd of men and boys went from the square where the major's things were burning to the church and set fire to religious objects, saints, vestments and anything they could lay their hands on. The church archives were burnt among other things. It was barbarous what they did, but the whole village was enraged, no one could stand in the people's way. Anyone who had tried, even I who had a certain influence, would have been pushed out of the way. There was no stopping them. All I could do was to publish an edict the following day which I worded very strongly ordering anyone who had taken religious objects from the church to hand them in to me at the town hall. Many hundreds of things, gold chalices and plate, priests' vestments and saints' robes, were handed in and I kept them in safety in the town hall which is where they were found when the nationalists took the village.

But many things disappeared. Among the people who were burning things there were some who were just pretending. They'd throw on a rag or two to burn and make off with the precious objects. They were there to mark down those who were really doing the burning to be able to denounce them later. 'So-and-so was the one. . . .' And when so-and-so had been jailed or shot the religious objects began to reappear. Things for which people served long sentences were now being sold. Since I came out of hiding I've seen many of these things in an antique shop that's been set up in the village. The owner has become a friend of mine and one day he showed me what he had been buying locally. And immediately I recognized many of the objects, sculptures of angels and saints, and I said: 'That was in such and such a place in the church, this one came from there. . . . For burning those many village people have been in jail.' Now no one remembers and these people can sell them for cash. This happens, has happened and will happen in Spain as long as there are charlatans who beat their breasts and go to church every day and don't have enough faith even to believe in themselves.

The things that were done during those first days were bad. There was no need for them, they didn't serve the revolution. But there was no holding back the people, who were hearing the news of what was happening in the nationalist-held cities and country-side. The refugees came through the village with the stories. Overhead bombers flew to drop their bombs on Málaga – more to frighten the population than to do serious damage. At night everyone waited for the planes and all the lights in the village were put out, and by day the people remained in the streets in a state of excitement and fear. The front was close, the nationalists had advanced as close as Estepona by the end of July. Seville, Cadiz, Córdoba, Granada had fallen. The front was in a state of flux everywhere and the republican forces were weak. And yet the faith of the people in victory was inexhaustible. The major industrial centres and above all the mass of the people were behind the Republic. The only thing missing for victory was arms. Where were they? Without a regular army, without officers – those who weren't hostile were indifferent by and large to the republican cause – we needed arms. With them the uprising would have been put down in a few weeks or months at the most. But it wasn't we but they who got the arms. Mussolini and Hitler sent everything that was needed for them to win, they won the war for the nationalists. While we, the Republic and legal government, had the Non-Intervention Committee imposed upon us by those gentlemen Chamberlain and Blum. Léon Blum, a socialist comrade – a hypocrite rather, whose actions didn't save France from Hitler either.

After the first few weeks things began to calm down a little. The nationalist offensive didn't advance and the most 'revolutionary' of the extremists here began to join the militia and go to the front. Then the communist party and the CNT were formed locally and they tried to stir things up again. Less the communists, who were only a few of the young and who had no concrete ideas, than the CNT. I helped the communists establish their branch and went to Málaga to get the necessary papers and things for them from the civil authorities, because I had better contacts than they.[23]

The CNT was a different matter. To me they were counterrevolutionaries who were seeking to split the working class. They were always going round saying that the socialists were a bunch of *señoritos* and the communists were tyrants and that they were the only revolutionary proletarian force. And with that sort of propaganda they managed to get members, including some of those *exaltados* who had been in the UGT. But they never had more than a hundred or so.

Fernando, the bourgeois I've mentioned, was again the organizer of the CNT. This gentleman had a plan which he tried to put into effect: nothing less than trying to appropriate the agate quarry for himself, with the help of the quarry-workers who were unconditional supporters of his in the CNT and whom he manipulated as he wished. They had no idea, but I could see what he was after. 'The quarry belongs now to the municipality,' I told him, 'no one is going to lay their hands on it. What it produces belongs to the town hall and to the workers. You may be the manager of it and get paid for managing it, but boss? Not in any way while I am here.'

I was backed by my party and the union, indeed the whole village. And he knew that and gave in, because he saw that otherwise we would take over the quarry and throw him out. I formed a small committee of the quarry-workers in which the town hall was also represented and over which I presided. It was this committee which administered the quarry and to which this gentleman had to present his accounts and reports. We didn't let him get very far with his plans.

The sort of stupidities these *exaltados* of the CNT got up to was seen one day when they all got excited and cut down the trees in the square. As though there wasn't firewood enough in the sierra for the taking! There was firewood everywhere but not for these people, no, they had to cut down trees that had been planted for everyone's benefit. 'Firewood for the militia, firewood for the trench-diggers,' that was the cry. There was a beautiful row of full-grown trees that gave shade to the square in the summer-time. But they didn't care, no, they just got an idea in their heads and that was enough; they'd get the people worked up that this was something important to do – without any thought of the consequences or anything like that.

In villages where the CNT dominated much more happened than happened here, that I know. In Ronda and other places they abolished money, for example, and the committee issued vouchers in its place. What's the good of doing these things in one or two places? To have any meaning it must be done on a national scale. Here, nothing like that happened.

By early September the government was beginning to take charge of the situation and my position was strengthened by a new agricultural law. This named the mayor the local delegate of the Agrarian Reform Institute, to take charge of all abandoned farms. Almost all the farms belonging to the land-owners had been left uncultivated, even when the landlord was still living here. Without some measures the crops were likely to be lost. The law was very necessary, though provisional, and I put it into effect. I had to draw up lists of farms where the land was unworked, and inventories of everything that was on the farms. I gave these in to the union which then took charge of bringing in the crops or whatever had to be done. Depending on the size of the farm and the nature of the work, the union assigned fifty or twenty or ten men with a foreman to do the job. The work was done collectively. All the produce, however, continued to come to the committee which paid the workers in produce and distributed the rest to the village. There was a great deal of wastage, as I've said. I was opposed to this way of doing things; to my mind the product of their labour ought to have gone to the workers directly, leaving a portion over for the committee's maintenance of village administration. But the committee never saw it that way.

In October there was a second agricultural decree which was a different matter. This was put through by the communist Minister of Agriculture, Uribe, after the formation of Largo Caballero's government which included communists. This decree expropriated all land belonging to people who were implicated in the military uprising.[24] A commission which, as mayor, I presided over was set up of delegates from both unions, the UGT and the CNT, two members of the committee and two municipal councillors. The UGT delegates included members of the smallholders' section I had created.

I wasn't at all happy about this law because it was open to all sorts of dangers. The extremists could come with a *denuncia* saying so-and-so is a fascist, his land ought to be expropriated, and I'd think, 'Yes, that's your opinion of the man but . . . to expropriate him just on an opinion, no.' Moreover, the law said that a landlord could be declared a fascist only for some concrete reason, like having given money or made propaganda for the nationalists. The extremists didn't pay attention to that, it was enough for them to say that someone was a fascist to demand his expropriation.

In the face of these difficulties I delayed putting anything into effect, and since I presided over the commission I could convene it when I wanted. Moral scruples prevented me from giving in to the extremists, it didn't seem right to brand anyone with so infamous a seal – 'for being a fascist – expropriated'. A seal for life that no one could erase if the Republic continued in existence.

During the winter there was some discussion in the union as to whether the land ought to be worked collectively or cooperatively. In Valencia, as I later saw, there were many collectives which were very well organized and lasted throughout the war, as well as land that had been distributed individually. But here so many other things were happening in such a short time. Moreover, by autumn the village was preparing its defence from the nationalist army, which by the beginning of November was at the gates of Madrid.

We had faith that Madrid would hold out but it was a critical situation for the Republic and we were close to the front. There were three or four hundred *trincheristas* here at first digging trenches round the village, in particular at the most easily defended points: the rock promontories on either side of the village and the Muralla on which the church stands. Later, both the Málaga CNT and UGT sent separate groups of *trincheristas*, and there were as many as fifteen hundred in all. It was complete confusion, no one knew what anyone was doing, and a lot of the *trincheristas* spent their time robbing the farms of food. They repaired the road to Benalmádena in case the front got that close, but otherwise it was wasted effort. In any case where were the forces who were to defend it? Almost from the start of the uprising the nationalist forces had advanced to about twenty kilometres from the Málaga–Almeria coast road – and that was the only road out of Málaga to the rest of the republican zone. It might be cut any day and we would be left caught here in a pocket. The defences of Málaga weren't well organized, it must be said. There were no units of the new republican army there, nor any of the International Brigades which were just starting to form. There was only the militia under the command of a Colonel Villalba, a regular army officer who was in Catalonia at the time of the uprising; otherwise he would have been on the nationalist side. All his brothers were. The city was still being bombed, and the militia lacked the discipline of a regular army. The CNT militiamen would leave the front lines for the rear whenever they felt like it.

Throughout the autumn we all thought that this part would be defended – what were the trenches being dug for otherwise? – but as winter set in there were plenty of peasants who began to say: 'What are we working for if it's only for *them* to have the crops when they come in? They're going to find all the work done and they're going to have it all. What are we working for?' The peasants were beginning to lose faith in victory, seeing the isolation of Málaga and this strip along the coast, nowhere much more than twenty kilometres wide.

In January the front at Estepona collapsed and the nationalists pushed forward to Marbella. The majority of the people still thought there would be an organized defence, but a few of us in the leadership of the party and union knew that the government had decided to abandon Málaga. This was about fifteen to twenty days before the nationalists began their major assault on the city. I was personally told of the government's plan by socialist leaders in Málaga who had it direct from Valencia which was then the republican capital. Largo Caballero was not only Prime Minister but also Minister for War, and General Asensio, also a socialist party member, was Under Secretary of War. It wasn't surprising that the party leadership in Málaga knew what the government planned. Of course, the bulk of the population didn't know. An important factor in the decision to evacuate the city was the disorganization caused by the militia.[25]

Although I knew what was going to happen, I kept waiting and waiting. I couldn't leave like someone who had no responsibilities here. My wife, who heard everything the refugees were saying and was frightened, kept pleading for us to leave. 'Not yet, woman, not yet,' I told her. 'I'm responsible to the village as mayor. You've got to understand that.' But by 4 or 5 February the situation was becoming critical enough to know that we couldn't wait much longer. Before dawn on the 7th we set out.

I had told about fifteen other people, the more responsible of the party and union leaders, that Málaga wasn't going to be defended and that they should come with me. I got them together in Osunilla, but they wouldn't leave. 'Let's go back to see our families, they haven't taken the village,' they said, and with one exception they all went back. Went back to their deaths, most of them, because the next morning a battalion of *carabineros* occupied the village and would let no one leave. My father-in-law, the old man who sits in the room by the door over there, wanted to leave and the *carabineros* refused him. 'Get back, you're too young to flee.'

This battalion, I heard later, had retreated from the sierra of Monda and reached Mijas via Alhaurin. Their commander thought they could stage some resistance here, which was ridiculous since Málaga itself wasn't being defended. All that he did was to stop a lot of people who might have been able to flee from saving their lives. They were all here at the *falangistas*' mercy the following day. The battalion itself got cut off but a hundred or so managed to break through the enemy lines from the rear and, by forced marches over the mountains, rejoin our side. A lot more were killed.

My wife, my mother-in-law and our eighteen-month-old daughter joined me and a young man, the only one who hadn't returned to the village, at a place we had decided on beforehand in the sierra. I knew it was no good my turning back, the only hope was to get out before those people came. Also I wanted to be in my own camp, adding my grain of energy to the defence of the Republic. At that time I couldn't imagine that we should lose everything. It was one thing if Málaga couldn't be defended – but I couldn't believe we should lose the war.

We had to carry my daughter in our arms, sometimes I and sometimes my wife. We walked all day over the sierra until we got to Alhaurin de la Torre on the other side. The mayor of Los Boliches had joined up with us while we were crossing the mountains. We went on down to the Málaga plain and at night-fall we arrived at a farm which was worked by people from Mijas. I knew already what I had to do. When we got there I said to my wife and mother-in-law, 'Where are you going? You haven't done anything. It'll be a tragedy for you to walk all the way to Almeria with me. And if we go on at this pace we'll all be caught. Alone I'll get out.' Carrying the baby was holding us all back. Nothing would happen to my wife if she stayed, I was sure of that, because she had never been involved in anything political. There was nothing they could hold against her. 'Yes,' she said, 'it's you who are in danger, you must go on.' I gave her fifty of the three hundred pesetas I had, we embraced and I went on.

To be safe I knew I had to get to Almeria which was the first city up the coast road in the republican zone. There was only the one road and that might be cut at any moment. We pressed on into Málaga, reaching there before midnight. All the lights were out, you couldn't see anything, all you could hear was women crying and calling out to each other, to their husbands, their children. People from the villages around, from Cártama and Alora and all the rest, were streaming through the town. And the people of Málaga with them, everyone was pouring out. Many had carts they were pushing, and others donkeys laden down with their belongings. I hadn't taken anything with me other than a lined coat and a blanket, so as to be able to walk faster without being burdened.

We walked all night without stopping and by daylight were at Torre de Mar. The road was black with people, there were hundreds and thousands of them all fleeing in the one direction, men, women and children. As it got light we saw ships out at sea and soon they began to get closer. We were on a stretch of road that runs right along the coast just beyond the lighthouse at Torrox. Soon the warships were so close we could see the sailors on deck and make out the name of the biggest ship, the *Canarias*. Its guns began to turn and aim and PAM! the first broadside was let loose at us. It was a massacre, people were falling to the ground all round us, dead and wounded, everyone was running and I with the rest. I ran into a field and from there scrambled up a watercourse which went up the mountainside and gave some protection. I lost my two companions as I went up and over the mountain, making a detour of several kilometres, before reaching the road again on the other side where it wasn't so close to the sea. But only men on their own could manage that sort of climb. Those who had women and children with them couldn't escape.

That day, too, at La Herradura, we were bombed. Two nationalist planes came over very low and circled round dropping their bombs. I don't know how I didn't get killed. I ran into a cactus plantation to hide. There were hundreds of women and children crouched and lying in there and the planes seemed to get lower and lower as they passed to and fro overhead. They were dropping bombs by hand and I said to myself, 'If one lands in among us you'll see where we and these cacti end up.' We were lucky, they missed us.

I got a ride only once the whole way, for a few kilometres on a mule. At Salobreña the bridge was down and the river in full flood. It was raining hard, and women and children were trying to wade across and being swept away and drowned. I saw a soldier riding a mule and, though he didn't want to, I insisted so hard that in the end he let me get up behind and that way I crossed the river to get to Motril.

All the farmsteads along the way were deserted because everyone had fled and people went into them looking for food. While I was hunting round in one of them I met three men I knew from

Fuengirola. They called to me to join them, they had found some rabbits. We skinned and boiled them and ate them like that, without bread or anything. That bit of rabbit and five dried figs that the young lad from Mijas gave me when I met him again just before reaching Almeria was all the food I ate in those six days of flight. I stopped only one night, my feet were beginning to swell and I said to myself that I'd better rest. Beside the road I found a lorry that had been left where it had run out of petrol and I got into the driver's cab. It must have been nine or ten at night and I was out again before dawn. All the time I was in there the people never stopped passing by on the road, filling it completely from one side to the other. Not an occasional person coming by but a continuous, unbroken flow! Thousands and thousands of people came by me that night and they were still behind me in their thousands when I set off again. Six days of walking it was, but I got to safety and to my own side.

JULIANA

I'll never forget that moment, not if a hundred years pass over me. Never. I can feel the pain now as I felt it then.

For weeks I kept telling him, 'Come on, we must leave here, come on, we must leave. . . .' Every day refugees from the areas the nationalists had taken were arriving here telling stories of what had happened. They came to the barber's shop to be shaved and they'd relate their stories. I'd be there and I'd hear what they had to say. People shot, others thrown into jail. . . . And I'd say to him, 'Do you hear? Are you listening to what they have to say about what is happening?' There was the mayor of Villamartin who escaped and reached here. 'Listen,' I said to him, 'that's the mayor of Villamartin who has escaped. You can believe what he has to say, can't you?'

There were refugees from everywhere, they were living anywhere they could find in the village, in the church, anywhere. We had three or four staying in our house. They all had the same story to tell. I believed them. If this is what they're saying it's because it's the truth. 'Listen to them,' I told him. 'Ech, people talk a lot, more than they should,' was what he replied. He didn't believe it could be as bad as they said, he thought they were exaggerating, he thought there was time. And when I insisted all he answered was, 'This woman is mad, you can't talk to her.'

Well, mad I may be, but not as mad as that. He's more intelligent than I am, compared to him I am nothing. But I'm always thinking of what might happen, I think of the worst, I'm on my guard. If it hadn't been for me he wouldn't have left at all. And there I was, day after day, 'We must leave, it's time, we must go . . .', and he couldn't see how late it was.

I could see the dangers all right. The day they burnt all the saints and sacked the major's house, he was in Málaga on official business. That's why they did it that day, knowing he wasn't here to stop them. I went through a bad moment when I saw what they were doing, because I don't like that sort of thing. Saints don't do harm to anyone, there was no need to burn them. When I saw the people going mad like that it made me feel terrible. I went up another street to avoid the savagery. In my house there has never been anything belonging to anyone else, thanks to God, not a pin. We never dirtied our hands in anything like that. And when he returned from Málaga and heard what had happened, he ordered the people to bring the things to the town hall, he managed to save a lot of religious objects that way, he saved all he could. But there was no saving what had been burnt. No, nothing good came out of the revolution, I don't like revolutions, and I knew there were people who were only waiting for the times to change to take their revenge. That was the danger I could see.

When the nationalists advanced, in mid-January it was, and reached Marbella, I told him again it was time to go. 'They've broken the front and they're coming this way, they're going to reach here. . . .' 'I've got my responsibilities,' was what he said. Responsibility! If he hadn't run in the end they'd have caught him here. When you see there's danger you get out quick, that's what I say. But not him. I wanted so much for us all to leave that I got together all the new clothes we had – the little any poor family has – and made a bundle of it and took it to my sister's house in

Málaga. My idea was that we could leave here quicker that way without being burdened down. As it was, my sister left before us and put the things on her cart and set off for Almeria. Not that she got there either, come to that.

At last – too late – he realized it was time to go. They were attacking Málaga, it seemed they might cut it off. He came and told me we were leaving. I thought for sure we had left it too late, that we couldn't get through. Two days earlier everything would have been all right. But I had waited for him, I didn't want to go on my own with my child, I didn't know where I would find him afterwards. Two days – even a day – earlier. . . . If I had been alone with him and hadn't my child to carry I could have done what he did, I can walk as fast as him, I'd have got to Almeria with him. But with a child it was impossible, we were going too slow.

He left the village that night and told me where to meet him in the sierra at dawn with the child and my parents. It was a good thing he left while it was still dark because in the morning the republican forces turned everyone back. My father was sent back when he came with us; he escaped up a watercourse and by a track into the sierra but we missed him. We had taken another path. He waited for us and then came back to the village on his own.

As soon as I knew we were going I emptied the mattress of its wool and took the empty cover to carry things in. A blanket, my child's clothes and a dress for myself which I wrapped in a bundle was all the rest I could carry. Some kitchen things I loaded onto a donkey belonging to a gypsy who had been turned back and who told us to take the animal and wait for him.

We set off straight away on the road to Benalmádena. We hadn't got further than Osunilla when the donkey fell down in a watercourse and couldn't get up. It was such a weak beast that we couldn't move it, so we left it there with all our things. All my china and kitchen utensils and even a basket of dried figs – the people of Osunilla benefited all right, they took the lot, the gluttons!

We were running all day, taking turns carrying the child. We hardly rested at all. It was a clear day and overhead the planes were flying to bomb Málaga and each time one came over we'd flatten ourselves on the ground. I was very frightened, but they didn't shoot at us. When we got to Benalmádena we went up into the sierra to cross over to Alhaurin de la Torre. We were worn out when we got down the other side to a farm close to the Cártama–Málaga road. It was nightfall already. At the farm the father of the man who lived there came running and said, 'They're coming, they're coming from Fuengirola. . . .' And someone else said that Málaga was already cut off and no one could get through. Then my husband said, 'For you and the child to come means they'll catch us all', and I said, 'You go, you go quick. . . .'

I'll never forget that moment, not if a hundred years pass over me. Never. I can feel the pain now as I felt it then. To be there, at this farm with only my mother and small daughter and having to say to him, 'Go.' Not knowing whether I would ever see him again, and the people saying, 'They're coming, they're killing as they come. . . .' It was dreadful, it's something one can't talk about.

I had to persuade him. 'I can't go, I can't go and leave you behind,' he said. 'Go, go quick and save yourself.' He had to flee, I wanted him to be safe. It was different for me. Whatever I had to go through, with more or less hardship, I knew they wouldn't touch me because I hadn't been mixed up in anything. But he had been mayor and a political leader, and for him there was all the danger I knew.

We were together at the farm only a few minutes. He didn't eat anything, none of us did. He gave me fifty pesetas, we embraced and then he was gone.

We stayed the night at the farm: the woman let us sleep there. I spent it crying with sorrow, and all the next day. For two days I couldn't eat or drink anything, thinking about what had happened.

We spent the next day at the farm; it was the day Málaga was captured. The following morning we got a man with a donkey to bring us back. We were frightened to go by the main roads and came back over the mountain tracks we had taken two days before. When we got here we found the *falangistas* in command. They knew Málaga had fallen and they didn't have to wait for troops to come to take over the village. Some soldiers came the next day to take the village officially, but they didn't stay. By the time we got back the square was packed with people, a lot of them in the blue shirts and uniform of the Falange. They had

had them hidden away a long time. We passed through the crowd and I saw who they were. I wasn't surprised, I had expected that. I knew who was who, whatever they said. They saw us pass but they didn't do anything, and I went to my house.

MANUEL

If we could hold out until our war became part of a general conflict everything would be changed. . . . If we were to die anyway, better to die fighting. . . .

I was a few days in Almeria not knowing what to do when the friend I had left Mijas with met a man he knew who was in business selling clothes and the like. This man, who came from somewhere around Málaga but had been living in Almeria, my friend and another young man who had also fled from Málaga soon went into business together. They asked me to join them. 'You come in with us,' they said, 'and we'll give you a day-wage.' So for a couple of months I helped them out selling. But I didn't like it much and, as there was a barber's shop close by, I went in one day and asked for a job. There was a shortage of barbers because many had been called up and there was no problem about getting a job. I worked there all summer.

One day in September or October, after the usual evening glass of wine with the boss of the barber's shop, I was standing in the square when a lorry drew up. 'Manolo! Manolo! Are you here too?' It was my niece's husband. 'Yes, I'm here too.' 'Jump in,' he said, and I got up into the lorry. We spent all night talking. He was in the army as a lorry driver stationed in Barcelona, and it was by complete chance that we met. The next day he came with me to the barber's shop and told the boss, 'I'm taking this man with me to Barcelona.' The following day we set off. 'You can live at home with us and you'll find yourself some sort of job or other,' he had said to me.

Earlier that year, in May, there had been a civil war in Barcelona between the communists and the anarchists. A civil war within the civil war, a power struggle.[26] Say what one will about the communist party, it was always loyal to the other forces on the republican side in the fight against fascism. But the anarchists – they'd leave the front in order to fight the communists in the rearguard. Imbeciles! As far as I'm concerned, there were only two anarchist leaders who were loyal and intelligent – Durruti and Ascaso – but they were both dead by then. Durruti was killed in the defence of Madrid and Ascaso in leading an assault on a Barcelona barracks during the military uprising. Though they were idealists, and I didn't share their ideals, these two weren't traitors like so many other CNT leaders, but firm in their political beliefs.[27]

By the time I got to Barcelona in September the worst was over, but there was still killing going on. I remember one day in a house almost opposite my niece's, a young communist was sitting in the doorway. There were other people around, the street was full. Suddenly a group of FAI men appeared, caught hold of the young man and shot him dead. Without a word, without asking him anything, nothing. Just shot him like that. There were days of terror when one couldn't go out in the street for the shooting that was going on. I wasn't sorry when my niece's husband got his orders to leave there for Valencia a month or so after I had arrived. . . .

We went down to Valencia and I was there only two or three weeks when I learnt that my *quinta* was about to be called up. The republican army was now being organized on military lines, the government was calling people up by their age groups. On the republican side more *quintas* were mobilized than on the nationalist side because those people had more than sixty thousand Italians, as well as Moors, Portuguese and Germans to win the war for them. We had a little more than thirty thousand volunteers in the International Brigades – real volunteers who came through political and trade-union organizations, not sent by their governments like the Italians and Germans.

I volunteered for the *carabineros*. They wanted to make me a political commissar, but I didn't want that. 'When my turn comes,' I said, 'I'll go wherever I'm sent as an ordinary soldier.

I don't want stars on my uniform or political duties. I'll do my bit without any of that.' Though I hadn't had any political duties since leaving Mijas, I had of course kept up with the political situation and with my party's provincial and national organization whose headquarters were in Valencia. And I kept up with my friends. At that time in Valencia there was a café where all the socialists went, so if I wanted to meet someone I had only to go there. And there was another café where all the Malagueños met, so if I wanted to see someone from anywhere in the province of Málaga I had only to go there. Between those two cafés I could find whoever it was I was looking for.

I was well enough known at the party headquarters to be able to get the necessary papers to guarantee people who had escaped from the nationalists. People I knew, of course. I'd take them to the headquarters and say, 'This is so-and-so, make him out a guarantee', and there'd be no more questions asked. One day I met a Mijas man in the street, a neighbour of mine whom I had known since he was a child, and he said, 'Manolo, I'm here and because I don't know anyone who'll guarantee me they're going to throw me into a concentration camp.' He claimed to have escaped from Mijas.

I thought there was something suspicious about it. If he had really escaped he wouldn't have been threatened with being sent to a camp. Though I didn't believe it, I swallowed his story. 'Come with me,' I said, and I took him to the party headquarters. 'Make this man out a guarantee,' I said, and they made him out the papers and that was that. He was free, no concentration camp or anything. But as his *quinta* had already been called up, he was ordered to report for army service. And as soon as he learnt that, he disappeared and turned up again in Mijas. He put me in a ridiculous position, though there was nothing I could do about it. I received a warning from party headquarters, but with the war going on and so forth nothing happened.

I didn't have time to see very much in Valencia before I joined up, but what I saw impressed me. Despite the war and the shortages – everything was rationed – and the difficult economic situation, there wasn't the chaos there had been here in the first months after the start of the war. The land was divided up and worked either collectively or individually. The factories were collectivized and the bosses replaced by committees of workers.

The same with the trams and public transport. The workers were a lot better off in so far as the war allowed. It was a sort of war socialism, it couldn't be pure socialism as I understand it, of course, because there were a number of forces which were all pulling in different directions. But all the same, it was a step in the right direction.

I wanted to join the *carabineros* because this was the vanguard socialist corps. All the political parties had their own forces and the *carabineros* were the socialist party's guard force. Before the war the *carabineros* had existed, of course, but as frontier guards. It was Negrín, Treasury Minister before he became Prime Minister, who created them as a socialist fighting force. This was why we were called '*hijos de* Negrín'. 'We are *carabineros*, we are sons of Negrín.' It was possible for Negrín to do this because, as frontier guards dealing with customs, the *carabineros* came under the Treasury, just as the Guardia Civil at that time belonged to the Ministry of the Interior. He formed three divisions, one of which was stationed on each of the three major fronts – Madrid, Catalan and Levante, which was where I was.[28]

We were shock troops, made up of volunteers only, convinced socialists who knew what we were fighting for. There were very few young men in the corps and those there were belonged to the Young Socialists. Most of the *carabineros* were mature men in their thirties, many of whom had left other units to join. Before you could enlist in the corps you had to have party clearance guaranteeing you as a party member, police clearance and a certificate of good conduct. Without those, you couldn't even apply to volunteer.

Apart from the political reasons for wanting to join, there was another reason – the pay was better. We got sixteen pesetas a day, food and clothing. As a matter of fact the whole republican army was better paid than the nationalist army, with an ordinary soldier getting ten pesetas a day. Like the Guardia Civil, who got the same pay as us, we wore an olive-green uniform.

As I had many friends in the party and the army as well, and knew something about it, I was made a medical orderly. The *carabinero* medical training school was in a small village in the province of Valencia and that's where I was sent. I was there a little under a month being instructed because, of course, one can't know everything. I could give injections and that sort of thing which I'd learnt in my youth in the village, but there was a lot more to learn.

I joined my battalion, the 19th, which had been newly formed, and a few days before the battle of Teruel we moved into the front line. It was a couple of weeks before Christmas 1937, and the weather was terrible, the temperature below zero all the time and snowing hard. Everything froze up, lorries, tanks, and for those of us from the south who weren't used to this, it was even worse. Teruel is one of the coldest places in Spain and that winter it was even colder than usual. When the republican offensive started we moved straight towards the city while other army corps advanced in a pincer movement to cut off the city and trap the nationalists. There was very fierce fighting on the flanks as the enemy tried to avoid being trapped; but as our forces advanced their resistance crumbled. Twelve thousand prisoners our army captured there.[29] My battalion advanced into Teruel against very little opposition. In the town itself the military commander, the bishop and other military and civilian leaders took refuge with the *falangistas* and Guardia Civil in the seminary and other buildings and turned them into a fortress. You couldn't pass through any of the streets dominated by these buildings for the hail of machine-gun fire. They were in there for a couple of weeks before surrendering because of lack of food and ammunition.

But I didn't see that because, after about a week in the city mopping up, my battalion was moved to a height called Muela de Villastar, twenty to twenty-five kilometres to the south-west. This height commanded the Teruel–Valencia road on the left flank. My battalion was dug in there and we remained even after the nationalists recaptured Teruel. As soon as Franco saw what we had done he got together all the men and weapons at his disposal – materially he was always stronger than us – and began a counter-offensive. It started at the beginning of February and by the end of the month the nationalists had recaptured the town. El Campesino and his division were the last to leave and they had to swim the frozen river at night to get out. There were great losses on both sides.

The loss of Teruel didn't strike us particularly as a disaster. The war was fluid and positions were won and lost. But when the nationalists continued to advance towards the sea and it looked as though they would cut off Catalonia from Valencia and split the republican zone, it was a different matter. By April 1938 they had reached the Mediterranean. The republican army suffered a severe setback then. Soldiers said, 'We can't win now, we can only resist, unless there's a change in the international situation. . . .' One battalion of my *carabinero* division was cut off and left on the Catalan side.

For my part, the loss of the north, of Bilbao and Asturias in the months before, had made me think we couldn't win the war.

There wasn't enough help coming from outside, anyone could see that. Our shortage of arms was so great that in my battalion, for example, the machine-gun company was never made up to strength. There was only one section with four machine-guns instead of the eight we should have had. Given the shortage, a captain and a lieutenant were sufficient officers to command the company. And this was how it was in many battalions. Others were complete but then very often with antiquated machine-guns from the First World War. Mortar sections were also depleted, if they existed at all. My company had none. And we were considered shock troops! Not that we were better armed than the rest of the army. Most of the rifles in my battalion were Czech, but other battalions had Mexican or Russian rifles. Still, the major shortage wasn't in rifles, it was in heavy arms, tanks and planes. For every artillery battery we had, the nationalists had four; for every plane of ours they had four or five. Those were the odds we were fighting against and that was the reason the war was so unequal, especially on the flat, on the plains.

The Soviet Union and Mexico were the only countries to sell us some arms, and we had to pay in gold for what we got from the Russians. If only France, with its common border, had sold us arms – for money if for no other reason – the outcome would have been different. But no, we were saddled with the Non-Intervention Committee. So all our arms had to come from a great distance by sea.

Of course, we couldn't have resisted for as long as we did if it hadn't been for the Soviet Union. This was the reason why the communist party grew so rapidly during the war. It was a very small party at the beginning, and people who had no firm ideological commitment and who saw that the Soviet Union was the only country helping the Republic, started to join.

But others like me – leaving aside the question of gratitude for

Soviet aid – didn't change our opinions about the Soviet Union. Stalin was a tyrant, and while communist ideology in social matters appeals to me, the political form of government, especially under Stalin, I have never liked. But as I say, the communist party became very strong by the end of the war – and it has been strong ever since. Ever since this regime has been in power, the communist party has been the strongest opposition party in Spain. And that is because they never gave up the struggle in clandestinity after the war, while all the other parties, including my own, disappeared inside Spain.

Our army, unlike the nationalists', was an army that had been formed in the struggle. At the front we had hardly any officers of the regular army. To begin with there weren't many who had stayed loyal to the Republic and those who had were mainly on our side because the war had caught them there. Most of these officers were kept in the rear for recruiting and jobs like that. The front-line officers all came from the militias formed at the time of the military uprising. They were soldiers who had proven themselves in battle. Or sometimes they were trade-union leaders, because a union – the UGT, for example – would form a battalion of its members in a locality and the union leaders became its officers. A great number of fine officers came up through the ranks. Lister, a communist, who was as good as if not better than any professional, was a quarry-worker who ended up as a colonel. Modesto was another communist, a carpenter and former corporal in the Foreign Legion who came to command a division. El Campesino . . . though he was a madman who didn't really know how to command, was very brave and firm in his political beliefs. . . . Fernandez who was a socialist, and so on.

Alongside the officers, there were the political commissars. At company level these were called political delegates, and only at battalion level and above were they called commissars. They had the same rank, though different insignia, as the commanding officer at each level, and they were the first to go into attack with their men. More so than the officers, who had to stay back to direct operations. The commissars had to inspire the men when they were at the front, to lead them into action. That was their place. After the fighting, or when there was no action, they held political meetings and discussions on the significance of the war, of this particular battle or the importance of defence, or whatever it might be. They were certainly men of great bravery, political or union militants – the first to be shot if they were captured.

In the *carabineros* we had no political delegates at company level. It probably wasn't thought necessary since we were all convinced socialists or at least UGT members. Only from battalion level upwards were there commissars. Our battalion commissar was a former UGT union leader from the Valencia docks. Frankly, I never thought it was necessary to have commissars at all; if I had been in charge I wouldn't have created them. All of us had belonged to political organizations before joining the army and we knew what we were fighting for. It's true that in the rest of the army, where there were many peasants and the like who didn't know the political reasons why they were fighting, the commissars may have done some good. But all the same, I don't think it would have made much difference if there hadn't been any.

In May 1937 we were transferred to a place called Alcalá de la Selva to the north-east of Teruel in Castellon province where the nationalists had launched another big attack. The front there was completely fluid among tall pine trees and our lines had been held by a brigade of El Campesino's division made up mainly of young recruits. When the nationalists launched their attack, these recruits panicked and fled, throwing away their arms. The *carabineros* were rushed up to hold the line, which we did, taking a great number of prisoners of General Aranda's Galician division. The Gallegos were scared stiff, having been indoctrinated with all sorts of propaganda about what the 'Reds' did to prisoners. Nothing happened to them, of course, but El Campesino, who had been a sergeant in the Foreign Legion, ordered a number of his men who had fled to be shot. He had their bodies hung in the trees as a reminder to the rest. That was rough justice – but discipline had to be restored, you can't have men in the line throwing down their arms and fleeing.

We held off the nationalists and broke their offensive. But a couple of months later, in July, they launched a new attack from Teruel in an attempt to break through to Valencia. Franco's armour moved down the plain towards Sarrión, leaving us trapped in a pocket to the north-east around Mora de Rubielos. It was a desperate fight to hold up their advance and then to get out.

I was lucky not to be caught there. The advance medical post was in an abandoned goat pen on a height and down below we could see the motorized columns which had broken through our front advancing on us, followed by infantry. Their air force was out in strength, there were never less than forty or fifty planes in the sky bombing our positions, and there must have been at least forty artillery batteries shelling us. The only position blocking their advance was a ridge held by our men – the *carabineros*. The planes came over, the bombs dropped on the ridge – pom-pom-pom-pom. . . . Then silence. Their infantry advanced to take the ridge and our men rose out of the ground and beat them off. It went on all day; our men beat back five attacks in all.

From our position in the goat pen which was little more than half a kilometre to the rear we watched the action. That night, at about 11 p.m., a messenger arrived from our captain ordering us to withdraw. Without our knowing it, our battalion, which we still thought was in front of us on the ridge, had been withdrawn and had left so quietly that we hadn't heard them. It was a good thing that the captain remembered to send the messenger and that nothing happened to him on the way, otherwise we would have found ourselves in the enemy lines in the morning.

I used to think that if I were captured I would try to fool the enemy by telling them I came from Almeria or somewhere still in the republican zone so that they couldn't check up on me. That was my idea – an instinct of self-preservation. Unless, of course, I had been captured by someone who knew me and who would have said, 'He doesn't come from Almeria, he's from Málaga.' The game would have been up then, they'd have got a report on me from Mijas – they always got reports where they could – and I'd have been shot.

That night we retreated without stopping and in the morning reached a promontory we called the Tabla. It was a good job the enemy didn't bomb us there that day, it would have been a slaughter. Cars, lorries, civilians fleeing, soldiers and *carabineros* looking for their units – it was pandemonium.

We found our battalion and there, on that promontory, one side of which gave onto the plain of Sarrión, we held out in a fierce battle that went on nearly three days. My battalion was decimated in the fighting and the withdrawal we had to make when the enemy took Sarrión on the main Valencia–Teruel road. More than half the battalion was lost, dead or captured, in the battle. The nationalist artillery was raining down shells on the road as we retreated across it. Once the enemy held the heights, there seemed nothing to stop them advancing into the plain where their motorized columns could strike down on Valencia itself.

I was posted to another battalion, the 24th, which was being re-formed. For two or three weeks we were in the rear while the battalion was brought up to strength. It was the first time since the battle of Teruel, nearly six months before, that my battalion had been out of the front line. We hadn't had a single day in the rear until then.

We were sent back up to the front south of Jérica on the main road. But here things were very different because strong fortifications had been built from Viver on the main road north of Jérica into the Sierra de Espadán – the Matallana line, as it was called, after the republican general who built it. Bombs, shelling, nothing could move it. The nationalists lost thousands of men in the attack, but they couldn't get through. The line held until the end of the war, the enemy never broke it to capture Valencia.

After six months at the front I was eligible for hospital duty in the rear. That was the rule: six months at the front. I was only a short time in the Matallana line when I was sent to a surgical hospital near Segorbe, about fifteen kilometres behind the lines. You could hear the artillery-fire far off in the distance – but we were well out of danger. During my time at the front – and we were never far behind the lines in our advance posts where we bandaged the wounded who were brought in on stretchers before sending them to the rear for attention – I was never really frightened. I was lucky, it depends on a person's nature whether he is frightened or not. But I always reckoned that in the front line you had time only to think of doing the job that had to be done. . . .

Life in the hospital was splendid in comparison to the front. We worked from eight one morning to eight the next – and then had the following twenty-four hours free. It was a hospital of about thirty beds for all types of surgical operations, and each medical orderly was on duty eight hours out of his twenty-four hours' service. In our free time we would go into Segorbe or one of the neighbouring pueblos, and on Sundays the girls would come over to see us. I always had plenty of money in those days because we were well paid and in addition I earned on the side as a barber cutting people's hair.

Earlier, while still in Valencia before joining up, I had heard that my wife and child were safe in Mijas. A young communist from Mijas, who had been imprisoned in Málaga after the nationalists took the village, gave me all the news. He had managed to escape and got to Valencia where I met him. He told me everything that had happened, the repression in Mijas and in Málaga – it had been very severe – and, of course, he was able to give me the good news about my wife and baby. Before that, I hadn't known anything and was worried all the time, but now I had no fears on that score. It was a burden lifted from me – and yet another was added by the news of the comrades who had stayed behind and perished.

It was a heavy blow when Barcelona fell in January 1939. But still the Republic held Madrid and a very large zone stretching from there to Valencia on the sea and including Múrcia, Almeria, Jaén, part of Córdoba and Ciudad Real. The Republic still had an army of 600,000 men. Negrín, who was Prime Minister, and the communists wanted to continue the resistance. They could see the international situation had worsened with Czechoslovakia and they said: world war will break out, we must continue to resist. I thought the same, if we could hold out until our war became part of a general conflict everything would be changed. Hitler and Mussolini wouldn't have been able to go on helping the nationalists with war material and it would have left our forces more equal. It was only arms that we lacked, not men. Moreover, we were fighting with faith in our cause. Had we held out, we would have provided a base for the Allies in their fight against the Nazis and Italians. Even if Hitler had taken over Spain, he would in the end have been driven out, as he was from everywhere else, and Spanish democracy would have been restored. A few months more – only until September – a year more we could have resisted. We would have lost a bit more ground here or there and gained ground elsewhere – we could have held them off. A republican offensive on the Córdoba front had just recaptured a lot of ground. Hadn't we fought on for a year after Catalonia had been split from the rest of the republican zone?

But in March there was the betrayal of Colonel Casado, the commander of the Army of the Centre in Madrid, who seized power to negotiate the surrender with Franco. Besteiro joined Casado's *junta*. I was very much surprised and disappointed in him when I heard this. I thought he was wrong. As always, he acted in good faith as a democrat – he was a man who valued democracy above everything – but he was mistaken in giving in. In the end he saw it himself; he had wanted to negotiate an honourable peace and instead he was taken in. But by then it was too late, the Republic had surrendered.

My division had been ordered to Valencia three weeks before. We had been sent there because it was thought communist units would take over the roads and railways and centres of communication to continue the war. We were to defend them against the communists if necessary. But we weren't needed.

When the surrender was announced in Madrid, an officer who had been serving with us came to the barracks and ordered us to fall in. It turned out that he was secretly a fascist and he had got in touch with the nationalists as soon as they entered the city. There was no resistance, it would have been useless, everything had been decided from above.

'All right, it's all over, they've surrendered,' he said. 'You can all go, back to your villages or wherever you like.' And so we disbanded, some went one way and others another. Those like me, whose homes weren't close by, spent our time running round in circles waiting to see what was going to happen. Thirteen or fourteen days, as I've said, before going to the bullring to report. Little did I think as I waited for the cattle trucks that thirty years' suffering still lay ahead.

JULIANA

When the war ended, I was full of fear. I wanted to see him again and at the same time I didn't want him to come back.

They came looking for him as soon as I got back to the village. The Guardia Civil came at three in the morning and banged on the door. 'Who is it?' I called out. 'The Guardia Civil. Is Manuel

Cortes there?' 'No, señor. He left the house three days ago and I don't know anything of his whereabouts.' 'All right, don't open the door', and they left.

The next day they came back and were talking and smoking a cigarette with his foster-father. Garcia was one of them; he was in charge. He saluted me. 'We came to your house last night, but as you said Manuel had gone I didn't want to bother you.' 'Look,' I said, 'he left, the way things were going. . . .' I told him what had happened, he believed me, the people had seen me coming back to the village with my mother and daughter alone. 'You know,' he said, 'Manuel did well to leave because the first moments are very bad.'

The Guardia didn't behave badly towards me that day. Later, when they used to call me to the barracks, it was different. But the fault lies with the people here, as I've said: the *camarilla* who put pressure on the Guardia to interrogate me. The Guardia weren't interested really in looking for him, they got the same wage whether they found him or not. It was the *falangistas* who wanted him.

Two or three nights after the Guardia's visit they came to search the house. They were the only ones who ever did. In all these years the Guardia never looked for him in the house; they came only looking for esparto. The *falangistas* were in uniform, blue shirts and berets, and with their rifles on their shoulders – they were on duty, it was after two in the morning. A relative opened the door to them. I took my daughter in my arms and put a blanket round us and stayed in bed. I saw them pass, one of them had the nerve to look under the bed as he went by. Some of them I recognized and others I didn't because I had no wish to know them. They were all from here, from the village. 'We've come to see if he's here,' they said, 'so that he can report to the authorities. Nothing will happen to him.' 'Yes,' I said, 'that's very good, but he can't report because he isn't here.' I was quite calm knowing that he wasn't here and at the same time full of grief at his having gone.

They searched only my house that night. Though I knew them and knew what they wanted, when I saw them in the street afterwards I never gave a sign of anything. I wouldn't show them what I felt, I kept it inside me as I still do.

Those first months were bad, very bad. They didn't care

whether someone had done anything or not, all they cared about was their ideas. They began rounding them up from the start; six or seven of them they took out to the watercourse and shot them there. Then they started on the women. They rounded up some of them and shaved their heads and paraded them through the streets. I was terrified they would do the same to me. Not because I had done anything, but because of him. I shut the door and with an eye to the keyhole I saw them pass. I was sick with fear, sick, and I said to myself, tomorrow it'll be my turn, because there was a list of twenty or more put down. For nothing. One of the women was shaved because she lived with a man, a stranger from outside the village who had fled as the nationalists advanced. What difference did it make to them what she did? And others because they had taken part in demonstrations or for personal reasons because someone had a grudge against them.

I went to the clerk of the town hall and said, 'Don Lucas, they say they've got twenty on the list, I'm sick with fear, I'm going to leave. . . .' 'No, not you, no one is going to trouble you, because you never troubled anyone,' he said. That was true, it was worth a lot, because otherwise they would have come for me too.

Don Lucas helped me a lot. He remembered how my husband had saved his life the night those people came to shoot him and the rest. He often used to say that Manolo had never done anything wrong, that he happened to be mayor at that time and that was all.

There was a gentleman in Málaga who helped me too. His house was one of the first where I sold eggs. I told him the Guardia were always questioning me and threatening to put me in jail. He said they couldn't do anything to me. 'If your husband was on the left that's one thing, but you tell them you've got nothing to do with ideas of that sort. You tell them you understand nothing of your husband's ideas.' And then he said they had to have a signed *denuncia*, supported by two witnesses, saying that I knew where my husband was, to be able to put me in jail. The next time I told the Guardia that. 'You're a legal force, not a political one, you're here to catch criminals not political people. In political matters you've no right to interfere.' That stopped them a bit.

Sometimes it would be the sergeant and at other times an ordinary *guardia* who questioned me. One day when I was walking along the Calle Nueva in Málaga I felt someone tugging at the parcels under my arm. I thought it was a thief and started to run. 'No, it's me,' and I turned round and saw this young *guardia* there. And he said, 'That time I had to question you – you haven't got it in for me because of that, eh? I was ordered to do it by the sergeant.'

'Have it in for you?' I said, 'why should I?' 'Because I gave you so much trouble. It wasn't my fault, I was ordered to do it. And you always replied the same thing, that you didn't know anything.' 'That's right. What else should I say? Since I don't know anything, I can't say anything.' 'That's right,' he said, 'you always say the same thing. But don't hold it against me.' 'I don't hold anything against you or anyone else, you're in the service and have your job to do.'

I was thinking all the time only of covering up any trace of my husband. The night I spent on the farm outside Málaga after we'd parted, I burnt a picture of him I'd taken from its frame and rolled up. I burnt it because I heard that they were looking for pictures and papers. As soon as I got back I went round to everyone I knew and, on any excuse I could think of, asked if they had a picture of him. One of the women had a picture and gave it to me. 'You keep this,' she said, 'what with the trouble that's going on.' All the pictures I had I put in a box and placed in a hole in the wall and sealed up. I was frightened they would want a picture of him for their police records in Málaga and that way they would catch him.

I wasn't wrong. A *guardia* came to my house and asked for a picture. I said I hadn't got one. A short time after he came back. 'You haven't got any pictures? Well, the postman's wife has just given me one, I've got it here.' 'Who?' I said. 'The postman's wife.' 'Ah,' I said, 'she's done very well to give you that, I would have done the same if I had had one.'

I didn't show a thing, but inside I was boiling with anger. Imagine that! She was the only one I hadn't thought of – and now she had given the picture to keep in well with those people. Her husband had been secretary of the trade union for a time, that was the reason. The *guardia* had gone from my house to collect the post and had mentioned to her that I hadn't got a picture. 'Oh,' she says, 'I've got one here, you take it.' Just like that. It was a picture of him and her brother with a group of others when they were doing their military service. The *guardia* made a cross beside my husband on the picture to show which one he was, and took it away.

Such a hatred of that woman came over me that I couldn't stand even to see her. It lasted for years. Every time I saw her I remembered that she had given him away. If he came back and they had a file on him, he'd be caught because of her giving the picture, I thought. But I don't think they ever sent it to Málaga, otherwise they would have arrested him at the station when he arrived.

For a year or more after he left I didn't know whether he was dead or alive. It was sometime in 1938 that I got a letter from him through the Red Cross. It came from Albacete, I think it was, and I wrote back and sent him a picture of my daughter. He got that one, but he never received a second one I sent because by the time it got there he had moved somewhere else.

As the war went on I didn't believe in anything any more. I didn't know who would win. Now they would say, 'The reds are attacking', and plenty of people were frightened. And then they would say, 'Our side is advancing', and so it went on. There's no end to this, I'd tell myself. It wasn't safe to talk openly. You'd hear something, but no one dared ask, because if you did they'd say, 'She wants the others to win.' Work and keep quiet and that was that; it was dangerous otherwise. When I went to the countryside for eggs there were many farmers on the left who would say, 'Our people are winning, our people are winning!' 'Yes, winning they may be, but I don't see it,' I'd answer. I didn't dare talk to anyone about anything because if I did they'd have me up at the barracks for questioning again.

When at last the war ended I was full of fear. I wanted to see him and know that he was all right, and at the same time I didn't want him to come back. And yet, I thought, he'll try to come back. Every day the trains were bringing back people from both sides and every day I went to the station in Málaga to wait. The trains were packed; there were always crowds waiting for them. My plan was to take him to my sister's house and tell him what was happening. He mustn't come back here, they were waiting for him, he mustn't report. I thought, he must have some idea but he won't know the worst, he doesn't know they're waiting to liquidate him. If he does, he won't come back. That was my hope, that he had escaped, had got abroad. Think of it – thirty years of anguish and suffering we would have been spared if he had escaped. He could have lived his life freely, and sooner or later I would have joined him. Yes, I would have gone wherever he was. Once things calmed down here it wasn't impossible to leave, for a woman anyway; they wouldn't let men out. There was a woman in the village whose husband was in France and after a while he sent her money and she went to join him. I would have made a new life wherever it was. Here I had to be working – why not abroad? Whatever the life was like it would have been easier than these last thirty years. . . .

But no, with his calm, his way of thinking, he didn't try to escape. He stayed to the end and then it was too late. He had an easy conscience, he was confident because he knew he hadn't done anything and they said that anyone whose hands weren't stained with blood would be all right. All he thought was that the war was over and everything was finished. So he came back.

The one day I couldn't go to the station – the only one I missed – that was the day on which he arrived.

Four

IN HIDING
Twenty more years
1949–69

Now [1960], after twenty years, Spain
enjoys a prosperity greater than it did before
the Civil War. The death-rate has
decreased and the country enjoys a *per capita*
increase of real income of about thirty
per cent higher than in 1931–5; that of
agricultural and industrial workers may
not be much more than six per cent.
(Real agricultural wages . . . were almost
precisely the same in 1958 as in 1935.) But
freedom of speech is limited. No political
parties are permitted – save for the Falange
as organized in April 1937. Many linger in
prison for criticism of the regime. The
Nationalist authorities continue to believe
that these measures are essential if the
explosion of another civil conflict is to be
avoided. In some areas, poverty remains a
horror and a reproach to all who see it.
Spain thus remains in travail.

– HUGH THOMAS, *The Spanish Civil War*

MANUEL

My faith – not so much in socialism but rather in democracy – has never diminished. I have and always have had faith that in the end democracy will triumph. . . . The tyranny of dictatorship, wherever it is . . . cannot be lasting.

Memories of the good times and the bad – how often they came back to me in my time of hiding. The cities I had seen, the friends I had made, the things that had happened during the war. . . . Not that there were many good memories from my time in the front lines – but in the rear it was different. Shut up in my room, I often used to remember those times at the hospital when we would go out on our days off. Theatres, cinemas, cabarets, girls . . . in the rear you hardly knew there was a war on. But above all, one memory always returned to me, a bad one. And that was the fighting between the anarchists and communists in Barcelona while I was there. I've never forgotten that, it is as clear to me today as it was thirty years ago, that young communist who was assassinated in front of my eyes. Yes, there were good memories and bad.

Still, being shut up in the prime of one's life after having seen the best part of Spain, it was good to have any memories to help me live. I was thirty-four when I came back here. Between thirty and fifty are the best years of a man's life, before that he isn't formed and after that he begins to go downhill. I've spent those years shut up and it saddens me. I was lucky to have a good wife and daughter, otherwise I couldn't have survived. The family is always important, but to me hidden here it was even more so. When you're free you love your family, naturally, but it's not the same thing. I was completely dependent on them. When they were good, well, then things were good, and if they were anxious and upset, well, it had its repercussions on me. Sometimes I used to feel like another child in the house, to be looked after when it suited and if not. . . . Someone useless, really. Normally the man is the head of the family, but here it was the other way round – it was my wife who had to go out to work, who had to look after us, who was head of the family. It had its effect on me, especially in the first years. Although I have never been one of those patriarchal type of men who allow their wives and children no freedom, I have my dignity and pride as a man and it affected me to be kept down in this way because of the circumstances I was in.

But as I say, my wife and daughter were very good. There are couples who don't get on, there are some women who are worse than others – and if that had been my case it would have been impossible to remain in hiding all these years. Once I was out of my father's house and in my own house with my wife I could lead something like a normal life again. Every night I could sleep in my own bed with my wife and, though we kept a bed upstairs for the few times I was ill, I didn't have to use it much.

I would have liked more children, three altogether, a son in particular. But one has children if one wants them, not otherwise. I know, there are plenty of people who say the contrary, and that's because of the poverty in which they live. They've got nothing else but that in their lives. For us it would have been a scandal for my wife to have got pregnant and it would have been dangerous for me. The people have tongues that never stop wagging and they'll say anything for the pleasure of hearing themselves talk. So I said, if we can't have more children we won't have any. As in everything else, you've got to have a certain talent, keep a cool head. . . .

My foster-father died in 1949 or 1950; I don't remember exactly which. His death came at a time when I thought there was no more hope. There had been one or two amnesties but they were always partial. It was clear now that the regime was going to continue in power, all my hopes at the end of the war had come to nothing. Soon the United States signed a military agreement with the regime – an injection of oxygen which gave it more strength. That was the final blow for the few democrats who were left here. This is for life, I thought in despair. So when a cousin of mine came to Mijas for my father's funeral I told my wife to invite him to the house for a meal afterwards.

He and I had practically grown up together. He went to live in Málaga where he worked in the docks only in his twenties. He wasn't political, never joined any union, even when there was one to join. But that didn't matter, I trusted him entirely. A question of blood and family. When he came to the house and the doors were shut, I suddenly appeared. He was overcome, he didn't know what to say! He didn't know I was here. At last he managed to get over his surprise. Then we started to talk; it was the first time in over ten years that I had been able to talk to anyone outside my immediate family. And out of this came a plan for my escape.

My cousin knew a docker in the port who he thought might be able to help. 'He's a friend of mine, very loyal – more on your side than mine because he's a socialist,' my cousin said. This docker had had to suffer a lot and had been jailed for his past. He was released with one of the first amnesties and came to Málaga to get away from Seville. My cousin said he would see what he could do and a few weeks later my wife went to see him. She came back and said that this docker couldn't do anything himself: he was too closely watched. But he had an idea of approaching someone else. He told my cousin the name of the young man in question. My cousin knew him too but without knowing what sort of man he really was. This young man appeared very friendly with all the authorities who looked on him with great favour – a good *falangista* in fact. But actually he was a communist – one of the new generation that came of age after the war – and he had a job as a clerk or something of the sort in the docks. I told my wife to ask my cousin to come up to Mijas on one of his free days, and when he came we had a long talk. I told him that, if he had confidence, he should let the docker approach this young man to see if there was some way of getting false papers so that I could reach Barcelona and from there France. I told him not to tell anyone, though, where I was.

Of course, all these moves took time. I suppose it was a year or more after my cousin came to my father's funeral before we got to this stage. It was worth taking time to be sure everything was all right. I had full confidence in my cousin and, moreover, by then he had got to know this young man through the docker.

It all seemed all right, there seemed no chance of a trap, and so the docker had words with the young man. He agreed to help. 'Although I'm to the left of you,' he said to the docker, 'the people here look on me as a fascist. I can go into any of these offices and be attended to. I'll go to the police and get an identity card and passport for this man. I'll need his photograph, that'll be all, because they'll fill out the documents in any name as long as there's a photograph. . . .'

Although my wife pretended she had destroyed all photographs of me, she had kept one hidden. She took it to Málaga to have it copied and made to size.

My plan was for my cousin to come up to Mijas in a taxi late at night. I would be waiting down on the road somewhere to be picked up. From Málaga, I'd take the bus to Almeria, a town I know well. Once there I planned to go by train to Barcelona. I hoped before leaving to have an address to go to in Barcelona where there was a clandestine organization that got people out to France by sea. That was safer than crossing the border, but it could be done only from close to France, not from down here. As long as I had an identity card with a false name I could get through a police check on the bus or train.

All the arrangements were made and we were waiting only for the young man to get the papers when he was killed. A terrible thing happened, a crane crashed on him in the docks and crushed him to death. A tragedy for him – and for us the end of our plans. We had no other contacts.

In other times I could have put my wife on to a number of people, but I didn't know any longer who had been killed or who was alive. Moreover, my wife is very cautious, she would never seek out someone who might help, even if he had been a comrade of mine.

To try to escape without papers to Africa or Gibraltar would have meant finding a boat. And my wife couldn't do that without knowing people, people who could be trusted. Moreover, she didn't have time, she had her business to look after. No, once that chance had passed there was nothing else for it but to stay hidden here. I was disappointed, naturally, but from then on I knew that I had to continue the struggle as best I could, sometimes with more courage and sometimes with less, but without thinking of escape. And that's how it was. I got so used to the monotonous life that I paid no attention to what was going on outside, unless there was danger in it for us. The only thing I waited for every evening was my radio, you couldn't drag me away from that.

After ten years of living in No. 5 we had some money saved and my wife wanted to buy a house of her own. She found this one, No. 11, in the same street and, though it was dilapidated and needed a lot doing to it, we decided to move.

We had to get the new house repaired and done up. We didn't have enough money to do it in one go and in any case we had to be able to go on living in it while it was being repaired. So the first year we did the ground floor.

While the masons and labourers were in the house I spent the day in a room off the stairs which led to the second floor. Behind a locked door, of course. I had to keep very quiet because the workmen were all over the place, and I had to be specially careful not to cough. But that was all right until one day, when my wife was in Málaga, one of the labourers decided he needed to go upstairs for something. He found the door locked and started to shove at it. It was only a thin door and one or two more shoves and he would have broken it down. On the inside I was saying, 'That son of a whore, what's he doing? He'll have the door down and I'll be found.' There was nowhere to hide, there was nothing I could do. He was rattling the door when, happily, my daughter came in and told him to stop. She said her mother had taken the keys with her to Málaga and he couldn't go upstairs. So the man gave up and went away. My wife gave Maria a good talking to that night.

The main improvement I wanted made was to have the staircase changed from the front to the back where you see it now. This was so I could go straight down to the kitchen from my room upstairs without being seen by anyone who might be downstairs in the house. Once we had made the change we always kept the door to the stairs locked from the inside, and so my freedom to move around was increased. While the workmen were rebuilding the stairs I hid in our bedroom down here. It was only normal that we should keep one room locked while work was going on so that dust and dirt shouldn't get in. I know now that the workmen who spent so much time in this house say, 'How is it possible that Manolo was hidden there? We've been in every single room while we were rebuilding the place. . . .'

It was the same with the women my wife used to have in to clean the house thoroughly and whitewash once a year. Before they arrived in the morning, my wife would arrange things upstairs, take out the radio and anything else that might give me away, and I'd hide in the bedroom downstairs. When the women went for lunch I'd come out to eat. My wife always thought it out carefully, so that all the work was being done either upstairs or down but never both at once. When they were working downstairs I was in my room on the first floor. They were never suspicious about our having a bed upstairs since they knew that we had family who came to stay like my cousin from Málaga. Having all these people in to work lessened suspicion because they would always tell anyone who asked, 'We've been in every room in that house, there's no one there, that's for sure.'

Otherwise the days and the months went on the same, without a break, weighing and binding esparto. Being in hiding seemed normal in the end, one year after another until thirty in all passed. Two years, the worst, in my father's house, ten years in No. 5 and eighteen here.

The major danger of being discovered now was if I fell ill. I was lucky. Except for some spells of 'flu which I got over with penicillin my wife bought in Málaga and rheumatism which I've got from the war, I had only a couple of days' serious illness.

The thing that plagued me most was my teeth. The number I've pulled out over the years! Nine or ten, it must be, including some of the molars at the back. With my fingers. What else could I do it with? As soon as I got a toothache I knew that the only cure was to get the tooth out. I'd kill the immediate pain with an aspirin or something and then I'd sit down in front of the mirror and catch hold of the tooth and begin. *Tras-tras-tras.* . . . I'd try getting the tooth to move from one side to the other, gripping it so that it would shift, looking to see what I was doing in the mirror. Sometimes they were already a bit loose and that would help. I'd keep at it then, pulling the tooth back and forth until, with one quick grip of my fingers and a twist, I'd have it out. But often the tooth wouldn't move at all, especially if it was a molar. Then it would be days before I could start to shift it. *Tras-tras-tras* . . . gradually I would feel it moving. If the pain was too great, I'd leave it for the time being and start again the next day. You've got to have patience for this sort of thing. I always got it out in the end, however long it took. It would bleed a lot and I'd stop it with peroxide and wash out my mouth with white wine. When you have to, you can do anything! And it was no good leaving a bad tooth in because the pain is always sure to come back.

One morning I woke with a terrible pain in my left side. It was so bad that nothing I could do would stop it. I had to get out of bed down here and go upstairs lest anyone heard me crying out. My wife and daughter were frightened, they didn't know what to do; the pain was so great I thought something was going to burst. I knew it couldn't be appendicitis because it was on the wrong side, but I didn't know what else it might be. I was lying upstairs with the pillow stuffed in my mouth so that no one would hear. Nothing we had in the house did any good; it was clear that I had to have medicine of some sort or other.

All that day and the following night the pain kept up and I thought, 'I'll have to get to a doctor or I'll die here.' My wife was already thinking of ways to get me to Málaga to a doctor. By then we had bought a taxi and my daughter's *novio* was the driver. But he didn't know I was hidden here, we would have to tell him and then get him to drive us at night to Málaga. It was very critical – and on top of the worry there was the pain. We thought that if we went to my cousin's in Málaga and got him to call a doctor we might get away with it. If the doctor said an operation was necessary, we'd try to get to a clinic where I could pose under a false name. That wouldn't be too difficult because all they're really concerned about is whether you've got enough money to pay.

Then my wife had this idea that she or my daughter could go to the local doctor, Don José, in the morning and pretend she had the pain and get him to prescribe medicine. . . . 'Let it be me,' my daughter said.

I could barely wait until morning when, very early still, my wife went to call Don José and tell him our daughter was ill in bed. She asked him for morphine but he refused. He came to the house to examine her. I'd told her exactly where the pain was and how it felt and she put on the act. She did it well, though the doctor said it was strange. He couldn't feel that she could have as much pain as she said. All the same, he didn't disbelieve her and pre-scribed some suppositories and injections. My wife rushed to the chemist's to buy the medicine and bring it back. I took the first suppository and that calmed the pain a bit, but it started to come back. A couple more and the pain was relieved. By evening, when we thought we would have to go to Málaga, it was gone for good. I've never known what caused it or what it was. It may have been food poisoning because, otherwise, in a few days or months it would have come back, and I've never had it again. It was very lucky that my daughter was capable of doing what she did and that the doctor was able to prescribe the right medicine, otherwise I don't know what would have happened. It was a very anxious twenty-four hours for all of us with only one thought in our minds: to try to get out without being discovered or stay here and take the risk.

By good fortune we never had to make that choice. The fact of owning the taxi would have made it easier to get to Málaga, but all the same I didn't want to run the risk if I could help it. We bought the taxi – an old pre-war Studebaker it was – from the man who had been running it here, to give my future son-in-law a fixed job. Later we bought a second one too. But I was never tempted to go out in it, even after my daughter married and my son-in-law was let into the secret. Once in a while in the last few years he has said to me, 'Come on, I'll take you to a bullfight in Málaga, no one will recognize you', but I've always refused. It would be just my luck to run across someone who knew me if I went out. And after all these years what was the point of taking a risk? Sooner or later something must change, there might be an amnesty which would allow me to come out. I kept listening to the radio.

When the regime celebrated its twenty-five years in power – the twenty-five years of peace as it was called – I had hopes. That was in 1964. Perhaps they would remember at last. But nothing happened.

By that time my daughter had got married. The day of her wedding was a sad day for me. I upstairs and the house and the patio full of people celebrating. All the rooms downstairs and the patio, where my cousin from Málaga put up a tarpaulin as awning, were packed with guests singing and talking. People from all social classes, friends of my wife in the village and Málaga, relatives of hers and mine from all over – a hundred or more guests at least. For a father not to be present at his daughter's wedding – that's a sad thing to happen to a man.

Before my daughter left for the church I came down behind the locked door at the bottom of the stairs. Crouching down I put my eye to the keyhole. My wife and I had planned this. As our daughter came out, my wife moved the others aside so that through the keyhole I could see her for a moment in her bridal gown. She stood there for a second or two, as though looking at something, then she was gone.

Upstairs my wife had brought beer and food and while the others were celebrating down here I was having my celebration up there. I made up on the beer for the lack of company; I've always liked beer, it's my favourite drink. A beer and a cigar – until I gave up smoking because of my cough – that's what I've always liked best.

Before she left on her honeymoon my daughter slipped away from everyone to say good-bye. She pretended she had something to do and very quietly she came upstairs to see me. She was already in her honeymoon clothes, the car was waiting outside and she and her husband were off to Madrid. Another instant and then she was gone.

It was only on her honeymoon that she told her husband I was here, until that moment he had never known.

She needed no telling that until she was married she shouldn't give the secret away to anyone, however close. She was always a good girl. When she was young her mother and I warned her often enough and since then there's never been a moment in which we feared she would say anything.

It's been the same with her children – never a word! They'd come to play with me upstairs almost every day, they'd warn me if someone was at the door – '*abuelo, abuelo*, get upstairs quick,' the eldest would say – and never a word to anyone outside. Not even their paternal grandparents knew, neither from their son nor from their grandchildren. Of course, my daughter was on top of them all the time to make sure they wouldn't talk in the street, and we took the precaution never to give me a name. I was 'grandfather' to them, so that if they talked about me they might be thought to be talking about their other grandfather or even about their great-grandfather, my wife's father, who lives here with us.

A derelict house next to ours was for sale; it was about the time we bought our first lorry. Our regular daily taxi service to

Málaga had been forbidden because the bus company in Málaga didn't want competition for its new service to Mijas. The power of monopoly! So I said, we'll get rid of the taxis and buy a lorry, a small one to start with. Tourism was beginning to expand and there was a shortage of transport. I wanted the house next door for a garage but my wife insisted that we build a house for my daughter and son-in-law. While it was being done up we gave them our bedroom downstairs. So that they could get in from their house, we broke through the adjoining wall. Although that wasn't the intention, the connecting door turned out very useful because it meant I could get to my daughter's house without going outside.

After a time they bought a TV set. Then every night it was, 'Come on down and watch television.' But I preferred my radio. With a radio you can tune in anywhere. I want to listen to New York, I turn a dial; I want to tune in to Peking, the same. But on television all you get is what they want to put on. You've got no choice.

However, after a while even I got hooked, because of the films and plays they put on TV. And the bullfights! Then there is all the sport, football matches and cycling especially. I can't even ride a bicycle myself, but cycle races like the Tour of Spain and of France – there's no sport I like better watching. Who's wearing the yellow jersey and who's king of the mountains – all that sort of thing I'd follow night after night.

I never liked Westerns – all that shooting and punching, there's not much that's instructive about that. What I liked were films and plays that dealt with social matters. *Death of a Cyclist* and *Calle Mayor* are two of my favourites. They've got an atmosphere, a spirit that's very Spanish. Also I've seen a number of English films dealing with social problems that I've liked a lot. But mainly they put on Westerns – on television and in the cinema. That's what's in fashion now because Spain has become yankee-fied. In the past, when something else was in fashion, when Hitler was the great man, the Americans were materialist devils and nothing else. But now they're the best in the world and the same people who were once against them are 'eating' their dollars.

Some afternoons when there was a bullfight I wanted to watch, my wife would have to make all sorts of excuses to keep the neighbours out. 'No, Maria isn't putting the television on today because she's got a headache. . . .' And then, with the doors locked and the shutters closed, I could come down and put the television on very softly. If anyone ever came to the door I could get out quick enough through the passageway which led straight into our bedroom.

But I never stopped listening to the radio. Especially on Fridays when the cabinet meets in Madrid. There was never anything and my wife thought I was a fool to go on listening. She was always pessimistic, she thought there was no end to this. I stuck to my radio, a good one it is, though in the last few years it developed a defect which couldn't be fixed. Only if you turn up the volume does the sound come through. So there were times when people next door or downstairs could hear the sound from my room. If anyone asked, my wife would say, 'Oh, that's in Miguel's house, or across the street.'

Otherwise life just went on, monotonously. Days and days passed without my thinking of the past or the future. I had my work and that was all. There was nothing else. A fiesta once in a while, for my saint's day, on the first of the year, Christmas, May Day. I always celebrated 1 May and I liked my wife and daughter to do the same. We'd have something special to eat, a chicken perhaps when we were better off, and some beer and I'd smoke a cigar. In the past few years they've declared 1 May the day of Saint Joseph of Workmen, or something like that. I'm not sure if that's the name, but it is a saint. For me it has remained what it has always been, an international working man's holiday.

There weren't many distractions in this sort of life, what could there be? About the only one I had was looking out of the window. Especially at the women who go up and down the street on their way to the market each morning. I got a lot of pleasure out of that. By opening the window a fraction – always with the lace curtain across the window itself – I could see quite a way down the street. I saw so many people that I got to know them, even if they were too young ever to have known me. I would work out who they must be, I'd say to myself, 'That must be so-and-so's daughter, so-and-so's son.' Sometimes I'd ask my wife if I couldn't make out who the person was, and she'd tell me. I think I know all the village by sight as a result – and there aren't that many left who ever knew me.

Others I'd see when they came to the house. I'd go down behind

7*

the locked door at the bottom of the stairs and look through the peephole. I've seen some things through that door when the women thought they were on their own! And I got so I could recognize the voices of people when they came to the house for materials and things like that. Even some of the foreigners I've come to recognize.

One day I watched the civil governor of the province and all his official party go down the street. They had come up here because Mijas had been awarded a prize as the most improved and beautiful village in the province for the year. It's one of those tourist things, each year another village gets the prize. All the money that was spent on cars bringing up those officials, a band and one thing and another – they'd have done a lot better to spend the thousands of pesetas on improving the village drains and things of that sort. . . . Anyway, from up there behind my window I was able to watch all the provincial and local dignitaries, the civil governor and the mayor, pass down the street.

Even at times when I wasn't thinking about it my situation must have been causing me anxiety because I used to dream about it. My wife dreamed more than I, often I had to wake her up from a nightmare in which she dreamed that I had been caught. I had nightmares also, though less often than she.

There was one in particular that used to come back. I was walking down the street and suddenly someone shouted, 'Look, there he is', and I'd start to run with everyone running after me, people from the village and Guardia Civil. I'd run and run and run and it seemed as if it would never finish, I'd try to escape down one street and find the people there, down another and they'd be there again. . . . Stupidities really, but there you are. Sometimes I'd be caught and sometimes I'd escape, but always I'd wake up frightened and relieved that I was still safe in bed. These nightmares reflected the state of anxiety I was in, to be sure, even to the end.

After saying that, it may sound strange when I say I always also had hope. My faith – not so much in socialism but rather in democracy – has never diminished. I have and always have had faith that in the end democracy will triumph because it is a more human form of political system than dictatorship. The tyranny of dictatorship, wherever it is, on one side or the other, cannot be lasting.

This faith has helped me live through these years, though I won't hide the fact that I've been more than disappointed by socialism – or rather by socialists – inside and outside Spain in the last thirty years. There's only one socialist party in Europe that has done anything, and that's the Swedish. For the rest, none of them have been firm in their ideals.

I had great hopes for the Labour government in England after the war when it was swept to office with such a large majority that it seemed it had enormous power. I can't judge its internal policies, but as far as its foreign policy was concerned it did very little to favour democracy that I know of. In particular for Spain. All it did was talk and take a few platonic measures which it might not even have done if it hadn't been for the Soviet Union. With its power, the Labour government could have done a great deal more. We Spanish are different – either we do something to the end or we don't do it at all.

Worse than the British has been the French socialist party. As for the German socialist party – what sort of socialism do you call that? Allying themselves with the party of Adenauer they've betrayed the proletariat, they've wiped off every postulate of socialism as I understand it. There's nothing socialist about them except the name.

None of these parties has put into practice the socialist aims that I have believed in and still continue to believe in. When they came to power they didn't carry out those aims which, in opposition, they claimed they would do. And the reason for that? To my mind it lies in one cause. None of them has ever properly attacked and conquered economic power, without which socialist ideals cannot be put into effect. I've said it before, it was the lesson we learnt under the Republic before the civil war. It seems to me, from the little I know, that the same thing happened in England after the war. The Labour government took political power but economic power remained where it had always been. And so the enormous strength that it had gained in popular support inside the country, I believe, and also abroad, was slowly lost. If they had had the firmness to put into practice their socialist principles, to be much more socialist than they were, things would have turned out differently, I think.

Sometimes I wish I had been born a Swede! More than an Englishman or any other nationality. As far as politics are

concerned anyway. Sweden has the only socialist – or social-demo-
cratic – party that has been able to achieve something. A high
standard of living, good social services and social security – but,
above all, democracy! There, everything isn't imposed from above
but comes from the mass of the population. The party has been
in power twenty-five years and it seems to me it is the only one
that is on the right path. It has managed to maintain its neutrality,
not to play the role of one or other of the big nations, but to
develop its own path. Of course, having the Soviet Union as
neighbour has prevented its leaning too much to the West, has
meant that it has had to keep a balance between East and West.
I know – there is still capitalism there, and even a king, but that
hasn't prevented the growth and spread of democracy.

Above all, because it was mine, my disappointment has been
greatest in the Spanish socialist party. It was the strongest party
in Spain[30] and yet it completely lacked the ability – which the
communists showed – of setting up an underground organization
here. Its leaders went into exile and there all they did was follies,
so that today no one would follow them as leaders any more.
Though I've had no contact with anyone – and nor do I intend to,
because I've suffered too much from politics – I know there are
new socialist elements in the country, a new socialist party here.
But it lacks the power – and especially the desire – to go out and
fight; it lacks a revolutionary spirit. Look at the communists!
Within a few days of the end of the civil war they had a clandestine
organization in operation. Today, indisputably, they are the largest
proletarian party in the country. In all those places where the
socialists were strongest – in Córdoba, Seville, Jaén and Málaga
too – they dominate today. In Córdoba and Seville there have been
whole villages which have come out on strike in defiance of the
landlords and authorities – villages which have had to be repressed
by the authorities. The communists are always the first to come
out. Kill one and there's another in his place. Put one in jail and
there are ten to replace him; they never surrender, they seem made
of steel. No wonder the other parties admire their strength!

If tomorrow there were democratic elections, the communist
party would, in my opinion, emerge as strong as, say, the Italian
communist party – or perhaps even stronger. All the other parties
and movements – socialist, anarchist, etc. – disappeared with the
war and are only very slowly re-emerging. What do I think of the

Italian CP? Well, it remains communist, of course, but it hasn't been particularly faithful to Moscow, which is a good thing. It has its own national guide-lines which it adheres to rather than taking orders from outside. And that is correct, any party must set out to resolve its own national situation first.

I remain – and shall die – a democratic socialist. Nothing will change my convictions on that score. But to come out of hiding after thirty years and find that my party, along with the other socialist parties in Europe, has not been up to the level of the tasks that confronted it has been a great disappointment.

JULIANA

For him everything is always going to turn out all right in the end. . . . But I never believed it.

One day after another, one after another . . . ten years, twenty, thirty. A lot of people don't believe it, they say it's impossible. But it's not impossible, it's the truth. Half a lifetime that has passed, bitterly.

I never thought it would end, I couldn't see how it could unless everything in the country changed. And I couldn't see that happening, so I told myself, this is for life. After so many years I even forgot that an amnesty could be granted, all I thought about was if he fell ill. *Dios mio*, what shall we do if he falls ill? If he's dying? I didn't expect anything else, neither amnesty nor release.

He always had hope, he never gave up. That's why he read so much and listened to the radio every evening. 'Every evening stuck to your radio, what do you want to listen to that for?' He'd get annoyed then and say I only had bad thoughts. That was true, I couldn't see anything clear. Sometimes it got so that I quite despaired. At other times I'd manage to forget it a bit, what with everything I had to do, all my work.

Often I had terrible nightmares. I'd hear it said that he had been out of the house and I'd cry out, 'They've seen you. You've been out and the people have seen you.' He'd be ever so quiet, trying to hide. But the people knew. I'd be so frightened I'd wake up. Ay, how happy I was then when I saw it wasn't true, I'd only been dreaming! He dreamed a lot, too, we'd go to bed thinking of nothing but these things, that's why we dreamed. Not even asleep could I be free of my worries. It doesn't seem possible, but that's how it was. Ay! I haven't been free of anxiety for so many years.

It would have been better if we had moved to Málaga, there I could have thrown people off the trail. But he didn't want to. So I decided to buy a house of my own. I got this one at last, seven months it took. The heirs were squabbling so much among themselves about dividing up the property they had inherited they couldn't agree on a price. At last things got so bad between them they agreed to my offer. I paid ten thousand pesetas down and the balance of four thousand five hundred a month later. There were plenty of others who wanted the place but at that time people didn't have that sort of money.

It took us five or six summers to do the house up. Sometimes the men were here working for as long as three months at a time. As there wasn't any work in the village then, the masons would drag out a month's work into three.

Having them in the house made the people less suspicious. I know they used to question the mason Romero who did most of the work here. 'Juliana must know where her husband is, look at the money she's got and. . . .' 'Well, she may know where he is but he's not in that house. We've been working there these three months, upstairs and downstairs and all over, and there's no one there. He's not in Mijas, that's for sure.' The other workmen said the same. Neighbours used to come in to have a look at the work. 'Ay! what are you going to rebuild now? What are you doing this time?' They'd go upstairs to have a look, they'd come down and look, wherever the work was. And no one saw anything of him.

There were some bad moments all the same. One noon I thought they had finished upstairs and when they went for their lunch he moved to the room up there. That way we could leave the door of the bedroom down here open and they wouldn't be suspicious. Soon after they came back to work, one of the labourers, Pepe it was, came in from the patio and said he had to go upstairs for a basket of tools. Ay! We hadn't noticed the basket. 'No, no – wait a minute, Pepe, wait, I'll get it. . . . I've shut the window up there and it's dark and you're sure to fall. . . .' I ran up the stairs and whispered to him, 'Give me that basket quick, Pepe is coming up . . .', and he handed it over and I brought it downstairs.

The workmen made a hiding place for him without realizing it. I got them to block up a cupboard that was next to the chimney so that he could break through the ceiling from upstairs to get into it. The hole we always kept covered with something or other. I got the mason to build a shelf where the cupboard had been so that no one would remember there had been anything there. The shelf was my husband's idea. 'What do you want a shelf there for?' the mason kept saying. 'All this trouble for a shelf to keep a few plates on.' My husband never had to use the hiding place though; in the eighteen years we've been here, they never searched the house.

All the same, there wasn't a moment when I wasn't worrying whether everything was all right. If things had been as they are today, I'd have gone to the bank and borrowed the money to do all the work at one time. But in those days there wasn't a bank here.

To throw people off the trail even more I used to get women to come in and clean and whitewash nearly every summer. The women cleaning would call out to passers-by, 'Look, here we are in Juliana's house whitewashing.' Then those who liked to think they knew where he was would go away satisfied. 'When we went by Juliana's today the women were all over the house cleaning again. There's no one in there, she can't know where he is,' they'd say.

The key of the house was never out of my pocket. When the women were cleaning I made sure not to be out. If only he had always been as cautious as me, but no! One day he came saying, 'I think the neighbour's girl saw me in the patio this morning.' Ay! I was always warning him not to come out of the angle of the wall we had had built and where, in the early mornings before sunrise, he sat and weighed esparto. But he didn't listen, he's always been stubborn. He had come out from behind the wall to pick up some esparto. Now, though, there was nothing he could find to say except, 'I don't know, I don't know, I think Maria Mercedes saw me this morning.' Then he went quiet and that's how he stayed for several days, worrying over it. Sometimes he'd say, 'No, she won't have seen me, she won't have. . . .' But he wasn't sure. There was nothing we could do but hope. I couldn't ask the girl because that would have given everything away. I didn't say a thing, and nor did she or her family. To this day I've never asked.

She wasn't the only one who saw him, either. In the last few years two other children saw him too. One noon he was eating in the kitchen when a young girl suddenly appeared. I'd forgotten to lock the door because I had already eaten! 'What do you want?' I said calmly, as though there were no danger. 'Nothing,' said the girl, 'I'm just looking.' 'Well, you've had a look now, so you can go,' I said. I acted as though there was nothing strange in her coming into the kitchen and seeing a man there. I knew that if she said anything I could always tell her parents that my brother had come.

Not so long ago my nephew went upstairs by himself and found my husband there tying up esparto. My husband growled at him to get out. I told my nephew that he was a man I had got to come and tie up the esparto. 'He told me to get downstairs quick or he'd kick me down,' my nephew complained. 'He hasn't the right to talk to me like that, I've more right than him to be upstairs in my aunt's house. . . .' I got a good laugh out of that.

But all the same, what a good thing it was that only children who were too young to have known him ever saw him. I don't know how more people didn't see him the way he used to look out of the window.

It was bad for him, of course, being shut up all day, and it was even worse when he couldn't have the house to himself in the evenings because my daughter's *novio* was visiting. 'Every night the *novio*'s here, every night. . . .' What could I do?

The *novio* had to be able to visit, there was nothing we could do about that. He'd come at ten or half past or eleven, and while he was here my husband was suffering upstairs. Other times, if he wasn't feeling well, he'd go to bed early in the bedroom down here. Though I knew he had the pillow wrapped round his face, the sound of his cough could sometimes be heard in here where we were all sitting. What a fright I used to get each time I heard that. But the *novio* never seemed to hear it. It was probably that I was just waiting for it.

One day I had an idea. We had just made some money out of

allowing our land to be used as a site for a new water 'mine' the people were digging. I had been given twelve hours of water for the right and with the first hour I sold for five thousand pesetas to a foreigner I went to Málaga and bought the best radio I could find. That was what he wanted more than anything else. Until then we had had only a small and bad radio which he used to listen to down here. It was a nuisance because every time some-one came to the door he'd have to go upstairs and miss whatever it was he was listening to. He was always complaining about that. So when I'd had the new radio a day or two downstairs I told him to take it upstairs. 'That way we won't have all this business of when people come and the *novio* and all that. . . .' So he took it upstairs and after that he was happier and didn't complain so much. He'd have his supper and go straight up to the room and be listening there until midnight.

One morning he woke up saying he had a pain in his side. Looking at him I could see it was bad. Suddenly all my worst fears seemed to be coming true. We got him upstairs – it was one of the times when we were having work done in the house – and he lay there all day trying to keep from crying out with the pain. I didn't know what to do, the medicine I bought at the chemist's didn't stop the pain, nothing relieved it. I kept running up and downstairs. The pain was so bad he couldn't do anything but lie there with his face in the pillow to stifle the moans. A day I'll never forget, with the workmen all over the place and him lying suffering upstairs, a day bad enough to die of worry.

The next morning the pain was as bad as before. He had had it twenty-four hours by then. At seven o'clock I was at the doctor's. Don José was still in bed when I knocked on the door. I told him my daughter had spent the whole night with a terrible pain. I was so desperate at that moment that I asked him to give me morphine. 'Morphine,' he said, 'for a young girl! No, I can't prescribe that. I'll come round and see her and give her something else.'

He came to the house. My daughter put on that she was in terrible pain in the left side behind the kidneys. Don José examined her carefully. 'I can't find anything that can cause such a sharp pain,' he said, 'all I can find is that you're suffering from indiges-tion.' And that was true, from all the worry and fear of the past day and night her stomach was in a bad state, her nerves have been in pieces since she was a child with all she has had to go through. But she went on pretending and the doctor prescribed some suppositories to relieve the pain and injections for I don't know what, and I ran to the chemist's. I bought more than was needed, just in case. They did the trick. Those were two of the worst days in my life, two of the worst in his. It seemed as if it might be the end of everything.

Not so long ago, after he came out of hiding, I saw Don José and he said to me, 'Ah, now I know why you came to call me in such a hurry that day. How right you were to come!' Well, that's true, if we hadn't thought of it, who can say where we would be today?

Through all these years my daughter has had a lot to suffer, and yet she's never complained. When things go well she's happy and when they don't she suffers and keeps quiet. All these years she has been a great comfort to me, to us both, she has always been very good.

The day she got married was a day of happiness but also great sadness – our only child becoming independent and leaving us. Afterwards my friends said to me, '*Chica*, what's happened to you since your daughter got married? You've changed, you're like someone else.' Yes, since then I've been sad, I've lost strength. If we had been able to have more children, perhaps the suffering would have been less. One or two more. We could have had another, our daughter was eighteen months old when my husband left the village. If I had known what was going to happen I should have had another child then; there would have been time. Not a lot of children, I didn't want that; for the poor to have a lot of children means that they are all looked after badly. But one more, yes, I should have liked that. But who was to know what was going to happen?

The day of her wedding I fell into a panic nearly as bad as the day he was ill. Imagine your only daughter's marriage and the father unable to be present and take part! All the wedding guests enjoying themselves as is natural down here and him hidden upstairs! I couldn't eat or drink anything, not a thing passed my lips for the sorrow I felt. And for him too, because he was suffering like me. All the guests saw how sad I looked and they thought it was because that's what is required on such a day and because her father was missing. But it was much more than that.

A sad day, a day of happiness and sadness for me and for him. We've had our fill. The day my mother died was another sad day. The house was so full of mourners that I hadn't the chance even to cook something for him upstairs. He had to make do the best he could. The day my granddaughter died – a day of even more sorrow and suffering. My daughter's first child. She was born with an incurable blood disease. But we didn't know that, the doctors wouldn't tell us.

She was a lovely child, full of affection. She spent more time with us than with my daughter in the end. My husband was mad about her. We would have her cot next to our bed and in the mornings he would play with her. Then one day, on the way to the doctor in Málaga, she died in the car. Ay! it was horrible.

My husband suffered a great deal. He saw us leave with the child alive and when we came back she was dead. And he couldn't come down to see the child again because the house was full of people. He couldn't go to the funeral, nothing. He was shut up in his room and there was nothing he could do. He suffered more than any of us then, though there was suffering enough for everyone.

Our two remaining grandchildren always gave him a lot of pleasure. Although I was frightened they would give the secret away, I couldn't keep them from him. He couldn't be living crucified upstairs without anything to do and not see his grandchildren. They went up to play with him very often. He enjoyed being with them and it made life more bearable for him.

We had to be on top of them all the time, just as I had been on top of my daughter when she was young. Neither of them ever breathed a word. They had it instilled into them so much that, even after he came out of hiding, they didn't want to talk. The *practicante* came one day to greet my husband. 'What granddaughters you've got,' he said, 'all these times I've been here to give them injections and not a word out of them that they had another grandfather here. . . .' Then the youngest, who wasn't yet three, stood in front of the *practicante* and said to him: 'Because that's something that cannot be said. . . .'

All the same, it's a rare thing for a child not to blurt out a secret when they're too young to understand. If they had – my daughter or hers – it would have been the end of us.

Yes, in these thirty years we've been through everything, most of it bad. Anyone who hadn't had his calm wouldn't have been able to get through the years the way he has. He has borne his cross with great patience. He has his moments of temper, his moments of despair, but generally he doesn't lose control. For him everything is always going to turn out all right in the end, if not today then tomorrow. And when I used to tell him, 'This is for life, this isn't going to change', he'd always reply: 'Woman, what bad faith you've got. This will change one day. You only think of the bad things that happen, but you'll see – one day there'll be an amnesty, the government will have to grant one.' But I never believed it.

MARIA

I'm not like my mother, she's always been pessimistic. . . . It's never too late to keep hoping. . . . And sometimes . . . it turns out true, doesn't it, in the end?

As I came to the age of having a *novio* there were some problems for me. My father never laid down the law about what I could do; he was very good like that, he left me free. But my mother nearly went out of her mind when she thought I might become the *novia* of a stranger in the village. The people told her quick enough that this man liked me.

'If I catch you talking with that stranger . . .' my mother said. 'I don't want any strangers round here, marrying my daughter and taking her away from the village.'

Because I was young I was delighted to meet someone new, but on account of my mother I didn't become his *novia*. He wrote me letters, and when my mother saw one she said she was going to tear it up. She was frightened I'd answer it and come to like this young man and marry him. If I had I would have had to go and live wherever he was and that's what she didn't want. My father never said anything, but my mother – uh!

I expect he would have said something if one of his enemies' sons had tried to court me. Sons aren't responsible for what their fathers have done, are they? All the same, I'm sure my father would have warned me. To have had the son of one of his enemies, of a man who had wanted to see him killed, coming to the house – no, I couldn't have done that. An only daughter causing such grief to my parents – I couldn't have consented to that.

My father never talked about politics directly to me. But I used to hear him discussing things with my grandfather and sometimes my mother and I knew well enough what he thought. Also I knew very well who was who in the village and what their fathers had been. I didn't want a political enemy of his in the house.

It wasn't until after I married that I told my husband the secret. During the several years we were *novios*, I didn't need to be told to keep the secret to myself. Though I loved him and I could see he loved me, *novios* can always fall out. And then there would have been someone who knew – and who could tell what might have happened? But how my *novio* didn't hear my father when he came to see me in the evenings I don't know. One night there was a fearful crash from upstairs. 'What's that?' my *novio* asked. I didn't know what to say. 'Oh, it must be the cat that's knocked something over.' I was waiting for another crash but happily there wasn't one. Later my father admitted that he had tipped the brazier over as he got out of his chair.

My mother talks about the time when she was my father's *novio* and the things her mother wouldn't allow her to do. Well, I can't say she was all that different! She wouldn't let me wait for my *novio* on the doorstep, and when he left the house I couldn't leave with him. When I went out on Sundays with him, my mother came too, and when we went to the cinema she would wait at a friend's close by to accompany me home. Today things are quite different; there's a different sort of respect. If I wanted to go somewhere with my *novio* I would never dare ask my father straight out. I'd go to my mother and say, 'Tell him I want to go with my *novio* to this place or that. Ask him if it's all right with him. . . .' My mother would come back with the answer. Not that my father ever said no as long as he knew we were going with respectable people, but I couldn't accept until he had been asked. My *novio* used to wonder why I couldn't give him the answer straightaway.

Once we had moved to this house I wasn't so frightened of my father being discovered because the Guardia didn't come here to search. What frightened me most now was that he would fall ill. That terrible day when he got the pain, I never want to live through another day like that, not as long as I live.

I got married in 1960. My wedding was as much sorrow as joy because my father wasn't able to be present. I nearly went wild trying to think of a way to slip away from my friends to say good-bye to him. They wouldn't leave me alone a minute. 'Maria, you're going to forget this. Maria, have you packed that?' I got as far as the door, the suitcases were already on top of the car when I turned back into the house and managed to escape. I ran upstairs to kiss my father and when I got back my husband was waiting for me. 'Where have you been?' 'Oh, I forgot something, I went to the bedroom to fetch it.' 'No, I saw you going into the kitchen,' he said. Happily the car was leaving and in the excitement nothing more was said.

All during our honeymoon I kept saying to myself, I've got to tell Silvestre. . . . I didn't know where to begin. On the last day I got up the courage. We were in the pension. 'There's something I've got to tell you,' I said. 'Ah, what's that?' 'I don't know where to begin. . . . Well, look, my father is in the house.' 'Ah.' He didn't look surprised. 'I don't know,' he said, 'I thought I noticed some strange sounds once in a while. Why didn't you tell me before?' I told him the reason. He wasn't angry. He said we should have had more confidence in him, though. He told me he had thought my father was probably in Málaga. A barber friend of his who had known my father had often told him my mother must know where he was. And he had thought that was true because my mother went every week to Málaga. But he had never seriously believed that he was in our house. Now he knew the secret and he lived with it like the rest of us.

Rosamari, my first daughter, was born in 1961. She had leukaemia, but we didn't know. Her first haemorrhage happened the day my second daughter was born. I didn't even know about it, because I was in hospital in Málaga. My mother took her to the doctor here. All he would say was that it was something rare. Without my knowing, my mother took her the next day to a nose specialist in Málaga because she had haemorrhaged from the nose. He told her a blood analysis was necessary. From that moment until her death five months later she was put through torture and agony by the doctors. She was nineteen months old when she died.

The doctors never told us what was wrong; they always pretended she could be cured. When I came back from hospital with my second daughter, Rosamari was too heavy for me to lift from her cot. All my children have been Caesarian births and my mother was frightened the stitches would open if I tried lifting her. That was when she took Rosamari with her and she and my father looked after her almost all the time until the day before she died. She loved my mother and father more, I think, than she loved me. She would rather be with them than with us here. Sometimes my husband would say, 'Rosamari, aren't you going to stay with papa?' and she'd answer, 'No, no, I'm going with grandfather and mother. . . .' My father loved her a lot, he was always playing with her and keeping her amused.

Poor child, what she was made to go through! Five months of blood transfusions, injections, blood samples. Three times a week to Málaga to the doctor, who kept on saying that she would be all right. Usually my mother took her because I had the baby to look after, but one day my husband and I went. My husband asked the doctor to tell him straight out what was wrong with Rosamari. 'She'll get better; it'll take time, that's all. Doing what has to be done and giving her the right medicine. The child will be cured.'

She died in my arms in the middle of the night as we were rushing her to the doctor. She had been to Málaga only two days before, but I could see how worn out she was. The last night I wouldn't let her stay with my parents, I kept her by my side. If the doctor had told us the truth, she wouldn't have died like that in the car. It was terrible, it would have been terrible anyway, but it would have been different for her to have died in our house.

In the taxi I couldn't cry. My mother kept saying, 'Keep quiet, keep quiet, if the motor-cycle Guardia stop us you'll have to leave her here. Keep quiet. We won't get her back to the village otherwise.' I had to try to hold in my grief, I couldn't cry, I had to sit there with her as though she were still alive. If the police had stopped us and found her dead they would have insisted that she be buried there. All the way back from Los Boliches and through

Fuengirola and up the road I had to hold back my tears. Ay! my nerves went to pieces and I've never properly recovered.

Thanks to God my other two daughters have been well. They've both been good girls. When Rosamari died she wasn't old enough to have talked about my father outside. But as soon as my second daughter, Maria de la Peña, was old enough to understand I was on top of her all the time. 'Daughter, if you talk about your grandfather being here and the Guardia hear they'll take grandfather away. They'll put him in prison. They'll come for me, they'll come for grandmother, they'll take us all.' I put the same fear into her – and later my youngest daughter – as my mother put into me. Of course, my daughters haven't gone through the things I went through; they haven't known the fear that I lived with as a child when the Guardia used to come searching, when my mother was being questioned all the time. I had to give them this fear. 'They'll take papa away too, they'll put him in prison.' I kept after Maria all the time. 'You're not to say anything to anyone, not to auntie or your grandfather' – my father-in-law – 'or anyone. Do you understand?' If there had been the slightest sign that she might talk I was ready to stop her seeing my father. I was watching her all the time.

My mother was worried. Often my sister-in-law came to take Maria out. 'Daughter, don't let her go,' my mother would say to me, 'she'll get to talking there and something will slip out.' 'But if I don't let her go they're going to think that I don't want them to see her,' I had to say. I couldn't not let her go. Each time I'd warn her, 'Maria de la Peña, remember! Just a word out of you!' Never, not a word did she breathe. I had to be on top of her even more when she started school at the age of six. At last she said to me one day, 'Mama, do you think I'm going to tell the children *that*?'

It was my father's idea that he shouldn't have a name. It was a good precaution. Maria de la Peña was always after him to say what he was called. When she didn't believe that he didn't have a name he'd tell her he was called Caratarama, and she'd say, 'That's not a name. What's your real name?' 'Caratarama,' he always replied. Of course, she was right, what sort of a name is that?

It was a joke but a useful one after all. Only last Christmas my youngest daughter nearly gave the secret away. Every Christmas there is a television show for the benefit of the poor. Franco's wife is in the audience, and it is one of the best programmes of the year. We always like to watch it because of the stars who take part, the flamenco groups and that sort of thing. Before it started the neighbour from across the street came and said, 'Maria, are you going to put the television on?' 'I don't know,' I said. If she came, my father would have to miss the show. Ever since we got television I've had this problem, the neighbours were always wanting to come to watch. The first few weeks the house was full of people all the time because we had one of the first private sets in the village. The worst was when there was a bullfight which I knew my father would want to watch. Then I'd pretend I had a headache and was going to lie down. My mother would stand watch in the doorway of her house and, if she saw anyone coming to knock at my door, she'd tell them I wasn't feeling well and that the children were asleep. I was always having to tell the neighbours, 'Oh, I don't know whether I'll put the television on', and my reluctance made them think I was stuck-up and cold. 'Ay! we'll go, Maria doesn't want us here,' they'd say.

Anyway, just before the programme started last Christmas Eve, this neighbour arrived and settled down to watch. My father couldn't come down. Suddenly my youngest daughter came in and said – 'and grandfather, isn't he coming to watch?' It just slipped out like that. 'Grandfather?' I said, giving her a warning look. 'No, grandfather can't come today, he's got to work mending shoes.' I meant her to understand that I was talking about my father-in-law. I gave her another look behind the neighbour's back. 'No, grandfather can't come today, he's working,' I repeated, and she understood.

It was a close thing – but during all these years there have been so many close things that could have meant the end. Yet somehow we survived. I never gave up hope that one day my father would be free to come out of hiding. I'm not like my mother, she's always been pessimistic, she's always thinking of all the terrible things that might happen. She thinks of things that might happen three months before they could happen! I'm nervous but I don't worry about what might happen until it happens. It's never too late to keep hoping – even when my daughter was ill I kept my hopes till the end. And sometimes, if you keep hoping, it turns out true, doesn't it, in the end?

Five
_____

RELEASE

MANUEL

The news had gone round and everyone came forward to welcome me . . . the working people of the village, those who really cared and felt glad.

28 March 1969 – a Friday, the day each week that the cabinet meets in Madrid. As always I tuned in to the news at ten that evening. Apart from the occasional flamenco programme, the news is about all I've been accustomed to listen to on the national radio. That evening, as usual, the Minister of Information and Tourism, Fraga Irribarne as it then was, announced the cabinet's decisions. Among them he said that the head of state and the cabinet had approved a bill amnestying offenders or supposed offenders for the period of the civil war, from 18 July 1936 to 1 April 1939. Although I didn't get the exact words, that was how I understood it. If it was true, they couldn't touch me. But I had to see it with my own eyes in the Official Gazette before I could believe it.

I came down and said to my wife, 'I've heard something on the radio that the cabinet decided today. I've got to know the complete text of the decree. See if you can arrange it. Talk to the porter at the town hall, he's a friend, and tell him you want to see the Gazette when it comes. Get him to lend it to you. If he doesn't trust you with it, get him to read the decree to you.'

What I didn't know was that the Gazette isn't published until Tuesday and wouldn't get here for a couple of days after that.

I didn't allow my emotions to run away. Until I had read the exact text, I couldn't be sure. There had been amnesties before, but each time they had left room for *denuncias*. There was one at the end of the Second World War allowing people to return from abroad, but when they got back they could be denounced in their home towns and villages. . . . There was another at the time of the referendum on the Organic Law of the State a few years ago, but that still left room, in my opinion, for someone to denounce me. And as in villages like these we depend on our enemies or on anyone who has a grudge, a *denuncia* and two witnesses and it's all tied up. I knew they wouldn't liquidate me but that I'd be sentenced to prison for a shorter or longer term. In prison I'd be condemned to a slow death because my health isn't good. It would be worse than being put to death straight away.

In the meantime, though, everything that I heard made me think that for once the door had been closed to *denuncias* by the latest decree. A man who had been head of the local branch of the trade union set up by the regime confirmed it to my son-in-law. They're relatives – his wife is a cousin of my son-in-law's – and he told him: 'Your father-in-law, wherever he is, can come back to the village now, there was a decree approved by the cabinet in Madrid today. . . .' My son-in-law came to tell me. 'Yes, I know that already,' I said to him, 'but first I want to read the decree. You're not to tell anyone I'm here, there's time enough for that yet. . . .' A few days, a few weeks come to that – what did it matter after waiting thirty years?

The following day the newspapers published the decree. When I read it I was convinced that it was what I thought, but still I wanted to see it in the Gazette. My wife went to the town hall and talked to the porter. 'No, it hasn't come yet.' In fact it didn't arrive until Thursday or Friday, a week after I first heard the news. Then my wife was able to borrow it for a moment, telling the porter: 'I think there's a decree favouring those who are abroad. . . .' She brought the Gazette to the house and I read it. 'That's it,' I said, 'I can come out now when I want.' I was very happy, of course, although it has come very late.

I told my wife to talk to the mayor. My son-in-law had already had words with him and he had said that, wherever I was, I could come back now. My son-in-law only answered, 'We'll see what he does, whether he comes back or writes a letter from wherever he is.' Now my wife went to see him.

He wasn't altogether surprised, I think. He had thought I was around here somewhere, in Málaga perhaps. Between them they made the arrangements and decided that I should report to the authorities in Málaga. It would have spared me a lot of publicity if they had let me report here, because none of the papers would have got to know about it. But they decided on Málaga.

On Saturday 12 April my wife, son-in-law and I left the house before sunrise. It was arranged that we should go in our lorry and meet the mayor in Málaga. We walked up the street here towards the Compas where the lorry was parked. The street was completely empty, we met no one at all. Absolutely no one! The bars were just opening as we drove through the village and I saw it again for the first time. One or two people looked at the lorry passing but I don't think they saw me. We made for Málaga as quickly as possible. It was thirty years, less four days, since I had gone into hiding.

The mayor had made all the arrangements. We met outside the Guardia Civil headquarters. I didn't recognize him – I'd seen him in the distance from my window several times but not close enough to – and of course he didn't know me. He said he was pleased to greet me. I should have come out much earlier, ten years ago, he said. Nothing would have happened, he was there to stand guarantee for me. . . . That sort of thing, what else could he say? Then we went into the Guardia Civil headquarters and the lieutenant-colonel welcomed me. 'You are completely free,' he said. 'If anyone troubles you, you have only to come with the mayor to me and I will take care of them.' He spoke to the Civil Governor's office and with the police to arrange for them to give me an identity card. At the police office they made me go to the head of the queue and I got a temporary identity card because the proper one has to come from Madrid. Then we came back to the village with the mayor in his car.

The square was full of people when we arrived. The mayor parked the car outside the bank he represents and I got out. The news had gone round and everyone came forward to welcome me, the women kissing me and the men shaking my hand and clapping me on the back. All that sort of thing – the working people of the village, those who really cared and felt glad. Though I'm not sentimental and don't let my emotions get the better of me, I was deeply affected, as one is when one sees that the people appreciate one because one has done nothing bad. . . .

I came back to my house with my wife and the people started to come to the house. They didn't leave me all that afternoon and all night and the next day – for a month at least. People from the village and from the countryside, some I had known and others whose fathers I'd known. And not only from here, but from Alhaurin and Fuengirola, from Málaga and Benalmádena and from all the villages round here where I had friends. . . . And on top of this, reporters and photographers from all over the world.

For the first two or three weeks there was a Guardia Civil patrol every night in this street. The Guardia had received anonymous letters attacking the government for pardoning people like me and threatening my life. I received a number also which I was ordered to pass on to the Guardia here. These letters were never postmarked from anywhere near here, but from Granada and towns even farther away; yet I'm sure they came from people not very distant from here. I also had a great number of letters congratulating me. Because of the threats, the Guardia head-quarters in Málaga ordered the patrol to keep watch on the house. They said they feared an attempt on my life by the left, who would use my assassination to say – 'Look, they let him out only to kill him.' It didn't frighten me, but it did my wife. Even now she worries about my going out. She shouldn't, there's nothing to fear. But you don't lose the habits of thirty years in a week.

MARIA

I was able to say to my daughter, 'It's all right, there's nothing to fear. We can talk about grandfather to everyone now.'

I couldn't believe it. My father free and able to leave the house! It didn't seem possible. 'But why not?' my husband said when my father told us what he had heard on the radio. And I said, 'I'm wanting so much for him to be free, and at the same time I'm frightened.' I wasn't sure it could really be true.

As we waited for the Gazette to come, my mother began to put fear into me; she was frightened it was a trap. 'I don't trust anyone, no one, I don't trust anything,' she kept on saying. I began to worry, too. 'Jesus, you and your mother, what a way of thinking you have!' my husband said. '*Chiquilla*, what can happen to your father now?' He brought back the newspapers with the amnesty reported in them, he told me again what he had been told by his cousin's husband. And yet I still had that bit of fear.

We didn't celebrate in the house, we kept our joy and fear to ourselves. At last the news was confirmed in the Gazette. The arrangements were made. He was really free!

In my joy I went, the evening before he came out, to tell our neighbours across the street. My eldest daughter, Maria de la Peña, came with me and when we got back she started to scold me. 'What were you doing talking about grandfather in Luisa's house?' she said. 'You're not supposed to talk about him.'

I laughed. I told her it was all right now. The next morning, at sunrise, I watched from the door as my father took his first step outside. My mother held him by the arm; after all those years he had difficulty walking in shoes. There was no one in the street, they walked away to where my husband was waiting with the lorry for them. I saw them disappear. . . .

When I went out later, the whole village seemed to be waiting for me, the people running up to embrace and kiss me; there was such a crowd I couldn't move. My friends wouldn't leave me. 'Ay, Maria! how did you manage it? All these years. . . .' 'And the children – imagine that, never to have said a word. . . .' The house was full of people; I couldn't do anything. No one seemed to be working that day. I heard one of the workmen say, 'That woman, Juliana, deserves a monument built to her', and another replied, 'Thirty years without leaving his house – how did he do it? I can't take more than two days at home!' Everyone was happy, everyone went to the square to wait for their return, there was real joy.

But my joy was greatest the evening before when I was able to say to my daughter, 'It's all right, there's nothing to fear. We can talk about grandfather to everyone now, he's free at last.'

I.H.

8

JULIANA

I look back and I say, is it possible that all this really happened? But it did. You can't describe it, you've got to live it to know.

I still can't believe it. I worry very often that something could happen, I don't know what. I'm on the look-out all the time. The anxiety of thirty years doesn't pass in a day or two. I never expected it to happen, that's why. At best, I thought, if they ever give an amnesty it'll be when we're dead – and what good will it do us then?

When he came down that night and said he was coming out of hiding I looked at him as though he had gone mad. 'Are you crazy? You're going to come out so that they can catch you now? Are you out of your mind?' 'No,' he said, 'it was on the radio just now. They've given an amnesty.'

He didn't lose his calm even at that moment. The thought filled me with fear. I ran out of the house to all the neighbours who have radios. 'Have you been listening to the news?' One of them said yes. 'Well, did you hear anything about an amnesty for all those who can't come back?' 'Ay! No, no, I didn't hear anything. . . .' That's how it was in all the houses, no one had heard anything.

I came back thinking he was suffering from a delusion. I didn't trust it. There had been amnesties before and he had always said, 'It's of no importance, it doesn't affect me.' And now he was saying he was going to be free. After thirty years. No, it wasn't possible!

The truth was he didn't really believe it himself until he read it in the Gazette. He wouldn't let anyone say where he was until he had read the decree. 'When the Gazette publishes it, I'll come out, not before,' he said. I asked the porter at the town hall to keep a watch out and let me know when it arrived. I told him only that I wanted to know if the decree meant that all those who hadn't been able to come back could now return. In the meanwhile the newspapers published the decree and my son-in-law was told that it meant he could come back from wherever he was. I half believed it was true, but I still wasn't sure.

At last I got the Gazette and he read it. 'Yes, that's it, I can come out,' he said. 'Go and talk to the mayor.'

I went immediately. I knew it was true now but I was still cautious. The mayor wasn't at his house; his wife told me he would be back at half past nine or ten. When I returned I found him there. 'I've come to find out if it's true that the Gazette has published a decree granting total peace after thirty years?' 'Yes, there is a general amnesty,' he said, and he asked if I wanted him to fetch the Gazette and read it to me. I thanked him and said it wasn't necessary. I came back and told my husband. 'All right, tell him I'm here and I'll report to the authorities whenever he wishes.'

When I saw him again he was very surprised. 'In your house all this time! Well . . . imagine being shut up for thirty years for nothing, just for an idea! If through force of circumstances things changed here I wouldn't consider myself guilty as mayor. The same thing happened to him, he didn't do anything. . . .'

He was very kind, he made all the arrangements in Málaga with the authorities. He wanted to take us in his car, but as he wasn't leaving until nine it seemed better for us to leave before the people were up. If they had seen us we might never have got to Málaga on time.

When I knew for sure that he was coming out I had to see if any of his clothes still fitted him. Over the years I had bought him a suit, a sports jacket, a nylon shirt. He might have needed them if he had fallen ill and we had to go to Málaga in a hurry. Not one of them fitted. He couldn't do the buttons up on any of them because of the weight he had put on!

There was nothing to be done about the jacket or suit, but I took the shirt back to the shop in Málaga. 'Look,' I said to the owner, 'I bought this shirt four years ago and now the owner has given it back because it's too small. I want to change it for a size larger.' 'Yes,' he said, 'after all the years I've known you I'll change it for you.' So I got a shirt that would fit and I bought trousers, a suit, a pair of shoes, everything he needed to come out of the house. When he tried on the shoes he didn't know how to walk in them. All these years he's been wearing sandals in the house so as not to make a noise and he wasn't used to shoes any more! The morning we left I had to hold onto him because he kept slipping. Even now he doesn't walk the way he used to. I look at him and can see he takes very long strides as though he isn't sure of himself.

When the owner of the shop read the newspaper the next week he realized straightaway whom the shirt had been for. We had a good laugh together about it later on. Four years was a long time to keep a shirt and let it get too small!

The idea of having to go to Málaga with him to report worried me. 'Perhaps they're going to ask questions, there'll be an interrogation,' I said to my daughter. 'Who knows what they might ask?' But no, they were very polite and asked nothing, and that was a relief.

When we got back the square was thick with people come to see him and congratulate him. The house was full of people; it went on for weeks. Almost everyone in the village has come to greet him and pay their respects. But for some it's only on the outside, inside they feel differently. There's one who said to me not so long ago, 'I haven't come to greet your husband because I don't know him, if only someone would introduce us. . . .' 'Well,' I replied, 'Franco, thanks to God, has given an amnesty and he's here now, you can meet him any time. If not today then tomorrow.' I was laughing to myself as I said it. He was one of those who came to search my house after my husband left. He tried not to show himself but I saw him.

He's not the only one to think we hold a grudge. They think that way because that's how they are, and they think I must be the same. I'm not. Yet I'm worried, even now, four months after he came out. Every time I see a stranger in the village I get upset. There was one last night when we went out with our grandchildren to the *feria*. He was standing close by us at the merry-go-round staring at my husband. I didn't take my eyes off him, off his hands, his face. He kept on staring. I couldn't wait for us to get away from there. You never know who a stranger might be. Someone who has a grudge against my husband might pay a stranger to come to – no, I don't trust anyone, no one at all. Whenever I see a face I don't know I'm all eyes. . . . I'm happiest when we're here in our house together in the evening. Go out, yes, but not stay out late, eleven thirty or midnight, that's the latest. If he comes back after that my nerves go to pieces.

But they're not all like the man I just spoke of. The other day another one of those who searched my house came up to me and said, 'I've just seen your husband and he recognized me!' He was happy about it. 'Have you seen him?' I said, 'that's good then.' He's one of those who has no grudge at all. He was a young man at the time and, like a lot of them, came to search my house because they were told to.

I hold no grudges at all, for me everything is forgiven, everything is finished. I've suffered a great deal but I hold nothing against anyone. The important thing in life is not to harm other people, isn't it? For the short time that we're granted to live before we die, what is the point in doing harm? Our time on earth is only loaned – one has to be calm and let the world go by. . . .

We're old now and what has passed is passed. He is finished with politics. When people ask him, he says, 'I'm old now, I don't know anything about politics any more.' That's the truth, he's seen what's good for him at last. Politics brought us nothing but slavery and ruination, for him, for me and for my daughter. I know, I'm a woman, but if I'd been a man I'd say the same; I'd never have let myself get involved in politics. Never. Work – work to make enough to eat – that's what the poor like us have to do, nothing else.

Now he's free, the last thirty years weigh on me less. When I think of it now I wonder how we endured all those years. I look back and I say, is it possible that all this really happened? But it did.

Six

TODAY
Manuel

MANUEL

I don't regret for a moment having been active in the struggle to create a better, a socialist world. . . . Though I'm finished with politics, my convictions will remain till I die.

The first days of freedom I felt abnormal. I was so used to being in hiding, to the routines and rhythms of hiding, that nothing else could feel normal. To be able to go where I wanted, to talk to people, to live without fear of being seen, was something strange and foreign to me. It's not that easy to change after thirty years.

So much had changed around me, too, while I was in hiding. I'd heard from my wife and son-in-law of the hotels and apartment blocks in Fuengirola and Benalmádena and Torremolinos, but I couldn't imagine it. The countryside round here, where there used to be only goat tracks, is now full of roads and cars going to new villas built by foreigners. I, who used to know Fuengirola like the back of my hand, lose my way there now. It has become a capital, and Torremolinos too! It's extraordinary. And here, in all these summer months, to see five, seven hundred cars coming up each day full of tourists – it's beyond belief. When I was a boy we'd be lucky if we saw a car once every three months. To begin with, I imagined that all these tourists who came were rich people, but now I can see that they are from the working classes as well. Their standard of living is very different from what we know here – it must be for a working man to be able to afford to come so far for a holiday of a fortnight or a month. That wouldn't be possible in Spain.

Tourism has brought work and a higher standard of living here, indisputably. But it's also transitory, in my view. When all the villas and hotels and apartments that are necessary have been built, what then? The people here think the boom will go on for ever, but sooner or later it must come to an end. Will all the building workers have to emigrate to France, Germany, Belgium or Switzerland to earn a living then? That could hardly be called a triumph for anyone. No, what is needed here is industrial development and an agrarian reform that will build up a strong agricultural sector. Otherwise we are living on an illusion.

I don't mean that the improvements in the standard of living haven't impressed me. There has been a great change in the past ten or fifteen years. I was aware of this in hiding, and I've become more aware of it now that I can see what is going on. Things are very different where there is no tourism away from the coast but here people have work, there's money about, and from Saturday noon everyone can lay down their tools. When I was young Sunday was the busiest day of the week, you were a slave in those days, you hardly ever had a day free. Though this free time is unimaginable to me, it's progress, a benefit for all the working people.

Yet I still ask, is it a triumph for a country's economy to have to depend on importing tourists and exporting workers to other European nations in order to live? Is it a triumph for a country that has had a tradition of livestock breeding to have to import meat today? A triumph when, with the exception of the large capitalist farms, the land is being abandoned and the peasants going out to work for a day-wage or emigrating? I don't believe so. To live off the foreign currency brought in by tourists on the one hand and sent back by Spanish workers from abroad on the other – that isn't the basis of a solid economy in my opinion.

But more than anything else, it is the youth here which has struck me most since I came out of hiding. Tourism is partly responsible, but it's not just the fashions which the youth copies, it's more than that. There's an indifference to anything but having a good time, there's lack of thought and respect for anyone or anything else. I'm not against anyone having a good time, but it's more important to learn first how to behave in life with dignity and honour and respect for one's equals. All that, as far as I can see, has gone. Today's youth in the village is as different from the youth I knew as the back of one's hand is from the palm.

Since I came out of hiding, I've talked to plenty of young people because I've wanted to make friends with everyone. And the first thing that struck me was that they know absolutely nothing about anything except amusing themselves. They don't think about other things, about government, the nation or even the village. They stand staring at me with their mouths open when I talk to them, as though I were something extraordinary out of the past. They listen attentively, but I can see they don't understand. Most of them are between eighteen and twenty-five and all they've known in their lives has been the present regime. They've heard of communism and that's about all, they know nothing of its origins; they don't know what the words conservative and liberal mean; they don't know about the forms of government in England or France. They are completely ignorant and de-politicized.

When I was a young man, we all knew what was going on in the world, some more, some less, according to the culture of each, but all the same everyone had an idea. In the thirties, under the Republic, when there was democracy, political parties, assemblies and meetings, this was even more true. The youth was involved. The youth is a nation's future. But today when I talk to them about the civil war, about Europe, about the conflicts between the Soviet Union and the United States, they stand there gaping, not knowing what to say nor whether I'm right or wrong. They've just about heard that there is a war in Vietnam, but they don't know where it is or why there's a war. So I tell them, it's because the United States is a large and powerful nation that wants to hold all the key positions on the globe in order to dominate the world with its money and power. I tell them that Vietnam is a small country fighting off the most powerful nation in the world to keep its independence. I tell them that the United States thinks that by fighting there they are creating a bulwark against the Chinese in the north, when to my mind it's the opposite – the North Vietnamese with their own form of communism adapted to their national needs, rather than aligned to either Moscow or Peking, are the bulwark against the Chinese. If the United States recognized that and finished with the slaughter of thousands and thousands of innocent people it would be a good thing. . . . And they stand there with their eyes wide open looking at me. They don't come out for or against me, because they don't know if one thing or the other is better or worse.

Yet they have more formal education than the youth of my time and it continues longer because they don't have to go out minding goats or to the sierra to collect esparto. When I was a boy, fifty per cent of the village didn't attend school. Nowadays they all go, though there's still a shortage of schools. And there's the effect of tourism as well which, despite some aspects I don't like, has its good side in bringing in new forms of culture.

No, it's the climate in which the youth has been brought up. All their lives they've never heard anyone talk of anything, there have been no political meetings in which they could learn and be formed. The regime has its own youth organization but in its immense majority the youth hasn't participated. They haven't liked the way it was directed from above, and there have been no other forces which could show them other paths. So the youth has turned its back on politics and at the same time on everything else, including religion. They are less religious today than under the Republic even.

I'm talking of the youth I know here. In the large towns where there are universities, where there is culture, things will be different. The university youth is a promise for the future. It's not the same in a village like this.

I've come to know some of the sons of former comrades of mine. They're no better than the rest of the youth. I've reproached their fathers. 'What did you do, *hombre*, about forming your children?' None of them did anything. I can't understand that. Even if nothing could be done outside, within the family a father can see that ideas are kept alive, that there is continuity and that everything doesn't die with him. For me a child should always know what his father believes, should know from what source he comes. Though I have a daughter and have never forced her to my beliefs, I've always taught her to know what I believed in. But not the others, they say the future always looked too black, that for the smallest thing they could be picked up – in short, fear.

There was terrible fear. I know that as well as the next person. Some of the comrades whom I considered firm turned out the weakest, the most cowardly, in the end. Not because they were threatened but because of the fear. But the others, those who retained their convictions, did nothing to teach their children about their beliefs. 'And when you die,' I say to them, 'what's going to remain?'

This has been the biggest disappointment to me in coming back to the world. For today's youth is tomorrow's leaders – and what hope is there with a youth that knows nothing and cares even less?

I don't know why I should let it depress me. I'm finished, the struggle isn't mine. I'm an old man who has saved his neck, that's about all I can say, an old man without much health to whom eight or ten years of life remain. And yet, because I've never lost faith in the possibility of a better world – the faith that took me into the socialist movement when I was a young man – the state of today's youth depresses me more than I can say. For what can come of that faith if there is no one to carry it on after one is dead? What of the hardships of the past thirty years?

There have been plenty of hardships for everyone – and the worst, I think, have fallen on my wife. She has had to suffer more and work harder than anyone could have asked. I never forget the times when she had to walk to Málaga all night to sell her eggs in those bad years just after the war. To keep us alive she has had to work like a man.

I know, if she heard me say now, after all she has had to go through, that I don't regret for a moment having been active in the struggle to create a better, a socialist world, she wouldn't want to believe her ears. After everything we've been through, not to regret that! But I've never regretted it, nor shall I. I went into the struggle because that is what I believed in, and though I'm finished now with politics, my convictions will remain till I die.

For the rest – well, what more is there to say?

NOTES

The intention of these notes is to amplify and situate at the national level the local events described by Manuel; it is not their intent – for it would be beyond their scope – to provide a parallel history of the period. They are based upon the following sources:

GERALD BRENAN, *The Spanish Labyrinth* (Cambridge, 1943) and *The Face of Spain* (London, 1950)
GABRIEL JACKSON, *The Spanish Republic and the Civil War* (Princeton, 1965)
HUGH THOMAS, *The Spanish Civil War* (London, 1961)
STANLEY G. PAYNE, *The Spanish Revolution* (London, 1970)
FRANZ BORKENAU, *The Spanish Cockpit* (London, 1937)
BURNETT BOLLOTEN, *The Grand Camouflage* (London, 1961)
PIERRE BROUÉ and ÉMILE TÉMIME, *La Révolution et la Guerre d'Espagne* (Paris, 1961)

I am indebted to Mr Brenan for allowing me to consult his Málaga diary of the period July–September 1936.

*

1. (p. 25) Brenan (*The Face of Spain*) gives a vivid account of the hunger, poverty and despair in Andalusia ten years after the end of the civil war. Never, he wrote, had he seen such misery before. In some villages people were starving, women were dressed in potato sacks or scraps of army blanket, with their legs and faces caked in dirt they no longer troubled to wash off. In Málaga there were four times more street-sellers and beggars than before and an array of the armless and legless. A local *falangista* told him that things were much worse than before the civil war. 'Never has such poverty been known before. . . . Yet Málaga is one of the richest towns in Spain.'

2. (p. 47) Many stories are told in the village about the outlaws – banditry has a long history in Andalusia. But the stories never made clear to me whether these post-war outlaws formed any sort of *maquis*. In 1949 Brenan reported that outlaws dominated the Serrania of Ronda

(less than twenty miles from Mijas as the crow flies) and that the whole area was cordoned off by police. However, apart from an occasional kidnapping for ransom, there were no reports of any actions suggesting an organized *maquis* with politico-military objectives. It was to clarify this point that I asked Manuel to describe the outlaws.

3. (p. 82) In this respect Mijas was better off than many Andalusian villages and towns, especially in the latifundist regions of Seville and Córdoba, where anything up to three-quarters of the working population were landless day-labourers. Their wages and living conditions were the worst in Europe: on average they earned in 1930 from 3 to 3.50 pesetas (7½–9p.) for an eight-hour day during four to five months of the year. Unemployment was higher and real wages, allowing for inflation, lower than in 1905. But for credit given by shops, they would have starved during their spells of unemployment, which was made worse by periods of rain or drought. Any labourer against whom a landlord held a grudge would get work only during harvest time (*The Spanish Labyrinth*).

4. (p. 87) While socialist union and party branches were closed down at local level, this did not prevent top-level socialist collaboration with the dictatorship: Largo Caballero, then secretary general of the UGT, served as Primo's Labour Councillor. The dictator hoped to use the socialists, whom he admired, against the anarchists, whose revolutionary trades-union confederation, the CNT, he had proscribed. Caballero had much the same aim – to gain strength for the UGT from the CNT whose membership was traditionally strong among the agricultural workers of Andalusia. He used his position to foster the growth of the newly organized Landworkers' Federation which brought into the socialist trade union hundreds of thousands of previously unorganized small peasants and labourers.

5. (p. 88) In scores of villages the experience described by Manuel was repeated. Beginning in 1931 with 100,000 members, the Landworkers' Federation quadrupled in size in its first year of existence. Its 445,000 members then constituted almost half the total membership of the parent UGT, which rapidly began to be radicalized by this influx of small peasants and landless labourers. Created in 1888, the UGT, like the socialist party, had traditionally pursued a 'parliamentary' road to socialism. Its growth was slow: by 1918 it had 200,000 members, mainly miners, railwaymen, steelworkers and small groups of peasants in the south. The Casas del Pueblo, workers' clubs with free lending libraries which housed the local socialist party headquarters and which the party had started in many small towns of Andalusia and Levante, not only helped gain membership for the UGT but educated a generation of socialist militants.

With the expansion of the Landworkers' Federation in 1931–2, the UGT and CNT were of roughly equal strength nationally and in Andalusia, with approximately one million members each. The UGT's swing to the left corresponded to socialist disillusion in the republican government's slowness in tackling the country's basic problems, notably agrarian reform. By 1934 the Federation had ousted its original moderate leader, replaced him by an advocate of revolutionary strikes and was openly championing collectivization. During the civil war the Federation organized several hundred collectives either alone or – in those areas where membership was divided with the CNT – in collaboration with the latter.

6. (p. 88) The municipal elections were held to test the way the wind was blowing for King Alfonso who, having had to ditch Primo, was attempting to save his position by returning to constitutional government. Despite the fact that municipal elections were easier to rig than parliamentary elections, the results were an avalanche. All but four provincial capitals voted republican. The country districts, largely controlled by *caciques*, voted royalist, but this made no difference. 'No king or dictator could hope to hold Spain if the towns were against him' (*The Spanish Labyrinth*).

7. (p. 101) Estimates of Spanish illiteracy in 1931 varied between 30 and 50 per cent of the total population. Almost half the school-age population – estimated at between 2,500,000 and 3,500,000 – lacked schools to attend. The Ministry of Education estimated that 27,000 new schools were needed. In the first year of the Republic over 7,000 schools were built, ten times the previous annual rate (Jackson). But, after 1932, international depression and an economic boycott staged by the ruling class to make the Republic unpopular led to a sharp reduction in credits.

8. (p. 103) The government originally proposed a less radical article which, while separating Church from state, gave the Church a special position and allowed it to maintain its schools. Such an arrangement would have been accepted by the majority of Catholics. But the majority of the Cortes, angered by the Church's support of the dictatorship and monarchy – particularly the identification of the latter with the Catholic religion during the recent elections – found these provisions too lenient. In the Republicans' determination to attack the Church, which inevitably gave the reaction a rallying cry, and their evasion of a far-reaching land reform, can be seen the germs of their subsequent defeat.

9. (p. 104) The agrarian reform law was exceedingly complex and legalistic. While in principle it authorized the expropriation of millions of acres belonging to large land-owners, it made many exceptions. Payne estimates that of the 80,000 land-owners liable to partial or total

confiscation only 10,000 to 12,000 were in fact large owners. The rest were small- and medium-holders. Only the grandees lost their land without appeal. The extent to which the reform was sufficient can be judged by the fact that in its first two years of operation only 12,000 families received land. So complex was the reform that 'one would have thought the law written for an association of unemployed lawyers who wished to assure not only their own, but their sons' futures, rather than a law written for the peasants of Spain' (Jackson). Caballero was more succinct: 'an aspirin to cure an appendicitis', he called the reform. The question of whether expropriated land should be split up into individual holdings or collectivized was crucial. The republicans wanted to create a small-holding peasantry as a bulwark against revolution; the social-ists, by and large, wanted to prevent this. Their goal of collectivization was inspired not only by ideological reasons but by the fact that dry-farming areas, requiring large extents of land, modern machinery, fertilizers etc., lent themselves naturally to collectivization. Manuel's position should be seen in the light of the *irrigated small-holdings* which constitute a large part of the Mijas countryside.

10. (p. 104) Generally less well-known than either Caballero or Indalecio Prieto, the two major socialist leaders, Julián Besteiro's political trajectory is worth considering for the light it throws on Manuel's political perspectives.

Leader of the party's right wing, Besteiro was professor of logic at Madrid University and had been an intimate associate of Pablo Iglesias, the party's founder. In 1917, against Iglesias's advice, he urged the call-ing of a general revolutionary strike. Its failure led him to believe that the proletariat was insufficiently prepared for revolution. With the advent of the Republic he argued against socialist participation in government in opposition to Caballero. While believing in the necessity of the dictatorship of the proletariat, he feared the Republic had come a generation too early, 'before the UGT had had time to prepare a generation of politically educated workers with the necessary adminis-trative and self-governing experience' (Jackson).

Several times president of the UGT, he continued to command re-spect in the union and party during the early years of the Republic. However, as the party and union swung to the left – especially after the right won the elections of 1933 – Besteiro came under increasing attack and was forced to resign the UGT presidency. Attacking his thesis that revolution could come about only when the masses had been educated, the UGT declared: 'The education of all the working classes cannot precede the revolution but must follow it.'

As president of the first (constituent) republican Cortes, he attempted to restrain anti-clerical passions and also what he considered as Caballero's adventurist tactics in planning a national revolutionary uprising in 1934 which, except in Asturias, was a complete failure. Despite his moderatism, Besteiro refused to accept any deal with the rising fascist forces and, during the civil war, demonstrated his support of the Republic by remaining in Madrid under siege when the government and most party leaders moved to Valencia. Suffering from TB, he served throughout the war as a city councillor. In 1939 he was one of the *junta* which seized power in the capital to negotiate an end to the war. His hope of securing guarantees from the nationalists against political reprisals was short-lived. He was himself sentenced to thirty years in prison where he died of TB in 1940. Among the charges on which he was sentenced was his role in the 1917 general strike.

11. (p. 112) Founded in Barcelona in 1904 by Alejandro Lerroux, the radical party began as a violently demagogic, anti-Catalan, anti-clerical party which found its support among the petite bourgeoisie. With the growth of working-class organizations, which attracted many former radicals, the radical party rapidly moved to the right and, by the time of the monarchy's fall, it was an anti-socialist, anti-clerical party of conservative republicanism. Lerroux's personal prestige was destroyed by the financial scandal when he was Prime Minister of the right-wing government in 1935; in the 1936 elections which brought the Popular Front to power his party was virtually wiped out.

12. (p. 113) The CNT (Confederación Nacional del Trabajo), the anarcho-syndicalist trades-union confederation, was founded in 1910. Unlike the UGT at the time, its aims were revolutionary. It sought to overthrow capitalism and the state by the general revolutionary strike which would herald the advent of libertarian communism: a society without state or private property organized in self-governing collectives which would federate at regional, national and eventually international levels. Its refusal of the state led to its refusal to participate in politics: until the civil war, anarchists joined no government and – particularly in the 1933 elections which brought the right to power – the CNT urged its members not to vote. However, in 1936, while taking no part in the Popular Front electoral pact, it did not call on its members to abstain, justifying its stand by the necessity of securing the release of the 30,000 workers, many of them anarchists, who had been jailed after the 1934 uprising.

The CNT's structure reflected anarchist goals for the future society: individual unions or syndicates were organized on a local basis, without distinction of craft, and federated at regional level; subscriptions were small, sometimes in Andalusia non-existent; there were no strike funds and none of its leaders or secretaries was paid. Traditionally strong in Barcelona and Andalusia, the CNT's membership in 1936 was perhaps two-thirds of the size of the UGT's, which then numbered one and a half million.

In 1927, with the aim of ensuring that the masses of workers in the CNT should be tempted by neither reformism nor communism, the FAI (Federación Anarquista Ibérica) was founded. This was a secret or semi-secret organization composed exclusively of anarchist militants, each of whom had also to be a member of the CNT. The anarchists had always extolled the criminal as the victim of bourgeois society: that many gunmen and criminals were allowed into the FAI's ranks is not open to doubt.

13. (p. 114) Brenan asserts that the CNT–FAI were supreme in the city and province of Málaga which, with the rare exception of certain villages like Mijas, they dominated at the expense of the UGT and socialist party. In the city, only the fishermen's union was controlled by the UGT. When socialists or communists were elected to the Cortes from Málaga it was with anarchist votes – often in spite of FAI orders not to vote (Brenan, *Diary*).

14. (p. 114) Gil Robles, leader of the right-wing Catholic CEDA, was a supporter first of Hitler and then of Dollfuss, the Austrian right-wing Catholic Chancellor. Robles advocated a corporate state on the Austrian model. 'We must move towards a new state. What matters if it means shedding blood?' He was hailed by his followers as a *führer* and with election slogans of 'All power to the Chief'. The CEDA's inclusion in the Lerroux government was the signal for the Asturian uprising.

15. (p. 118) At the national level, the government was formed of left republicans alone. Mainly on Caballero's insistence, the socialist party had decided not to renew the experience of participating in government – a government, moreover, which was committed to a minimal programme which included no socialization whatsoever. The Popular Front won the elections by only a narrow margin of votes cast – a large number of these anarchist votes – but under the electoral law which gave 80 per cent of the seats to any list obtaining more than 50 per cent of the vote, secured 278 deputies to the right's 134. The socialists had the largest single representation in the new Cortes with 99 deputies; the left republicans had 87, the Republican Union 39 and the communists 17. The latter represented a big gain for the communist party whose participation in the Popular Front resulted from a change in Comintern policy. Until then, in the so-called 'Third Period', Comintern attacks had been directed mainly against social democratic parties. Faced with the growing threat of fascism, the Comintern changed its line and called for the formation of Popular Front governments. The Spanish party followed the new line and appealed to the

socialists for collaboration, merged their small trade union in the UGT and later secured the fusion of the socialist and communist youth organization; during the war the latter went over *en bloc* to the communist party. During the 1936 elections, sections of the socialist party considered themselves so much to the left of the communists that they coined the slogan, 'To save Spain from Marxism, vote communist.'

16. (p. 119) Veteran secretary general of the UGT, Largo Caballero was, from 1934 on, the leader of the left wing of the socialist party. In that year, believing that the only hope for the masses lay in a socialist revolution, he swung the party and union behind a general revolutionary strike: in Madrid, where he was personally responsible for its organization, the uprising failed; but in Asturias, where socialists, communists and anarchists fought side by side for the first time, miners' soviets held power for a week before the army repressed the uprising. As a result, Caballero was jailed; at the age of sixty-seven he discovered the works of Marx, Engels and Lenin.

The champion of reformist policies until 1934, Caballero was immensely popular as a working-class leader – a plasterer by trade who had started work at the age of eight and learnt to read at twenty-four. His swing to the left represented the revolutionary aspirations of large sections of the UGT. Aspirations, however, were no substitute for revolutionary strategy and organization. Apart from asking, in vain, the President of the Republic, Azaña, to arm the workers a month before the outbreak of the war, Caballero appears to have had no other policy than to wait for power to fall into his hands. This it did in September 1936, when he appeared the only figure who could rally the Republic after its initial military setbacks. As Prime Minister he was quickly persuaded of the necessity of sacrificing the revolution, even if temporarily, for the support of Britain and France and much-needed arms. Advocates of this policy, the communists joined his government as did later, under different pressures, the anarchists. Banking on his personal prestige, Caballero believed he could hold the coalition together. His failure (see note 27) reflected the growth of communist strength, the indecisiveness of the anarchists and – by no means least – the declining strength of his own party which, split between left and right, lacked the communists' coherence, discipline and benefits of foreign aid.

17. (p. 120) The wave of assassinations between February and June are estimated to have cost more than a hundred lives. Not all the fighting was between the left and right. The Málaga assassinations were one of the worst outbreaks in this period of the conflict often latent between local branches of the CNT and UGT. The leadership of both unions condemned the violence which arose out of a dispute between

the CNT fish-vendors' union and the UGT fishermen's union which was seeking to get higher prices for its fish (Brenan, *Diary*).

18. (p. 125) The Falange Española was founded in 1932 by José Antonio Primo de Rivera, son of the dictator. It remained a very small party until after the 1936 elections, most of its members being university students; its few working-class members were mainly former anarchists. Outside Madrid, its chief recruitment area was Andalusia – Seville, Jerez and Cadiz. Its programme differed from orthodox Italian fascism on only one significant point: respect for the Church. The party's growth after the elections was largely due to Gil Robles's failure to win the election, which the bourgeoisie had confidently expected him to do. Fascism then became their riposte to the proletarian revolution that was threatening.

19. (p. 131) 'We CNT militants in Aragon made the crass error of never taking fascism or the Old Spain seriously. The sad and shameful reality showed us unprepared and with insufficient strength to tackle the danger that confronted us,' an anarchist militant wrote later about the fall of Zaragoza. In Barcelona, however, the anarchists were the main force which crushed the insurrection in bitter street fighting. As a result, the President of Catalonia, Companys, offered them power. Declaring that the hour of libertarian communism had not arrived, the anarchists turned down the offer and agreed to the formation of an anti-fascist militia committee in which *all* anti-fascist parties and organizations were represented.

20. (p. 134) Overnight, the republican state apparatus disintegrated and collapsed. Power lay in the streets with the armed workers and peasants. In the greatest revolutionary upsurge witnessed in Europe since the Russian revolution, popular committees rose to take over every area not under nationalist control. The central government's power was virtually non-existent outside Madrid. However, no working-class organization made a bid to seize power centrally. What existed was a situation of dual power (or powers) embodied in the local committees which exercised legislative and executive authority in each village or town. Under a variety of names – revolutionary, anti-fascist, workers', defence – these committees confronted the triple task of organizing militias to carry on the war, organizing the repression to destroy or intimidate the counter-revolutionary forces in their midst, and organizing war production and food supplies. Their revolutionary *élan* was enormous, diverse and – ultimately – fragmented. Throughout the country they took over and ran factories and farms, public transport, shipping, mines, electricity and gas works, cinemas and theatres, food-processing plants and breweries – an inexhaustible list which, in Barcelona above all, extended to virtual control of the entire Catalan

economy. They controlled frontiers, prices, employment and, through the militias, the conduct of the war. In Barcelona the committee fed 120,000 people a day throughout August in restaurants open to anyone carrying a trade-union card. Two days after the uprising, buses, trams and the underground were running as normal – though now under the direction of the workers themselves. Throughout the country, delegates to the committees, on which all Popular Front parties and working-class organizations were normally represented, were elected or appointed by their respective groups; it was rare for these delegates to be ratified by popular vote. The committees thus never became popularly elected and revocable soviets, for no party or organization supported such a transformation. The committees' power – almost always local – diminished after two to three months as the central government regained control and damped down the revolutionary upsurge.

21. (p. 135) This procedure was one of many adopted in villages throughout republican Spain. In Aragon, where CNT militia columns predominated and the CNT had created the only regional committee, collectivization prevailed. Some 450 collectives were organized there, totalling about 433,000 workers or 75 per cent of the population of the region which was still in republican hands (Thomas). Apart from collectivizing the land and abolishing private trade, anarchist collectives often abolished money; wages, usually a fixed sum agreed by the collective, were paid in vouchers. Describing one such collective in Andalusia, Borkenau reported that the villagers were almost certainly worse off than before. Stores were so low as to foretell starvation, the village bar was closed, coffee-drinking abolished. 'But the inhabitants seemed to be proud of this state of things. . . . Their hatred of the upper class was far less economic than moral.' An indefatigable observer of the revolution in the countryside, Borkenau reported that in the first months of the revolution the land question by and large remained unsolved and 'the greatest uncertainty prevails about the problem of how to solve it'. In as far as it was one, the solution adopted in Mijas appears to have been fairly general: nothing was done to alter the farm-workers' fundamental situation. 'The same hands work the same land, the divisions between the old estates are upheld, the old wages are paid, and the only difference is that they are no longer paid by the land-owner's estate agent, but by the committees and unions' (Borkenau).

22. (p. 136) Concerning the 'red terror' of the first two months, Brenan has written that it was 'a spontaneous movement, corresponding to the necessities of revolutionary war, where the enemy within may be as dangerous as the enemy outside' and, despite protests, was supported by all Popular Front parties except the republicans (*Spanish Labyrinth*). The victims were selected by Public Safety committees; in

Málaga no one was killed in cold blood until eight days after the uprising, and then mainly as a reprisal for the nationalist air raids and for
what was happening in Seville. At the same time, FAI terrorist groups
began to drive round the city and countryside looking for fascists.
With the exception of priests and a large mill-owning family in Málaga,
those marked out were often people who were disliked for their
tyrannical behaviour, rather than those who, on ideological grounds,
might have been expected to be shot (*Diary*). Reaction against the terror
began after 25 August when the news of the nationalist massacre of
Badajoz reached Madrid. A general massacre of political prisoners was
only averted by the republican government's creation of a Revolutionary Tribunal which, though it tried only cases of open treason or
rebellion, provided a safety-valve for public opinion. Irregular executions were gradually put down, 'the FAI itself lending a hand, so that
by the end of the year [1936] unauthorized "eliminations" had
practically ceased to occur' (*Spanish Labyrinth*).

23. (p. 145) Nationally, the Spanish communist party had been
founded in the early twenties by socialists who split from the socialist
party when it voted against affiliating with the Third International, and
by a number of anarcho-syndicalist dissidents. At the end of 1935 the
party claimed 25,000 members, but during the war its membership rose
phenomenally. Its opposition to the socialist revolution, which it considered endangered the Republic, brought it support from all sectors
opposed to the revolution and concerned with a vigorous prosecution
of the war. While denying that it was sacrificing the interests of the
revolution in order to win the war – 'We are fighting for a democratic
and parliamentary Republic of a new type, [not] a democratic Republic
such as that of France or any other capitalist country,' the party's
secretary general José Diaz said in 1937 – the party sought not to alienate
the petite bourgeoisie of Spain nor the bourgeois democracies of Britain
and France. 'Respect the property of the peasant', 'No interference
with the small businessman', 'No socialization of industry', were
among the party's slogans. This policy, as well as the vital aid provided
by the Soviet Union and the prestige of the International Brigades,
brought an influx of members. By March 1937 it claimed 250,000
members – nearly a third of whom were peasant owners – making it the
largest party in the republican zone. By June of the same year it claimed
387,000. The socialist party, the biggest working-class party at the
outbreak of the war a year earlier, now claimed about 160,000
members.

24. (p. 147) While the first decree merely gave formal assent to what
was already happening – the cultivation by the committees of land they
had taken over – the second was more controversial. It was the first

significant government intervention in the land problem, and expropriated land without indemnity in favour of the state. Expropriated land could be cultivated individually or collectively, depending on the majority decision of the beneficiaries; but the law also gave small-holders (with certain limitations on the size of the holdings) the permanent use of the land they had been leasing. The Landworkers' Federation demanded that the decree be extended to include landlords not implicated in the fascist uprising but who, in one form or another, had shown themselves enemies of the working class. It protested particularly about the small-holders' provision, stressing that the law gave tenant farmers 'who had accepted the new order of things, a desire to recover their former parcels'. The anarchists were equally bitter about the law and its restriction of expropriation to land-owners who had intervened in the nationalist uprising. Despite this, by spring 1937 nearly four million hectares had been taken over by the Agrarian Reform Institute (Thomas), a figure which rose by August 1938 to nearly five and a half million hectares – one-third of the republican zone's arable land, excluding Aragon and Catalonia (Payne).

25. (p. 149) The militia had had no experience against tanks and panicked at the threat of being cut off by the Italian armoured columns and Moorish and Spanish troops. According to Thomas, Caballero turned down a request for more arms and money for Málaga's defence, while Broué and Témime maintain that no aid was forthcoming because the Republic was about to launch an attack – pre-empted by a nationalist attack – in the Jarama valley to relieve Madrid. Manuel's assertion that the government had decided to abandon Málaga two weeks before the city fell is information apparently not known before.

26. (p. 157) The fall of Málaga precipitated a political crisis; anarchists and communists, now both in the Caballero government, accused each other of being the cause of the defeat. Their antagonism came to a head in Barcelona in May. There the unified socialist and communist party (PSUC) sought to reduce the still very significant anarchist gains which included control of the American Telephone & Telegraph Co. exchange. In an incident which still gives rise to polemic, the PSUC made an attempt to take over the exchange, the anarchists defended it and there followed three days of street fighting in which 500 died and 1,000 were wounded. The CNT, UGT and the central government all called for an end to the fighting. When it ended, the communists called for the suppression of the Trotskyist POUM, which had supported the workers who had taken to the streets. Caballero, whose relations with the communists had deteriorated rapidly as their strength grew, refused. The communist ministers walked out of the cabinet which then resigned *en bloc*. Caballero's term as Prime Minister, which had begun

the previous September, was ended. He was succeeded by Juan Negrín, a fellow socialist, who remained Prime Minister until the end of the war. Under his government, the POUM was suppressed, the anarchist regional committee in Aragon dissolved and troops under the communist commander Lister sent in to break up anarchist collectives in Aragon.

27. (p. 157) Durruti and Ascaso were legendary heroes of the Spanish anarchist movement. Inseparable friends from the Zaragoza working class, they robbed banks (including the Bank of Spain), assassinated a cardinal, participated in the preparations for killing a prime minister, planned an attempt on King Alfonso's life and were in the forefront of practically every anarchist uprising or strike, when they were not in jail. As soon as they came out, they returned to their trade as masons; none of the money they expropriated was kept for themselves. So much has been written about the terror exercised by the Durruti militia column during the revolution that it is of interest to note that Jackson reports having received many testimonials to Durruti's personal intervention in saving the lives of landlords who had not aided the rising but were of the right. Certainly on more than one occasion he threatened to shoot his own militiamen for looting. His revolutionary anarchist ardour was unquenchable: 'We haven't the least fear of ruins. . . . We are going to inherit the earth. . . . We carry this new world here, in our hearts, and this world is growing by the minute,' he declared before his death.

28. (p. 159) Negrín's creation of the *carabineros* as a fighting force during the first months of Caballero's government had a dual purpose: to assist the task of building a regular army in place of the militia system, and as a police force at the service of the socialist party. The question of the militia system, in which each trade union or working-class organization had formed its own columns under political command, was one of the major areas of dispute between the anarchists and all other parties in the Republic. While not agreeing on what sort of army was needed, none of them, after the initial defeats which had brought the nationalists to the gates of Madrid, continued to support the anarchist militia system which was broken up and replaced by traditional-style army units.

29. (p. 160) Faced with the threat of a new nationalist attack on Madrid, after the loss of the north with its heavy industry and mines, the Republic desperately needed a victory to divert nationalist attention from the capital. They chose Teruel, which was weakly defended; their initial success brought victory over the only town of size the republican army was to capture throughout the war. As before, however, they were unable to exploit the breakthrough; the nationalist forces were

materially and numerically superior. One of the bitterest and most bloody battles of the war, which raged for two months, Teruel has been seen as a turning-point. Until then there had been a certain equilibrium at the military level; but when the republican lines broke, the nationalist offensive became an irresistible force: 'the equilibrium was definitively shattered' (Broué and Témime).

30. (p. 188) Though the socialist party provided the prime minister and a large part of the cabinet throughout the war, its influence and strength relative to the communist party was in constant decline. Split between left and centre and lacking a coherent strategy, the party defined itself only negatively in the fundamental options presented by the concurrence of revolution and war. Against pursuing the revolution, it lacked the cadres, military expertise and aid – not to say collective determination – to prosecute the war as efficiently as the communists. Unable to match the latter, the party as a whole stood only to lose. At the same time, the left wing had nothing to gain from the revolutionary masses which it had mobilized – and subsequently demobilized – as a result of the party's change of policy.

CHRONOLOGY
1900–1970

	National	*Local*
1900	Constitutional Monarchy	
1905		Manuel born
1913		Juliana born
1917	UGT – CNT General Strike	
1918		UGT organized, calls strike
1923	Primo de Rivera becomes dictator	
1927–8		Manuel's military service
1930	Fall of Primo dictatorship	UGT and socialist party formed
1931	Fall of Monarchy, Republic declared	Socialist, radical and radical-socialist local council elected; Manuel deputy-mayor
1932	Agrarian Reform law	
1933	Casas Viejas. Right-wing electoral victory, Lerroux Prime Minister – November to February 1936: *bienio negro*	Landlords' boycott, UGT takes charge of grape crop
1934	CEDA enters government; Asturias uprising	Socialists evicted from local council, replaced by radicals and CEDA members
1935	Lerroux resigns	Manuel and Juliana marry Maria born
1936	February Popular Front electoral victory, Azaña Prime Minister May Azaña President of Republic, Casares Quiroga Prime Minister	Manuel elected mayor

National	*Local*
1936 July Military uprising, Popular Front committees take over in republican zone; military uprising in Madrid, Barcelona, Málaga, Basque country defeated	Committee takes over
July–August Seville, Cadiz, Córdoba, Granada in nationalists' hands	Front runs from west of Estepona through Ronda and Antequera to Granada
September Caballero government	
October Decree expropriating nationalist landlords	
November Battle of Madrid	
1937 17 January First phase of nationalist offensive against Málaga: Estepona, Marbella, Alhama de Granada captured	
3 February Second phase of offensive	
7 February	Manuel and family flee from Mijas
8 February Fall of Málaga	
9 February	Juliana and child return to Mijas; Manuel walks to Almeria
10 February	Token force takes Mijas
May Anarchist–communist fighting in Barcelona; Caballero cabinet resigns, Negrín becomes Prime Minister	
June–August Nationalists capture North	
October	Manuel volunteers for *carabineros*
December Republicans take Teruel	
1938 February Nationalists recapture Teruel	

National	*Local*
1938 April Nationalists reach Mediterranean and cut Republic in two	
July Nationalist drive to Valencia held up	Manuel withdrawn from front line
1939 January Barcelona falls	
March Casado *junta* seizes power in Madrid to negotiate with nationalists	
1 April Republic surrenders	Manuel in Valencia
16 April	Manuel returns to Mijas, goes into hiding
1940-42 'Hunger years'	
1941	Manuel moves from father's house to No. 5
1946 U N ambassadors withdrawn	
1950	Manuel's escape thwarted
1951	Juliana buys own house, No. 11
1953 US Military pact	
1960	Beginning of tourist boom
1969 28 March Amnesty for civil war offences announced	
12 April	Manuel emerges from hiding